# *The*
# *Gentle*
# *Art*
# *of*
# *Murder*

# The Gentle Art of Murder

## The Detective Fiction of Agatha Christie

Earl F. Bargainnier

Bowling Green University Popular Press
Bowling Green, Ohio 43403

# CONTENTS

# The Gentle Art of Murder

## The Detective Fiction of Agatha Christie

### Preface

"The queen of crime," "the mistress of fair deceit," "the first lady of crime," "the mistress of misdirection," "the detective story writer's detective story writer," and even "the *Hymns Ancient and Modern* of detection"—these are just a few of the epithets which have been used to indicate Agatha Christie's position as writer of detective fiction. In her sixty-seven novels and one hundred and seventeen short stories of detection and mystery, Christie created a body of work which made her the most popular writer of the twentieth century. The very fact of that popularity, as well as critical disdain for the genre in which she wrote, has prevented her work from receiving much serious attention. Supposedly T.S. Eliot once planned a study of the detective novel, with a long section on Christie, but it was never written. Most of the few works on her and her writing have been anecdotal and poorly documented, more peripheral chat than study of the fiction itself. Christie did not care; she was not concerned with criticism of her work, refusing most requests for interviews and repeating the same statements over and over in those few she did grant. Even her autobiography gives more space to other matters than to her fiction. Perhaps as a result of her influence, her husband, Sir Max Mallowan, has issued in his memoirs a stern warning to anyone presuming to be a critic of detective fiction, saying that such a critic is "under an obligation not to reveal the resolution of the story," so that he does not "ruin a book for the reader," adding, "I have the feeling, unfair perhaps, that the analytical critic of detective fiction is either a knave or a fool."

In spite of the risk of being called "a knave or a fool," my intent is a literary analysis of the detective fiction of "the queen of crime." I hope that I will not ruin any of her works for readers, but rather enable them to understand better the general skill of their construction as works of a particular genre of fiction. With Mallowan's warning in mind, I originally intended to reveal no resolutions, but I have found that to fulfill that intention would be both awkward and artificial. The murderers in thirteen novels and

1

two short stories are named,* and even when names are not revealed, the analysis of a work may "give away" the murderer or his method. But since this study is an analysis of Christie's technique as a writer of detective *fiction,* it is impossible for me to approach that fiction as mere puzzle, whose "answer" is its only importance. The serious study of detective fiction is relatively new, and there is no one critical method for that study. I have attempted to classify the major components of Christie's fiction and to illustrate and evaluate how she employs them. The plan is first to examine briefly critical comments on the nature of detective fiction as written by Christie and then to consider those major components: setting, character, plot and theme, as well as other narrative and stylistic devices. Recent formula criticism of popular fiction, as developed primarily by John G. Cawelti, has been of great help and is a significant contributor to my approach.

This study is not a defense of either Christie or detective fiction. I accept the view of Percy Lubbock that whatever course a novelist pursues, he needs only "to be consistent on some plan, to follow the principle he has adopted." Christie chose to write a specific type of detective fiction—why she chose it is not the question; rather how she accomplished it is. A reader who rejects the genre altogether, as Edmund Wilson and others have done, will not be interested in Christie's work, and it seems unnecessary to try to convince such a person otherwise. My premises are that detective fiction is worth studying as an enormously popular genre and that Christie's work is a significant body within that genre. At the same time, I have not forgotten Erik Routley's admonition that anyone writing about detective fiction will go astray if he does not recognize "the humbug-content" present in the genre.

Just as the study is not a defense, it is not a biography. Christie's *An Autobiography* and her husband's *Mallowan's Memoirs* can be consulted for the facts of her life which she and her family wished to be known. Of course, when biography elucidates the fiction, it will be used for that purpose.

Detective fiction, the detective story, mystery fiction, crime fiction, mystery-detective fiction and the whodunit are terms generally used interchangeably in discussing such writing as Christie's. In this study *detective fiction* will be used as the generic term, and *mystery fiction* will be used only for works in which a detective, amateur or professional, does not appear as the protagonist, works such as *And Then There Were None* and *Endless Night.*

Documentation becomes a major problem when dealing with such a mass of primary material. Rather than having footnotes for each chapter numbering in the hundreds, I have used key title words for Christie's works to allow for citations within the text. Footnotes are used for all other references, unless otherwise indicated. A Key to Documentation can be found behind the Index of Titles in the back of the book.

I would like to acknowledge the aid and encouragement which I have received from friends and colleagues, particularly Dr. Jane S. Bakerman, Indiana State University; Dr. Jeanne F. Bedell, University of Missouri-Rolla; Dr. George N. Dove, East Tennessee State University; Dr. Barrie Hayne, University of Toronto; Dr. Kathleen Klein, Indiana University-Purdue University at Indianapolis; and Mrs. Leiselotte Goodman, Dr. Dwight Langston and Miss Ann Munck, Wesleyan College. I am grateful to all the participants over the years in the sessions on detective fiction at the meetings of the Popular Culture Association, who have taught me much about the genre and in many cases provided me copies of the papers they presented. My thanks also go to Mr. Allen J. Hubin, editor of *The Armchair Detective*, and Dr. George Gerbner, editor of the *Journal of Communication*, for permitting me to incorporate material from articles of mine which originally appeared in their journals. My greatest debt is to my friend Mrs. Corawayne Wright, Associate Librarian, Willet Memorial Library, Wesleyan College; without her patience, energy and knowledge, I could never have completed this study.

*The Body in the Library, Crooked House, Death Comes as the End, Easy to Kill, Endless Night, Hercule Poirot's Christmas, Hickory Dickory Death, The Murder of Roger Ackroyd, Murder on the Orient Express, Nemesis, Remembered Death, Sleeping Murder, The Mirror Crack'd from Side to Side, "The Under Dog," and "Where There Is a Will."

# Chapter I

## Golden Age Detective Fiction:
## An Introduction to Christie's Genre

*...detective stories have nothing to do with works of art.*

**W.H. Auden**

*If you can grow lyrical over Proust's crumb of cake in the teacup, you can find charm in the ambiguity of any clue.*

**Jacques Barzun**

*Detective novels ... were no more intended to be judged by realistic standards than one would judge Watteau's shepherds and shepherdesses in terms of contemporary sheep-farming.*

**Robert Graves & Alan Hodge**

Though her books span a period from 1920 to 1976, Agatha Christie's detective fiction is essentially of the type called "Golden Age," or classic, that is of the period between the two world wars. She could and did change various elements within her work as time passed, but the basic form of her fiction did not change. Each new "Christie for Christmas" could be counted upon to be another surprising variation on the general pattern. Therefore, an examination of the nature of Golden Age detective fiction is a necessary first step in evaluating Christie's work.

Nearly every writer on detective fiction has resorted to analogy as an aid to definition or explanation. The analogies have varied considerably, from religious ritual to the minuet, but three large groups have been most prominent: games, logic and mathematics, and other literary forms. The analogies to games range from card games and jigsaw and crossword puzzles to football and other sports. R. Austin Freeman called the genre "an exhibition of mental gymnastics," and he was joined by Willard Huntington Wright, who not only described detective fiction as "a kind of intellectual game ... a sporting event," but even as "a complicated and extended puzzle cast in fictional form."[1] Numerous other critics have followed this line. Julian Symons' characterization of such fiction as "an exercise in logic" and Dorothy Sayers' statement that in "its severest form, the mystery story is a pure analytical exercise" are typical of the second group.[2] Often, however, blame is implied by such analogies, as in Mary McCarthy's view that the characters in such stories are "about as real as the A and B of the algebra problems"; on the other hand, John Leonard uses the same analogy

4

to defend Christie specifically: her stories "were elegant, as a balanced equation is elegant. Who complains about the x, or any other quantity, in an equation?"[3] Francis Wyndham even coined the phrase "animated algebra" to characterize Christie's work: "Agatha Christie writes animated algebra. She dares us to solve a basic equation buried beneath a proliferation of irrelevancies."[4]

The third group of analogies is, as might be expected, the largest, for the tendency to find resemblances between detective fiction and other forms of literature is natural; what is unusual is the forms most often chosen. As early as 1913 Carolyn Wells found an equivalent to detective fiction in the fixed forms of verse: the sonnet and the French forms, such as the triolet, the sestina and the rondeaux. Others have agreed, among them Sayers, C. Day Lewis, Richard Lockridge, Michael Gilbert, Hillary Waugh and John Cawelti, particularly as to the sonnet. Waugh's statement that "the mystery is to the novel what the sonnet is to poetry" is matched by Cawelti's "The formula of the classical detective story is as rigid and formalistic as that of the sonnet."[5] Michael Gilbert uses a double analogy to differentiate between the classic detective story and the thriller: "The detective story is the sonnet. It is precise, neat, satisfyingly symmetrical, constrained, but sustained, by the nicety of its form.... The thriller is the ode. It has no formal rules at all. It has no precise framework."[6] Among other literary forms to which detective fiction has been compared are the medieval morality play, Renaissance pastoral, Restoration comedy, the fairy tale, the comedy of manners and, of course, melodrama.

The point of most of these analogies, of whichever group, is the sense that form, pattern and even rules govern detective fiction. The attitude is summed up by Dorothy B. Hughes: "The mystery novel, like the theatrical play or the sonnet, is contained within a prescribed pattern. The writer may wander a bit but not far, not and stay within the form."[7] One may dislike the form, or the work of a specific writer using it, but one cannot help realizing that it is present; even Georges Simenon's comment on his detestation of Christie—"It's not literature, it's embroidery."—implies an awareness of an underlying pattern.[8]

Nowhere is the strict form of detective fiction more clearly indicated than in the numerous attempts to compile rules for the writing of it. The "Rules of the Game," by whomever formulated, have had the purposes of defining the genre, eliminating trite and hackneyed elements, and insuring "fairness," that is, how the "game" should be played. The 1920s were the great period of the rules, which were also at least partially the result of the desire to give the genre respectability, by distinguishing it from such related popular forms as the horror story, the mystery-adventure, and the spy thriller. The rules of the 'twenties were essentially based on the idea later expressed by Raymond Chandler: "The mystery novel must not try to do everything at once. If it is a puzzle story operating in a cool mental climate, it cannot also be a story of violent adventure or passionate romance."[9] S.S. Van Dine's "Twenty Rules for Writing Detective Stories" and Ronald A. Knox's "A Detective Story Decalogue" are perhaps the two most famous such lists of the 'twenties, and though most of their rules at first glance may seem commonsensical, they have all been successfully broken. Christie alone broke fifteen of Van Dine's twenty and seven of Knox's ten.[10] Van Dine and Knox were not, of course, the only ones to attempt to codify the writing of detective fiction. Every how-to-write-a-detective-story manual still includes such a list, however futile. But it must be noted that no writer would break all the rules in one work, for, as Hughes' comment indicates, if he did, he would be writing something other than detective fiction.

Later critics have been less rigid in what is permissible in the classic form. Howard Haycraft has only two commandments: "1) The detective story must play fair. 2) It must be readable."[11] John Dickson Carr goes even further, "Once the evidence has been fairly presented, there are very few things which are not permissible," and after giving his own "four golden maxims of Do's and Don't's," he says that all have been "shattered admirably," the reason being that "they are not really rules; they are only prejudices."[12] Carr's evaluation is accurate, for however well-intentioned, these absolutes are basically only their compilers' formulas for success. The repeated strictures on romance and overt comedy in detective fiction—which have so often been broken—are just two instances. It seems most sensible to view the rules, as Haycraft does, as simply the relationship between author and reader, for then his and Carr's demand for fairness, what is sometimes called "Fair Play," becomes an acceptable principle. However, one must admit that fairness is in the eye of the beholder. Christie claimed that she was always fair with her readers, even in *The Murder of Roger Ackroyd,* which was accused by Van Dine and others of being arrant trickery. Readers can argue long over the fairness of a particular work, but one basic test has been suggested by Marie F. Rodell: "Doubt about the fairness of any given point or situation can best be solved by answering the question: does the use of this point or situation make it impossible for the average reader to solve the puzzle himself without prompting by the detective? If the answer is yes, then cheating it is."[13] Of course, the words *impossible* and *average reader* still leave quite enough room for argument.

The question of fairness brings up the puzzle element of detective fiction. Most readers enjoy the duel of wits with the author: will he be able to fool me this time, or will I solve the mystery first? Nevertheless, it is too facile to say that detective fiction is just a puzzle to be solved, as implied by the already quoted statement of Wright that it is "a complicated and extended puzzle cast in fictional form." Rather, Julian Symons seems more nearly correct when he says, "The puzzle is vital to the detective story but it is not a detective story in itself."[14] A story that is only a puzzle would be as unreadable as a crossword puzzle—and as small in size; in fact, it would not be fiction. The content of a detective story is different in kind from the words which make up a crossword puzzle. A puzzle is always present in classic detective fiction, hence the term *whodunit*, but it is not the entire work. It is actually just the result of plot arrangement. Instead of telling the story so that the perpetrator of a crime is known, the author arranges the incidents to allow that perpetrator to attempt to hide his act, and, therefore, there is a process of discovery. In essence, the mystery of a detective story "is a narrative puzzle within a narrative development."[15] The puzzle is in the challenge to the detective, and the reader, to use his intellect to find the guilty among the innocent. The significance of the puzzle element is that it places the emphasis upon the contest between the detective and the murderer, rather than upon the actual deed and the victim. The effect is what John Cawelti calls "the aestheticizing of crime"—the removal of its horror—which he considers a major quality differentiating classic detective fiction from both earlier and later types.[16]

Also contributing to this aesthetic—some might say *antiseptic*—quality is the form's detachment. Some have found the detachment an irritant, if not a serious flaw. Typical is Symon's statement: "The fairy-tale land of the Golden Age was one in which murder was committed over and over again without anybody getting hurt."[17] This sanitizing of the ghastliness of murder, as in such euphemisms as "a neat bullet-hole," "a pool of blood," or "a dark stain," is a convention of classic detective fiction, one which must be accepted or the form left unread. Critics often label such stories "cosy," and Christie is usually said to be the doyenne of the Cosy School. She would not have objected. She disliked hard-boiled detective fiction, saying, "I don't find it very interesting—all that seems to happen is, first one side bashes the other side, and then the other side bashes the first one"; her preference is clear: "I like poison killings best. I don't like messy deaths."[18] Of course, many deaths are messy, and perhaps there are people who enjoy reading all of the gruesome details. They must, however, go to writers other than

Christie and her Golden Age colleagues, for they do not present sensational violence—the murders nearly always occur offstage—but rather a detached process of ratiocination.

Though most people think of detective fiction as principally entertainment, which it is, a case can be made for its being the most intellectual of popular literary forms, and this is especially true of the works of the Golden Age. This usually overlooked intellectuality is the result of the detective story's concern for the discovery of truth, however hidden or distorted it may be or appear to be. Many years ago H. Douglas Thomson stated, "Crime, however odd it may sound, is *not* the primary interest of the detective story."[19] The primary interest is the process of solution, and in classic British detective fiction that process is basically one of thought rather than action. Hercule Poirot does not continually speak of "order and method" for nothing; he is stating a principle which applies not only to the *modus operandi* of the classic detective, but to the nature of detective fiction itself, for the author as well as the detective must have analytical ability and acute reasoning if he is to compel the reader to follow the twists and turns of a complex series of events. The reader must be made to want to *know,* and he must be willing to bring his own reason to bear on these events. He may fail to solve the mystery, but he has to make an effort to solve it, and logic must be the method. The casual reader will miss clues which are minute or concealed, which provide the solution; the careful reader will be aware that everything may be important. Perhaps the major reason that classic detective fiction has appealed so strongly to the educated is that it is a form of entertainment which also enables a reader to test his intelligence and perception. If detective fiction is a game, it is an intellectual game; though the detective and the criminal are opponents, the real intellectual activity is between the author and the reader.

Formal rules, necessary fairness, puzzle element, intellectual activity—these would seem to eliminate realism from detective fiction, and perhaps no aspect of the genre has generated so many varying opinions as its realism or lack of it. Raymond Chandler condemned the classic form from the premise that fiction has always tended toward realism, but realism was a nineteenth century creation, a relatively recent literary mode. Nevertheless, since it has been the dominant fictional mode for the past hundred years, detective fiction's relation to it is an issue.

To present the many attacks on detective fiction for being unrealistic and having nothing to do with real life is unnecessary. The answers to such criticism have generally fallen into one of four groups. The first is best represented by Michael Innes, who proclaims that detective fiction should not be realistic, because the reader must not *care* about the events: "Nothing *real* must be allowed in. Let your guilt and misery, for instance, be real and you crack the mold of the form"; what is actually desired is "the highest degree of unexpectedness at all compatible with plausibility."[20] A similar statement is Sutherland Scott's that "the better the novel, the less absorbing the mystery," that is, the qualities of the realistic novel interfere with the process of discovery by emphasizing other things.[21] A second defense is that detective fiction creates its own "reality," which allows the reader to escape himself and identify with the given characters and action. Cawelti calls it "an imaginary world that is just sufficiently far from our ordinary reality to make us less inclined to apply our ordinary standards of plausibility and probability to it."[22] If this concept has validity, that slight difference from the actual world is probably the reason that detective novels of the 1920s and 1930s seem so little dated. They exist in their own world, which knows not change. A third and widely-held view is that detective fiction is really a combination of fantasy and realism. Eric Routley finds that "this constant tension between the far-flung remoteness of romanticism and the restrictions of reason tied down to physical particulars ... form the dynamic of the detective story."[23] Fantastic action in a realistically presented setting by characters who are at least recognizable types may not satisfy those who demand that all fiction be realistic, but such a view does provide a legitimate approach to what detective fiction actually is.

The last answer is that most often propounded in essays, introductions and reviews by Jacques Barzun, though others have agreed with him. Barzun believes that "detective fiction belongs to the kind of narrative properly called *the tale*. It is a genre distinct from *the novel* as we have come to know it since Balzac.... The tale, much older than the novel, appeals to curiosity, wonder, and the love of ingenuity."[24] He does not make any apology for the tale as a literary form: "A tale charms by its ingenuity, by the plausibility with which it overcomes the suspicion that it couldn't happen. That is art."[25] The concept of detective fiction belonging to the genre of the tale eliminates argument about its reality or lack of same, for tales have never been bound by the strictures of the novel or short story: *Don Quixote* is not *Portrait of a Lady* and "Hansel and Gretel" is not "The Prussian Officer." If the detective story is a tale, it is most like the fairy tale, in that the good and innocent are rewarded—if only by having suspicion removed—and the wicked are punished, with the detective acting as fairy godmother. (The problem with Barzun's concept is that writers of detective fiction call their works novels and short stories, and they are therefore judged as such—not as tales.)

Perhaps the best answer to the question of detective fiction's lack of realism may be found in the fact that, though differing in their defenses, Innes, Cawelti and Barzun all use the term *plausibility,* the implication being that it is a necessary factor in successful detective fiction. Surely it is more sensible to demand that a work of fiction be *plausible* than that it be *real*—an impossibility in any case. After all, every writer uses artifice to some degree, and no novel, whatever its type, is an actual slice of life.

Another criticism of Golden Age detective fiction nearly as prevalent as its lack of reality is that it is too conservative, even reactionary, in its social, political and moral outlook. Typical of such criticism is that expressed by a recent writer, who believes that Golden Age detective fiction

offers social stability and moral certainty to a world in which neither exists. In order to enable the detective to fulfill his traditional function, that of restoring the social and moral *status quo,* authors faced with a world threatened by economic and political chaos, rigorously excluded from their novels situations and characters which posed ethically defensible opposition to established values. But in doing so,...they bound themselves to a narrow and perhaps narrow-minded view of English society, a view based upon overt class bias.[26]

Without necessarily sharing the disparaging attitude of such a statement, one has to agree with the underlying concept that detective fiction is conservative. In fact, it seems doubtful that there could be a radical detective story, for the form consists of the disruption of community harmony by an identifiable person or persons and then the elimination of that disruption and a return to a tranquil and stable condition. The author's, and reader's, sympathies must be on the side of law and order, not on that of the lawbreaker; therefore, the society must be basically good and worth preserving. A continuously changing society, often confusing and frightening, is not one in which good and evil can be markedly differentiated as they are in detective fiction. There it is accepted that moral good *is* good and evil *is* evil. (Such an attitude is, of course, another reason for the charge of unreality.) However, the critics so often overstate their case that one wonders why they bother to read what they must know beforehand they are not going to accept. Colin Watson's *Snobbery with Violence* (1971) is an extended attack on the conservative assumptions of Golden Age detective fiction and presents all the arguments against the form, but by the last chapter one can only guess what he really expects from it. Classic detective fiction is a type of escape fiction, and no one wishes to escape into uncertainty, terror or poverty. The escape it provides is to a world of political and social order, moral certitude, and usually of wealth and culture. Though the peace of this world is broken, the reader can be assured that it will be restored or have a new birth by the end.

The charge of snobbery should be examined in light of detective fiction's relation to comedy. In his influential *Anatomy of Criticism*, Northrop Frye places the form under Comic Fictional Modes. He is undoubtedly correct, for in the strict literary sense of the word *comedy*—a genre in which, no matter the temporary difficulties, all things work out happily for the innocent—no form so fits as classic detective fiction. The most developed discussion of it as comedy is George Grella's "Murder and Manners: The Formal Detective Novel."[27] His basic argument is that detective fiction is a form of fictional comedy of manners:

> Once the comic nature of the detective story is revealed, then all its most important characteristics betray a comic function. The central puzzle provides the usual complication, which the detective hero must remove; and its difficulty insures a typically comic engagement of the intellect. The whodunit's plot, full of deceptions, red herrings, clues real and fabricated, parallels the usually intricate plots of comedy, which often depend upon mistaken motives, confusion, and dissembling; it also supports the familiar romantic subplot. And the upper class setting of the detective story places it even more precisely in the tradition of the comedy of manners.

To some the idea of murder and the tracking down of a murderer as subjects for comedy may seem at the least distasteful, whatever the setting, but as Cawelti has pointed out, "A basically comic literary universe ... can encompass a considerable degree of disorder and danger without destroying our basic sense of security."[28] The key phrase is "basically comic literary universe," one which, as will be seen, is the world of Agatha Christie's fiction. Nevertheless, there have been many objections to *overt* comedy in detective fiction, though it has been and continues to be present. A major problem for the writer of detective fiction is to find the proper balance between the form's comic universe and its serious action. Christie's usual method is to use comic characters, major and minor. They are comic both in presentation and conversation, whereas their actions are serious; Hercule Poirot is the most obvious example. To fail to see such comic, even satiric, elements which mock the foibles of the upper class as much as those of others socially beneath them in classic detective fiction is to misread the nature of the form.

The word *form* has appeared again and again in this discussion, both as a synonym for genre and for the nature or structure of that genre. The point has been repeatedly made that classical detective fiction has *form*. Because it does, the reader knows beforehand what to expect when he begins a detective novel or short story. He chooses to read it, because he has enjoyed previous ones, and he knows, though perhaps unconsciously, that it will conform to the expected pattern. The author provides what is expected and, at the same time, wishes to ring as many changes as he possibly can within the limits of the pattern, even to exploit the reader's expectations, to give his work its distinctiveness. This combination of predictability and variation is significant in detective fiction, for it involves the whole issue of form. Critics have attempted to explain, define or schematicize the general form of detective fiction by treating it as a process with distinct steps, by dividing it into principal compositional elements, or by explicating it from a particular literary-philosophical thesis. It is possible here to cover only a few such explanations, and those only very briefly. Those chosen are ones which are representative of different approaches to classical detective fiction and which, I have found, are helpful in understanding the logic and technique of Christie's fiction.

To begin with the simplest, R. Austin Freeman considers the detective novel a form of argument; there is a problem, data are given, and through logic working on those data, a solution is found. He divides the construction into four stages: "1) statement of the problem; 2) production of the data for its solution ('clues'); 3) the discovery, i.e., completion of the inquiry by the investigator and declaration by him of the solution; 4) proof of the solution by an exposition of the evidence."[29] This pattern presents only the absolute essentials of the form, the barest of bones, but it also implicitly directs attention to the variety of muscle and tissue which may be found to cover these bones. Another relatively simple analysis is that of Marie F. Rodell:

> The fact of murder presupposes: a corpse, a murderer, a motive; means and opportunity; a place.
> The factor of detection presupposes: a detective, the things on which he must work—clues, alibis, suspects; and the tools with which he detects—scientific techniques and mental ones.[30]

Her division of detective fiction into murder and detection denotes her view that the detective novel consists of two separate but connected conflicts. The second conflict, that between the detective and the murderer, is the major one, and she points out that the classic detective novel usually begins "with the inception of that conflict: the murder" (65). But always in the background is the first conflict, that between "murderer and victim which culminates in murder ... the murder is intended to be the solution" (60). The detective must logically, and imaginatively, recreate that first conflict if he is to be the victor in the second. As will be seen, much of the mystification in Christie's works is the result of her extraordinary ability to hide the true first conflict from the reader by presenting other possibilties.

A quite different approach, but one which repeats the predictability-variation concept, is that of Brigid Brophy; her interpretation is mythic: "The countless stories we generically call 'the detective story' resemble a group of myths, inasmuch as there is really only one skeleton detective story, on which detective writers invent variations consciously ... and more or less ingeniously."[31] The detective is the mythological hero who performs miracles, but he does not use magic or superhuman strength to perform them, rather "nothing but commonsense, which, however, the detective uses to an uncommon, heroic degree," and he uses it for the same purpose as the mythic "hero uses his magic powers and talismans— the deliverance of the population from a threat" (19). Perhaps "nothing but commonsense" should be replaced by "logic" or "reasoning," but in any case, it is *his mind* which enables him to deliver the innocent from suspicion and danger. Brophy also gives a rationale for the series detective. Much "as King Arthur and Robin Hood are the centers of their cycles," so the detective is the unifying force in his many cases; therefore, his eccentricities and idiosyncrasies are repeated from work to work, while the other factors, "the details and methods of the crime, must be fresh for each novel or short story" (20).

W.H. Auden's essay "The Guilty Vicarage" (1948) is also a mythic interpretation of detective fiction, but in a specifically Christian context.[32] He places much more emphasis upon the condition of order before the murder and after its solution than on the process of discovering that solution. His basic formula is another simple one: "a murder occurs; many are suspected; all but one suspect, who is the murderer, are eliminated; the murderer is arrested or dies" (400). More important to Auden than this formula is the state of the society and its members, in their relationship to Christian grace and secular law:

It must appear to be an innocent society in a state of grace, i.e., a society where there is no need of the law, no contradiction between the aesthetic individual and the ethical universal, and where murder, therefore, is the unheard-of-act which precipitates a crisis (for it reveals that some member has fallen and is no longer in a state of grace). The law becomes a reality and for a time all must live in its shadow, till the fallen one is identified. With his arrest, innocence is restored, and the law retires forever (403).

To effect this movement from grace to fall and law and then back to grace again, the author employs five elements: "the milieu, the victim, the murderer, the suspects, the detectives" (402). (As a similar organization is used for this study, comments of Auden on these elements, with the following exception, will be included if needed in the appropriate section.) For Auden, as for Brophy, the most important element is the detective, whose job it is "to restore the state of grace"; he may be of two types: "either the official representative of the ethical or the exceptional individual who is himself in a state of grace. If he is the former, he is a professional; if he is the latter, he is an amateur" (406). Christie prefers the amateur in a state of grace, Superintendent Battle being the only principal "official representative of the ethical."

In 1935 Dorothy Sayers delivered at Oxford University what might at first seem a whimsical, if not facetious, lecture entitled "Aristotle on Detective Fiction."[33] However, there is nothing facetious in her statement that "the *Poetics* remains the finest guide to the writing of detective fiction that could be put, at this day, into the hands of an aspiring author" (24-25). With the most careful reasoning, Sayers proves her case, and the result is one of the major critical works on classic detective fiction. It is so carefully reasoned that it is difficult to excerpt, but three of her points are relevant enough for the attempt to be made. First, like others, she emphasizes form. Noting Aristotle's dictum that plot must have a beginning, a middle and an end, she says, "Herein the detective story is sharply distinguished from that kind of modern novel which begins at the end, rambles backwards and forwards without particular direction and ends on an indeterminate note"; rather, the detective story begins with murder, its middle is "occupied with the detection of the crime and the various peripeties or reversals of fortune arising out of this," and it ends with "the discovery and execution of the murderer—than which nothing can very well be more final" (26). Her second point is concerned with the technique of misdirection, what she calls "The Art of Framing Lies" and Aristotle called *Paralogismos*: the ability to cause a reader to make unwarranted inferences or conclusions. Her example is worth quoting:

> Thus, at the opening of the story, the servant Jones is heard to say to his master, Lord Smith, 'Very good, my Lord, I will attend to the matter at once.' The inference is that, if Jones was speaking to Smith, Smith was also speaking to Jones; and that, therefore, Smith was alive and present at the time. But that is a false conclusion; the author made no such assertion. Lord Smith may be absent; he may already be dead; Jones may have been addressing the empty air, or some other person. Nor can we draw any safe conclusion about the attitude of Jones. If Jones is indeed present in the flesh, and not represented merely by his voice in the form of a gramophone record or similar device . . . ,then he may be addressing some other party in the belief that he is addressing Smith; he may have murdered Smith and be establishing his own alibi; or Smith may be the murderer and Jones his accomplice engaged in establishing an alibi for Smith. Nor, on the other hand, is it safe to conclude (as some experienced readers will) that *because* Smith is not heard to reply he is *not* therefore present (31-32).

Nothing could better demonstrate the wariness of thought the reader of detective fiction needs if he is not to be misled, for there is no prohibition on the writer's using multiple possibilities. Directly related to the same issue is the third point, which is Sayer's conclusive answer to the quarrel over fairness:

> Nothing in a detective story need be held to be true unless the author has vouched for it *in his own person.* Thus, if the author says:
> Jones came back at 10 o'clock,
> then we are entitled to assume that Jones did indeed come home at that time and no other. But if the author says:
> The grandfather clock was striking ten when Jones reached home,
> then we can feel no certainty as to the time of Jone's arrival, for nothing compels us to accept the testimony of the clock. Nor need we believe the testimony of any character in the story, unless the author himself vouches for that character's integrity (33).

All readers of Christie should remember this statement, for it is a kind of guidepost to her methods of mystification.

The last of the critics to be examined is John Cawelti, who has already been quoted several times. His *Adventure, Mystery, and Romance* (1976) is the most detailed and systematic analysis of detective fiction yet to appear. On a broader level, it is an exposition of a theory of formula criticism. One of Cawelti's definitions of formula fiction is "certain types of stories which have highly predictable structures that guarantee the fulfillment of conventional expectations."[34] As already indicated, classic detective fiction is a principal example of such writing. It would be futile to attempt a summary of such a long and important work in a short space, but, as with Sayers, a few of Cawelti's comments that bear directly on the nature of Golden Age detective fiction must be mentioned.

First, since by repeated reading of formula fiction, one gains a familiarity with its "world," what to expect, there is an ever increasing "capacity for understanding and enjoying the details of a work" (9). Therefore, two requirements for the success of a formulaic writer are "the ability to give new vitality to stereotypes and the capacity to invent new touches of plot or setting that are still within formulaic limits" (10-11). Needless to say, these are not easily accomplished in work after work. Christie's ability to find ever new mystifications through stereotypical characters and plots bound by the limits of the detection formula is a principal reason for her success for over half a century. Though Cawelti says that "a number of different situations, actions, characters and settings" may appear in classical detective fiction, he limits the minimal conditions for the formula to three:

> If a work does not meet these conditions, it is something else: 1) there must be a mystery, i.e., certain basic past facts about the situation and/or a number of the central characters must be

concealed from the reader and from the protagonist until the end...; 2) the story must be structured around an inquiry into these concealed facts with the inquirer as protagonist and his investigation as the central action...; 3) the concealed facts must be made known at the end (132).

Within this formula, the writer must find a balance between mystification and detection, that is, the reader may be mystified and unable to solve the crime, but he must be "able to follow the course of events with clarity and interest" (112). If the reader is excluded in any way from the detective's investigation, mystification becomes merely confusion. Cawelti uses Christie's *An Overdose of Death* as an exemplary illustration of proper and effective balance—and her *Third Girl* as an illustration of a novel which fails because of the lack of it. The final topic of Cawelti's to be mentioned is concerned specifically with the detective novel: "The major artistic problem of the longer classical detective story is how to develop additional narrative interests without dissipating the central line of the action. Or, to put the problem in reverse, how effectively does the writer construct a structure of detection-mystification that is strong and capacious enough to accommodate a variety of other interests?" (110). That additional narrative interest is the mark of the successful writer of detective fiction. It may take many forms, but whatever its type, it is what makes a reader ask for the work of a particular author. To examine Christie's methods of adding "a variety of other interests" to her fiction, while keeping its central emphasis of mystification-detection, will be a major part of this study.

A number of critics have been cited on varying elements of detective fiction. It is now necessary to draw some conclusions to serve as premises for this study. Classic detective fiction has already been defined as British detective fiction of the type written from 1920 to 1939, with the understanding that Christie, and others, continued writing the form after 1939. This definition provides limits as to place and, to a lesser degree, time. However, a more descriptive definition is required. Detective fiction includes novels and short stories written in a formulaic pattern of mystification-detection, that pattern having a high degree of predictability, but also allowing for wide variation among its elements, so long as the variations do not break the boundaries set by the pattern. The formulaic pattern of classic detective fiction differs from those of the thriller, the tough-guy or private eye novel, and the police procedural, but all of these are subsumed by the general definition: the differing patterns distinguish the various sub-genres. The pattern of classic detective fiction is characterized by *its emphasis on logic or reason* to solve disruptions in the community caused, nearly always, by single perpetrators. As corollaries to this basic pattern are ten principles (*not* rules) of the form:

1. Classic detective fiction has form.
2. The necessary characters of classic detective fiction are victim, criminal, suspects and detective. The necessary actions of the plot are crime (most often murder), investigation, and solution. The only other necessity is setting.
3. Classic detective fiction is intellectual in its construction and purpose. It requires logical thought from author, detective, and (hopefully) reader. Its intellectual nature gives it greater detachment or objectivity of presentation than any other form of popular literature.
4. Since there is a mystery to be solved, a puzzle element is always present, but it is not the totality of the work. It is a result of plot arrangement and can usually be explained, and is, in a few pages at the end. More important than the puzzle itself is the process of discovery leading to its solution, which generally requires three-fourths or more of the work.
5. The author is expected to be fair, that is, whatever is needed for the reader to solve the mystery should be available to him. This principle does not mean that the author cannot conceal, distort, or confusingly arrange the needed information; it has only to be present. The reader has the responsibility of discovering it.
6. The reader must suspect *everybody*. He must abandon trust when he enters the world of classic detective fiction. Nor can he be credulous as to apparent facts; verification is mandatory.
7. Classic detective fiction does not fall into the literary mode of realism; rather, it uses verisimilitude, realistic and plausible detail, to tell a story which more closely resembles the earlier tale than the realistic fiction of the past hundred years.
8. Classic detective fiction is basically a form of comedy in the original sense of that term. Whatever the perils of the events, all ends well, with the evil punished and the good triumphant.
9. Classic detective fiction is socially, politically, and morally conservative. It views society as fundamentally good and worth preserving for its members. When a member deliberately violates the order of society for his own purposes, it considers that that member should be rejected by the society and expelled from it.
10. The successful writer of classic detective fiction is able to develop additional narrative interests in longer works without destroying the central action of mystification and detection. These additions give a writer's work its distinctive quality.

The definition and its corollary principles provide an approach to Christie's fiction, but before that body of work can be analyzed, a few preliminary remarks on its nature and scope are necessary. Christie's productivity from *The Mysterious Affair at Styles,* written in 1915, to *Postern of Fate,* written in 1973, is astounding. She began when Conan Doyle was still writing the Sherlock Holmes stories—the last collection was 1927—and ended long after the deaths of such famous writers in the genre who started after her as Dorothy Sayers, Margery Allingham and Raymond Chandler. In the 1930s she produced seventeen novels and six collections of short stories, and between 1940 and 1945 there were eleven novels and two stage adaptations, as well as *Curtain* (publ. 1975) and *Sleeping Murder* (publ. 1976)—all in the midst of World War II. Ignoring other works of poetry, drama, romantic and supernatural fiction, and autobiography, she produced 184 works of detection or mystery, plus joining in the collaborative effort of The Detection Club, entitled *The Floating Admiral* (1932), for which she wrote the fourth chapter. Dividing her works of detection by the detective present, the distribution is as follows:

|  | Novels | Short Stories |
|---|---|---|
| Hercule Poirot | 33 | 52 * |
| Jane Marple | 12 | 20 |
| Tuppence & Tommy Beresford | 5** | 0 |
| Superintendent Battle | 4 *** | 0 |
| Harley Quin | 0 | 14 |
| Parker Pyne | 0 | 14 |
| No series detective | 13 | 17 **** |
|  | 67 | 117 |

*There are a pair of identical Poirot short stories published under different names: "The Theft of the Royal Ruby" and "The Adventure of the Christmas Pudding."
**The Tuppence and Tommy adventures in *Partners in Crime* are a series of related stories set in a frame. It is more practical, however, to consider the work an episodic novel.
***Superintendent Battle also appears in *Cards on the Table,* but there Poirot is the principal detective.
****Two other pairs of identical stories published under different names are "Mr. Eastwood's Adventure" and "The Mystery of the Spanish Shawl," and "Where There's a Will" and "Wireless."

As a *general* rule, Christie's novels are better than her short stories. She perhaps realized this fact, for she stated, "The short story technique, I think, is not really suited to the detective story at all. A thriller, possibly—but a detective story, no."[35] The space limitations of the short story do not allow for the complex mystification which was Christie's forte. Nor, since the crime in short stories is often something other than murder, does the problem and its solution reach the same level of intensity as in a novel of murder. Her longer short stories are almost always better than the shorter ones. A comparison of "The Submarine Plans" and "The Incredible Theft"—the same story, but in the second version quadrupled in length—provides a striking illustration of this tendency. At the same time, her novels are relatively short. Her preference was for them to be even shorter, but she bowed to her publisher's and her public's wishes:

I think myself that the *right* length for a detective story is fifty-thousand words. I know this is considered by publishers as too short. Possibly readers feel themselves cheated if they pay their money and only get fifty thousand words—so sixty thousand or seventy thousand are more acceptable. If your book runs to more than that I think you will usually find that it would have been better if it had been shorter.[36]

She could complete such a novel in about six weeks. During most of her career, she worked directly at the typewriter; in the last years the books were dictated into a machine given her by Collins, her British publisher. Her early writing was done for money; as she has ingenuously said,

The nice part about writing in those days was that I directly related it to money.... This stimulated my output enormously. I said to myself, 'I should like to take the conservatory down and fit it up as a loggia in which we could sit. How much will that be?' I got my estimate, I went to the typewriter, I sat, thought, planned and within a week a story was formed in my mind. In due course I wrote it, and then I had my loggia.³⁷

Later she came to take pride in her work, or at least in its success. She very rarely accepted advice about a work, refusing to make changes even when suggested by her immediate family. Similarly, when she was asked to allow an abridgement of *The Body in the Library* to be published, her reply was that "she felt making an abridged version of a creative author's book was like mutilating his brainchild."³⁸ Though she often told interviewers that "I am a lowbrow," she knew that she was also a craftsman and that her craft had made her the most popular writer of the century—no small accomplishment.

Her popularity and the mass of her works allow for numerous ways of dividing and classifying her fiction. The method used here, by the detective, is an obvious and simple one. Some years ago C.H.B. Kitchin presented a different classification, one which indicates the range of her work and provides an appropriate conclusion to this introduction.³⁹ Kitchin found five Agatha Christies: the seeker of thrills, the philosopher, the archaeologist and traveller, the sociologist, and the world citizen. Her thrillers, and the heroines in them, he describes as "daring, resourceful, absurd and not above a bit of burlesque." An accurate description; Christie herself refers to " 'the light-hearted thriller type.' These were always easy to write, not requiring too much plotting and planning."⁴⁰ The Tuppence and Tommy novels and all of those with "bright young people" as detectives (e.g., *The Seven Dials Mystery, The Secret of Chimneys, Why Didn't They Ask Evans?*), are works of this Christie, as are such spy novels as *The Big Four* and *Passenger to Frankfurt*. More overtly comic than the others, this Christie is the one most often disparaged. The second Christie is "the gentle philosopher—fey, melancholy and now and again Barriesque... she has no complete book to her credit, though she wrote the greater part of *The Mysterious Mr. Quin*. But she lends a hand to her more robust rivals." The Quin stories are engagingly unique, but personally I am glad that this Christie was usually recessive. An entirely fey detective novel would be intolerable. As for the travelled archaeologist, Kitchin says, "I think we must hold her entirely responsible for *Death Comes as the End* and *They Came to*

*Baghdad,* and we cannot ignore her collaboration in many books by her namesakes—such as *Death on the Nile, Appointment With Death* and ... *Destination Unknown.*" Christie's trips with her archaeologist husband to digs in the Middle East provided the background not only for these, but also such other novels as *Murder in Mesopotamia,* as well as a number of short stories. The fourth Christie is "the observer of English middle-class life—especially in the character of Miss Marple." Kitchin rather limits this Christie. This writer-persona is without question the most important, for in all the works which take place in England, and they are the majority, life in that country can be traced from World War I to the Swinging 'Sixties. Finally, there is "Christie, the cosmpolitan woman of the world. Unlike Mrs. Christie the Third, she is interested not in places but in people." Kitchin only mentions two works by this Christie: *A Murder Is Announced,* which could as easily be by the fourth, and *Murder on the Orient Express,* which was also the result of the trips to the Middle East. The fact is that the fourth and fifth Christies are really one, for it was her cosmopolitanism which enabled her to observe her own society so closely.

Kitchin's categories are partially fanciful and arguable, but they do demonstrate Christie's range of subject and emphasis—a range many more critically acclaimed writers might envy. His five Christies were contained in one person, a half-American English lady who for nearly sixty years in 184 works cultivated the gentle art of murder, and so succeeded that she has been read in 103 languages by hundreds of millions all over the world. Perhaps that success can never be fully explained, but the attempt can be made to understood what she did and—to an extent—how she did it.

# Chapter II

## Setting

*High-class advertisers have long known her rule of work: keep the background innocuous if you want your product to stand out.*

**Nigel Dennis**

*...nor do we want a description of scenery when the only thing that matters to us is to decide exactly how long it takes us to walk from the boat-house above the mill-race to the gamekeeper's cottage on the other side of the coppice.*

**Somerset Maugham**

*...she tells more about what happened to England since the First World War than* The Times— *either of London or New York. That quick and unerring eye for the homely detail is worth volumes of social history.*

**Emma Lathen**

Among critics of detective fiction, there is a clear division of thought on setting. One group desires a careful delineation of locale inextricably linked to the action; the other group wants as little physical description as possible. Christie's work has always appealed more to the second group, while being often attacked for its bland backgrounds by the first. In explaining why she gave up attempts to become a sculptor, Christie said, "I had no eye for visual forms.... I realized I couldn't really *see* things."[1] She was being modest, for she did *see* things. But certainly descriptions of natural scenery do not play a large part in her work. Her attitude is that of her narrator in *The Man in the Brown Suit*: 'I guarantee no genuine local color—you know the sort of thing—half a dozen words in italics on every page. I admire it very much, but I can't do it" (107). Nor does she often place her stories in specialized milieus—the lawyer's office, the theatre, the university—where the action is integral to the locale. The major exception is *Murder in Mesopotamia*, which takes place at an Iraqi archaeological dig, and that was the result of personal experience. Her usual method is to sketch the physical scene quickly, leaving it to the reader to fill in the details as his imagination desires. The setting is never obtrusive; it is not mere decoration or filler, which is allowed to distract from the central action of mystification-detection. She does not attempt, as some other writers do, "to conceal a shaky plot behind a screen of

21

scenery," the danger of which is "that what begins as a detective story wind[s] up as a travel guide."[2] Rather, in her work plot occurs in a place, but the place is never equal in importance to the plot occurring there. The atmosphere of her stories is much more the result of the societal milieu—made up of the characters, their level of society, their way of life, amusements, activities, attitudes, etc.— than of the physical locale. Though it is impossible to consider the two as completely discrete, they demand separate examination.

## The Physical Scene

Though the specific locales in Christie's work vary, her favorite type of setting is the isolated one, what has come to be called "the closed circle." She employs it within all five of her principal settings: foreign, in transit, London, the village and the country house. The advantages of a limited space isolated for the action of a detective story are several. It limits the number of suspects, for the murderer from outside—the ubiquitous "It must have been a tramp"—is easily excluded. At the same time, all of those present in the closed circle can become suspects, for generally known to one another, they offer a multiplicity of motives. In other words, the spatial boundaries of the problem are defined. Besides this almost classical unity of place, the closed circle also can, if the author desires, provide the classical unity of time; this occurs particularly when the detective is amateur, for the isolation frees him from the rules and regulations of official police procedure and enables him to solve the case much more quickly. The closed circle also emphasizes the abnormality of the crime by isolating it from the everyday matters of the world around it. The focus is solely on the crime and its detection. Finally, being out of that everyday world, cut off from usual concerns, creates tension and suspense. Nerves become frazzled, tempers flare and spirits flag, for a murderer is loose and "one of us."

Christie's closed circle settings range from an airplane in flight (*Death in the Clouds*) to an island off England's south coast (*Evil Under the Sun*), from a snowbound guesthouse ("Three Blind Mice") to a riverboat journey (*Death on the Nile*), from a London card party (*Cards on the Table*) to the numerous houseparties in the country (*Murder After Hours, Towards Zero, The Seven Dials Mystery*, etc.). Such a setting may be the result of a family gathering (*Hercule Poirot's Christmas*), geographic isolation (*Appointment With Death*), or a group of strangers brought together by *apparent* chance (*And Then There Were None*). In the last category is *Murder on the Orient Express*, but it also involves geographic isolation, a snowbound train in Yugoslavia, and, as it turns out, an unusual kind of family gathering. This novel is a perfect illustration of the following statement about the train in detective fiction: "The train is a universe of its own. It is confined, remote and comfortable.... The train journey has shape...: within a time scale the crime will be perpetuated, discovered and solved.... It is very tidy."[3] Very tidy indeed—the entire system of a closed society is encapsulated. The snow traps all persons on the train to its confines. The outside world is eliminated. The murderer has to be on the train. Evidence cannot be destroyed. Tension mounts. Hercule Poirot is in charge until help, and the police, arrive; the others can only submit to his interrogation and await his solution. Naturally, he solves the case before the outside world reenters the next day to end the isolation of this closed circle *par excellence.*

With this emphasis on the closed society, it is not surprising that Christie gives more attention to interior description than to exterior. Outside is the great world; inside is the world of death and detection. The natural world plays little part in the unnatural happenings of her detectival world. Therefore, time is not wasted on describing it. A scene is limned in a sentence: "Warmsley Heath consists of a golf course, two hotels, some very expensive modern villas giving onto the golf course, a row of what were, before the war, luxury shops, and a railway station" (Tide, 19). We know where we are; that is enough. On that sketch, we must imaginatively develop the fully colored painting. Similarly, though she is noted for her repeated use of country houses in her works, Christie does not linger over their exteriors: Garston Hall "was a large solidly built house with no special architectural pretensions" (*Christmas*, 153), "Enderby Hall was a vast Victorian house built in the Gothic style" (Funerals, 1), "Anstell Manor had a bleak aspect. It was a white house set against a background of bleak hills. A winding drive led up through a dense shrubbery" (Sleeping, 139). A few generalized details and then on to the events inside: such is her practice. She may even omit description altogether, as in *The Secret of Chimneys*: "It is also No. 3 in *Historic Homes of England*, price 21s. On Thursdays, char-a-bancs come over from Middlingham and view those portions of it which are open to the public. In view of all these facilities, to describe Chimneys would be superfluous" (73). When she does present more detail, the description still has a quality of generality; for example, the description of Sunny Ridge, a home for the elderly in *By the Pricking of My Thumbs*:

How Sunny Ridge had come by its name would be difficult to say. There was nothing prominently ridgelike about it. The grounds were flat, which was eminently more suitable for the elderly occupants. It had an ample though rather undistinguished garden. It was a fairly large

Victorian mansion kept in a good state of repair. There were some pleasant shady trees, a Virginia creeper running up the side of the house, and two monkey puzzles gave an exotic air to the scene. There were several benches in advantageous places to catch the sun, one or two garden chairs and a sheltered verandah on which the old ladies could sit sheltered from east winds (12).

The only exceptions to such slight exterior descriptions are those of her villages.

While more extensive, Christie's interiors are not just descriptive verbage. Although she enjoyed decorating houses and did so often, her fictional interiors are nearly always functional: they are used to characterize their owners. Occasionally the descriptions are mildly satiric, as in "ye olde cottage" of the Misses Tripp of *Poirot Loses a Client*, the chaotic parlor of Maureen Summerhayes of *Mrs. McGinty's Dead*, or the various tearooms, such as the Buttercup of *The Clocks*, which "lived up to its name by being violently and aggressively yellow. Formica table tops, plastic cushions and cups and saucers were all canary colour" (162). They may also be ironic, creating a kind of disjunction between the character and his domestic environment. The following description of a small city garden (admittedly an exterior, but certainly domestic) is hardly the surroundings one would expect for a man who turns out to be a villain: "It was indeed a model of suburban perfection in a small way. There were beds of geraniums with lobelia edging. There were large fleshy-looking begonias, and there was a fine display of garden ornaments—frogs, toadstools, comic gnomes and pixies" (Clocks, 62). Likewise, the description of the parlor of a successful satiric lady dramatist clashes with her shrewd nature:

The room ... had walls of a rather drab oatmeal colour with a fringe of labernum around the top. The curtains were of rose-coloured velvet, there were lots of photographs and china dogs, the telephone was coyly hidden by a lady with ruffled skirts, there were a great many little tables and some suspicious looking brasswork from Birmingham via the Far East (Tragedy, 187).

Obviously such irony can be used, and is by Christie, for authorial trickery.

More often the descriptions are straightforward presentations of character. Two examples from *Towards Zero* can illustrate (the first, of a schoolmistress's office, shows again Christie's liking for oatmeal-colored walls):

Her room was representative of the spirit of Meadway. Everything was of a cool oatmeal colour—there were big jars of daffodils and bowls of tulips and hyacinths. One or two good copies of the antique Greek, two pieces of advanced modern sculpture, two Italian primitives on the walls. In the midst of all this, Miss Amphrey herself...(22).

Thomas Royde's room was untidy, with clothes lying about. Pipes and pipe ash on the tables and beside the bed, where a copy of Kipling's *Kim* lay half open.

"Used to native servants clearing up after him," said Battle. "Likes reading old favorites. Conservative type" (148).

A final illustration is the elderly Miss Emily Arundell's drawing-room in *Poirot Loses a Client*. It indicates the greater amount of specific details in Christie's interiors, but also the fact that they are still brief and selective and that their purpose is to give a sense of the inhabitant's personality:

> The drawing-room conjured up memories of the past. A faint fragrance of pot-pourri hung about it. The chintzes were worn, their pattern faded garlands of roses. On the walls were prints and water-colour drawings. There was a good deal of china—fragile shepherds and shepherdesses. There were cushions worked in crewel stitch. There were faded photographs in handsome silver frames. There were many inlaid workboxes and tea caddies. Most fascinating of all to me were two exquisitely cut tissue-paper ladies under glass stands. One with a spinning-wheel, one with a cat on her knee (50).

Another aspect of setting is the employment of maps or plans. Emile Gaboriau was supposedly the first writer of detective fiction to include a map of the crime site. Christie followed the practice, particularly in her early work. The intent of such a map is to create greater verisimilitude: the place exists in space; here is where it happened. Again, most of the maps are plans of interiors: a house or a single room. The few exceptions are of such places as the village of St. Mary Mead in *Murder at the Vicarage*, the area around Sunny Point in *Towards Zero*, and Smuggler's Island in *Evil Under the Sun*, or of such conveyances as the boat *The Karnak* in *Death on the Nile*, the rear compartment of the airplane *Prometheus* in *Death in the Clouds*, and the Athens-Paris Coach in *Murder on the Orient Express*; these latter also interiors. The expedition house at the tell in *Murder in Mesopotamia*, Styles Court and Mrs. Inglethorp's bedroom in *The Mysterious Affair at Styles*, and the house (and grounds) and the library in *The Murder of Roger Ackroyd* are typical of Christie's floorplans. They are used to "help" the reader see the action, but they are also used to puzzle or confuse him by indicating the apparent impossibility of the crime having been committed as it actually was. The maps add to the sense of isolation and are, in fact, related to the locked-room ploy, for they pose the question: it was done, but how could it have been?

Still another of Christie's methods of verisimilitude is repetition of places. By familiarity from earlier works, the reader "knows" the scene. However, the more significant reason for such repetition is to be able to bring back characters from earlier works. The Miss Marple stories set in St. Mary Mead are the obvious examples, but there are others, such as the village of Chipping Cleghorn which is the site of "Sanctuary" and *A Murder Is Announced*. The town of Market Basing, which is supposedly one and a half hours by car from London and near both St. Mary Mead and Chimneys, must have a higher incidence of crime in its vicinity than any other fictional town in England. It appears or is referred to in both novels and short stories over and over. Also, the country houses of Styles Court and Chimneys each appear twice: in *The Mysterious Affair at Styles* and *Curtain* and in *The Secret of Chimneys* and *The Seven Dials Mystery* respectively. Combined with the repeated characters, the repeated places create a self-contained world, one with its own geography. Related to this technique is the number of pubs, inns and cafes which are so conspicuously present and whose names run together in a blur of colors and animals: the Blue Boar, the Golden Boar, the Three Boars, the Red Cow, the Black Swan, the Green Swan, the Ginger Cat, the Blue Cat, the Blue Dog, the Blue Tit, the Bluebird, etc. There is a sense of familiarity, if not *deja vu*, when one comes upon another of them. Perhaps this sense is one cause of Christie's work being labelled "cosy"; in any case, her England *is* a small and intimate one.

The intimacy is to a large extent the result of Christie's sticking to the world she knew. As Emma Lathen has written, "Refined creative instinct, or a lot of horse sense, saved Christie from the fatal error of sending Hercule Poirot to New York, or Miss Marple to Washington, D.C."[4] New York and Washington were not known to her; her five major settings were, and personally so. She had travelled in Europe and the Mideast, she had lived in London and among the upper middleclass of the southern counties. Her autobiography and her husband's memoirs provide the sources of many of her settings. She and her mother lived for a winter in Egypt, and she later visited it with Mallowan, thus supplying *Death on the Nile* and "Death on the Nile." "The House at Shiraz" and "The Pearl of Price" resulted from visits to Iran and Petra. The girl's school in *Cat Among the Pigeons* seems to be based on Caledonia, her daughter Rosalind's school. Bertram's Hotel is actually Brown's Hotel. Her first country home at Sunningdale, where luxurious modern houses were built around golf courses, became the Baydon Heath of *A Pocket Full of Rye,* the Swinley Dean of *Crooked House*, and Warmsley Heath of *There is a Tide.* Greenway House, her white Georgian home on the Dart River in Devon, was transformed into Nasse House of *Dead Man's Folly* and Alderbury of *Murder in Retrospect.* Mallowan says that the coastal scene of *Towards Zero* is "the estuary at Salcombe—the Yealme in which all the landmarks are discernible" (again in Devon, a short distance from Greenway House), and that the accursed field Gipsy's Acre of *Endless Night* "was pointed out to Agatha on a Welsh moorland and made a deep impression."[5] Typically, Christie moved Gipsy's Acre from Wales to southeast England. Even such a small scene as the smoke-filled room of Colonel Pikeaway, the intelligence chief of *Passenger to Frankfurt* and *Postern of Fate*, has its source in her husband's office at the Air Ministry during World War II, where smoking was incessant. These few illustrations demonstrate the extent to which Christie's fictional England was the England she knew. In fact, it was the England of London and the counties south and southwest of that city, especially her own Devon.

The works set in London are dominated by the Poirot novels. Eleven are set wholly or principally there, ranging from the early *Lord Edgware Dies* to the late *Third Girl*. Otherwise there are two early Tuppence and Tommy novels (*The Secret Adversary* and *Partners in Crime*), one Miss Marple (*At Bertram's Hotel*) and one other (*Remembered Death*). Many other novels are at least partly in London, and the short stories taking place there, especially those of Poirot and Parker Pyne, are numerous. Murder is rampant in Christie's London, even though, in actuality, as late as the 1950s, murders in London never numbered more than forty per year. The romance of the big city offers many opportunities for scenic development in solving the murders, but Christie rarely accepts that offer. She prefers to concentrate on a closed circle within the city, as with the student hostel in *Hickory Dickory Death*, the card party of *Cards on the Table*, or the restaurant gathering of *Remembered Death*. Miss Marple's exercise in nostalgia, *At Bertram's Hotel*, does allow for much description, but what is described turns out to be fake, in reality an element of the plot. Though there is more movement and more varied locales in these works than in those of the village or the country house, Christie still chooses to emphasize a small, particular world within the macrocosm of the city.

The second principal setting is the village of southern England, whose pastoral element fulfills the closed circle concept even more strongly than her London. The village is physically small; has a definite, often rigid, social structure; and is "isolated" from the great world. In addition, everyone is acquainted; when murder occurs, friends suddenly become threatening strangers, normal routine is shattered, and horror is engendered by the sheer outrageousness of crime in such a peaceful and bucolic environment. Additionally, the village as setting has an appeal of its own. Colin Watson has said of such a setting, "It offered not outward escape, as did books of travel, adventure, international intrigue, but inward—into a sort of museum of nostalgia."[6] A valid statement, but one must add, as Miss Marple so often does, that evil things can and do happen in that "museum of nostalgia," the village.

The Miss Marple stories form the largest group in this category; nearly all of the works in which she appears involve her village of St. Mary Mead to some extent, and many occur solely there. Perhaps surprisingly, the number of other predominantly village works is small. Poirot has only four cases in English villages: *The Murder of Roger Ackroyd, Poirot Loses a Client, Mrs. McGinty's Dead* and *Hallowe'en Party*. Tuppence and Tommy have two: *By the Pricking of My Thumbs* and *Postern of Fate*. There are only three others: *Murder at Hazelmoor, Easy to Kill* (particularly good for the description of Wychwood Under Ashe), and *The Pale Horse*. Of course, villages are part of a number of other novels, as well as short stories, but most of the time they serve as a backdrop to the English country house.

Christie's favorite setting is the country house, and she has been criticized for repeating it so often. Her answer to such criticism was firm:

> But the one thing that infuriates me is when people complain that I always set my books in country houses. You *have* to be concerned with a house: with where people *live*. You can make it an hotel, or a train, or a pub—but it's got to be where people are brought together. And I think it must be a background that readers will recognize, because explanations are so boring. If you set a detective story in, say, a laboratory, I don't think people will enjoy it so much. No, a country house is obviously the best.[7]

The phrase "Explanations are so boring" can serve as Christie's motto for setting and for her avoidance of the specialized in favor of the familiar. The familiarity of the country house lulls the reader by its beauty, its civility and its remoteness from the hustle and bustle of the everyday world. Murder in such a setting creates the same shock as it does in the village. Physically, the large house and grounds provide within a limited area many places for crime to be committed. (The library seems by far the most popular spot for murder.) There is also the space to collect an often disparate—and sometimes desperate—group of people for a weekend houseparty or family gathering. Like the village so often near it, the country house is the epitome of a stable society plunged into fear by crime and requiring the outsider, the detective, to restore its normality.

Omitting short sequences at such houses, there are still a great many major examples. The Miss Marple novels contain, for example, Gossington Hall (*The Body in the Library*), Stonygates (*They Do It With Mirrors*), and Yewtree Lodge (*A Pocket Full of Rye*). An even larger number appear in the Poirot novels; in fact, thirteen of his thirty-three cases take place wholly or in great part at various country houses. His first and last cases occur at Styles Court

(*The Mysterious Affair at Styles* and *Curtain*), and between these two are such others as End House of *Peril at End House*, Garston Hall of *Hercule Poirot's Christmas*, and Nasse House of *Dead Man's Folly*. Among the other detectives, three of Superintendent Battle's cases are at country houses: Chimneys of both *The Secret of Chimneys* and *The Seven Dials Mystery* and Gull's Point of *Towards Zero*, and there are several Harley Quin stories, but the country houses of the rich play little part in the Tuppence and Tommy or Parker Pyne works. Among the novels without a series detective, the three most significant country houses are Sunny Point in *Ordeal by Innocence*, Three Gables in *Crooked House*, and the house on Gipsy's Acre in *Endless Night*. The short stories are filled with them—far too many to list.

The works which take place in transit require little comment, as the already discussed *Murder on the Orient Express* is a prime illustration of this relatively small group. There are three other novels: *Death on the Nile*, *Death in the Clouds* and *The Mystery of the Blue Train*. The six short stories in which crime takes place or a mystery occurs in transit include four on trains ("The Girl in the Train"; "Plymouth Express," an earlier prototype of *The Mystery of the Blue Train*; "The Case of the City Clerk"; and "Have You Got Everything You Want?") and two on boats ("Death on the Nile" and "Problem at Sea"). It should be noted that these works overlap with the other categories, in that they take place either in England or foreign countries, but the emphasis of setting in them is more on the means of travel than on the place of travel. All fulfill the closed circle setting. There are also three other novels in which travel plays a significant part. A murder is seen as one train passes another in *What Mrs. McGillicuddy Saw!*; Miss Marple is on a coach tour of homes and gardens when murder occurs in *Nemesis*; and in the thriller *So Many Steps to Death*, a young woman travels from England to a mysterious scientific complex hidden in the vastness of North Africa—but in this last case the only murder has been committed before the novel begins.

The last principal category of setting includes those works set outside England. Some novels have extended sections occurring elsewhere, such as *The Big Four, Cat Among the Pigeons*, and *Passenger to Frankfurt*, but they do not really belong to this group, for the events in England are the core of the work. Aside from these, and such in transit novels as *Death on the Nile*, there are seven novels and seventeen short stories in the foreign group. Miss Marple appears only in *A Caribbean Mystery* and "The Companion"; the latter takes place in the Canary Islands while Miss Marple solves it sitting in St. Mary Mead. Poirot is in three foreign novels—*Murder on the Links* in France and *Murder in Mesopotamia* and *Appointment with Death*, both in the Middle East—and eight short stories, five of them in *The Labours of Hercules*, which occur in Switzerland, Belgium, France, Ireland, Greece and "Herzoslovakia." The Poirot "Triangle at Rhodes" is later moved from that Italian controlled Greek isle to the English south coast and becomes Smuggler's Island of *Evil Under the Sun*. Three Harley Quin stories occur in France, on Corsica, and on an unnamed Mediterranean island, and five Parker Pyne stories occur on his tour through the Middle East and the Mediterranean. Two thrillers are also included: *The Man in the Brown Suit* (South Africa) and *They Came to Baghdad* (Iraq). Finally, there is Christie's curiosity, *Death Comes as the End,* which is set in ancient Egypt.

France, the Mediterranean and the Middle East are the foreign areas most often appearing, and again Christie's use of the world she knew is evident. Her travels with Mallowan on his archaeological expeditions gave her the knowledge necessary to place her detective fiction in these locales. Her love of the Middle East, so enthusiastically evident in her autobiographical *Come, Tell Me How You Live*, makes the works set there the most significant sub-group of this category, for she provides more description in them than in any of the others. Yet, though the exoticism of these works is quite different from the familiarity of the English works, Christie still continues to create closed circle societies, no matter what the country.

To repeat, these five principal settings, the closed circle societies within them, the techniques of verisimilitude and repetition, the sketchy use of formal description—especially of external nature, and the use of only personally acquired knowledge make up the scenic element of Christie's fiction. It is a case of her limiting herself to the essentials, only what is needed for the action to take place.

## The Social Setting

Agatha Christie belonged to the English upper middleclass, and the world of this class forms the social scene of her fiction. As with physical setting, she avoided what she had not experienced. She once said, "I could never manage miners talking in pubs, because I don't know what miners talk about in pubs."[8] Therefore, she did not write about miners in pubs, but about the class and the social world which she knew firsthand. Her values were those of her class: trust in reason, desire for stability, belief in civilized conduct, faith in property and a strong sense of morality. Basically conservative in wishing to preserve its world, but almost

continuously having to adjust to drastic change, the English upper
middleclass provided Christie a known social structure for her
mysteries, and they are a record of both the attitudes of that class
and the changes with which it had to cope from the 1920s to the
1970s.

Social forms and attitudes are integral to the action of the
classic detective story. Christie uses them as a framework of cause
and effect to make explicable the actions of her characters. They act
as they do because of the social class to which they belong (this is as
true of the murderers as of any of the others).[9] The party of
*Hallowe'en Party* with its traditional games—broomstick
competition, flour cake, lover-mirrors, snapdragon and bobbing for
apples—is not just social background, but also an opportunity and a
means for murder. The charity fete in *Dead Man's Folly*, with its
booths and murder game, serves the same purpose. One of Christie's
better, but little known, short stories, "The Incredible Theft," opens
with an extended description of seven houseparty guests at dinner.
The dinner is used to introduce these characters, one of whom is a
spy, but in the midst of these introductions, the social forms are
described:

> As the butler handed round the souffle Lord Mayfield leaned confidentially towards his
> neighbor on the right, Lady Julia Carrington. Known as a perfect host, Lord Mayfield took
> trouble to live up to his reputation.
> \* \* \*
> Round the table, moving silently in the subdued amber light, a butler and two footmen offered
> dishes and filled up wine glasses. Lord Mayfield paid a very high salary to his chef, and was noted
> as a connoisseur of wines.
> The table was a round one, but there was no mistaking who was the host....
> \* \* \*
> The dessert had been placed on the table. The port had circulated once. Catching Mrs.
> Vanderlyn's eye, Lady Julia rose. The three women left the room.
> The port passed around once more, and Lord Mayfield referred lightly to pheasants. The
> conversation for five minutes or so was sporting (3 & 4).

Poirot's solution to the disappearance of bomber plans later the
same evening is the result of his understanding the social forms
followed by these diners; the same is true of many other cases.

Christie is not completely admiring of the social forms; there is
much satire, albeit mild, of the pretension or excess of them. In *Sad
Cypress* Poirot gains acceptance by Mrs. Bishop, a very snobbish
woman, by recounting his recent visit to the royal family at
Sandringham, and they then discuss "the selection of a suitable
future husband for the Princess [Elizabeth]" (118). The elegant
Abernethies of *Funerals Are Fatal* possess a fortune based on the
success of Coral Cornplasters. On a different level, there are the
newspapers and magazines read by Christie's characters, which

seem to be straight from Evelyn Waugh: the Daily Blare, the Daily Newsmonger, the Daily Flicker, the Daily Blague, the Evening Shout, the Weekly Howl, X-Ray News, the Low Down Review, and the indispensable North Benham News and Chipping Cleghorn Gazette. Also, as will be seen, many characters are satirized for rigidity in their social codes. At the same time, Christie obviously felt nostalgia for earlier times when life was simpler and change was not so rapid. Her grandson, Mathew Prichard, has been quoted as commenting on this nostalgia: "She was not really comfortable with the modern age.... She longed for the golden twilight of the Victorian era and its leisurely way of life."[10] There can be little doubt of the truth of this assessment, but it needs to be balanced by recognition of her sensitivity to change and her desire to keep up with the times. In 1970 she asked her publisher to send her a series of works by "Modern Masters," "because she felt that Alexander *must* have an intelligent great-grandmother. The series includes such writers as Freud, Fanon, Chomsky and Wittgenstein. Alexander's great-grandmother was then eighty."[11] Thus, there is a dual, even contradictory, quality in Christie's personality, which is reflected in her presentation of the social scene: a nostalgia for a gracious past, with a clear-eyed amusement at its follies, and an acceptance, however regretful, of the necessity for change.

Christie's acceptance of and amusement at her class and its social norms can lead to puzzlement by those separated by time and distance from them. With tongue in cheek, Emma Lathen, the pseudonym for a successful pair of American mystery writers, has expressed that puzzlement:

Who counts as young, who counts as old? Above all, when do people retire?...what is [an American] to make of all those fifty-year-old men, coming home to marry and start families as country gentlemen of leisure....

...What in the world do these people do, day in, day out? The men, including the ex-Empire-builders, are equipped with studies to which they regularly retire. For what purpose is never made clear. The ladies, lamenting the loss of pre-war domestic staffs, are all sustained by chars, foreign help and village girls.... As for children, apparently they pack their bags for school as soon as they can walk.[12]

The major reason for such questions is Christie's belief that "explanations are so boring." The characters are of their class, which defines them, and they are involved in a crime; for Christie, that is enough. Continued reading of her fiction generally transforms puzzlement to familiarity and acceptance of her characters' way of life, so that it becomes a "given" of her work. But even she commented on how different that pre-World War II society appeared from the perspective of a later time: "When I re-read those first ones I'm amazed at the amount of *servants* drifting about. And nobody is really doing any work. They're always having tea on the lawn like in E.F. Benson. It gives one great nostalgia for the past."[13] Nostalgia, yes, for that world is gone forever, but combined with the nostalgia is the realization, indicated by the reference to Benson's frothy novels, that it is the result of a rose-colored view of a past that was never quite as idyllic as she and so many others painted it.

Houses of the wealthy were staffed by a quantity of servants during the interwar period to a degree difficult to imagine today. Christie's autobiography is filled with details of her own family's servants, their coming and leaving, problems with some, and so on. In her fiction, the legion of butlers, cooks, gardeners, valets, chauffeurs, footmen and assorted maids—lady's, parlor, upstairs, downstairs, and kitchen—are the living embodiment of the country house; they attest to the social position of their employers. Rarely, however, do they play any significant role in the action. They discover corpses, scream and "go all queer," and undergo interrogation, but that is about all, unless, of course, they become victims. If so, they are barely mourned: "Can't even remember what the girl looked like, although I suppose she's opened the door to me dozens of times. Quiet, insignificant little thing" (Finger, 172). Admittedly there is a basic snobbery toward servants in such a statement, and it is present in nearly all of the upper class characters, probably a reflection of the real life situation, but snobbery is also present among the servants. In a number of cases, however, there is respect for and dependence upon a valued servant. Obvious instances are Miss Marple's Florence, Tuppence and Tommy's Albert and Poirot's Georges, the last being an even greater snob than his master. Because so many of Christie's works are set among the upper middleclass, one can trace the decline in the number of family servants in England as clearly as by a statistical table. The large establishments dwindle to one or two all-purpose domestics, even among the rich. The difference between the staff at Styles Court in 1920 and the single elderly servant of the Old Manor House of *Nemesis* in 1971 is representative of what happened to the upper middle class in England over that half century.

Snobbery and narrow chauvinism, even xenophobia, have been called characteristic of the interwar English upper classes, and the detective fiction of the period has been accused of fostering those attitudes. Certainly the lower classes are treated similarly to the servants. Working people—small tradesmen, landladies, yeoman farmers, etc.—often "talk funny," meaning ungrammatically. Education, or lack of it, was a part of class distinction, and, although it may make a reader of today uncomfortable, incorrect or non-standard English was an accepted sign of one's lower place on the social scale. Christie follows the practice and, therefore, can be accused of snobbery, but it must be noted that she never makes such persons guilty of murder; that is left to their "betters." In regard to foreigners, Christie allows her characters to express narrow prejudice, but nearly always with some attached disclaimer.[14] Seldom does she as author develop a character from what might be called xenophobia—the most flagrant and unpleasant exception is the racism inherent in the presentation of Mr. Akibombo in *Hickory Dickory Death*. More typical is the anti-semitism of the unlikeable Ronald Edgware in *Lord Edgware Dies*, where one expects prejudice from a character with so many other faults. When a sympathetic character is guilty of such an attitude, it is covered as individual animus. Inspector Bland in *Dead Man's Folly* provides an illustration: "Although he had none of Constable Hoskins' ingrained prejudice against foreigners, Inspector Bland took an instant dislike to Etienne De Sousa. The polished elegance of the young man, his sartorial perfection, the rich flowery smell of his brilliantined hair, all combined to annoy the Inspector" (81). Here snobbery is conjoined with both masculine and nationalistic chauvinism. Stereotyping is also prevalent in her early depictions of Americans. Though half-American herself, she knew few Americans. Those appearing in her early works are always rich and have such names as Julius P. Hersheimmer, Lucius C. Gott, Odell C. Gardner and Rufus Van Aldin. Happily, she gradually abandoned such caricatures, either replacing them with English types or creating less trite examples, such as the dignified Andrew Lippincott of *Endless Night*. Christie, like most of her major characters, was of her class; she never escaped from it—she neither wanted nor tried to—and so the prejudices of that class do occasionally appear in her fiction. What must be emphasized is that she was craftsman enough to suppress them to the extent that readers of all classes and nationalities have responded to other elements and never been troubled by those prejudices that do appear.

As simply a record of a half century of English life, Christie's fiction abounds with the small details which make up social history. As an example, the thoughts of Colin Lamb, in *The Clocks*, demonstrate Christie's careful observation of ordinary social habits:

There were few people about, a couple of boys on bicycles passed me, two women with shopping bags. The houses themselves might have been embalmed like mummies for all the signs of life there were in them. I knew why that was. It was already, or close upon, the sacred hour of one, an hour sanctified by English tradition to the consuming of a midday meal.... Either the windows were discreetly screened with nylon netting, as opposed to the once popular Nottingham lace, or—which was far more probable—anyone who was at home was eating in the "modern" kitchen, according to the custom of the 1960s (174 & 175).

Numerous other examples could be given of the same close observation, but it is perhaps as a record of change that her works will be most valuable to the social historian. She recounts the movement from Fred Astaire and Ginger Rogers to Eddie Presweight, a rock singer; from the Spanish Civil War and the Imperial Shirts, "they march with banners and have a ridiculous salute" (Overdose, 155) to terrorists and reefers, purple hearts, dream bombs, LSD and coke and talk of lesbians and indecent exposure, and from local telephone exchanges to computerized electric bills. Stately homes become youth hostels or boarding houses. The National Health Plan is introduced, West Indian emigrants arrive, people discuss ESP and buy toy space guns, power mowers, Fluffy Flakelets and Wonder White. There are the "bright young people" of the works of the 'twenties and the "mods" of the 'sixties of *At Bertram's Hotel* and *Third Girl*. Though *Third Girl* is weak as a detective novel, it is significant as a conscious attempt of Christie to be "up-to-date." The meaning of the title; the typical advertisement for a second roommate; the Borodene Mansions, with its ten "frescoes" available for apartments according to taste; and those young mods all demonstrate that, whether she liked them or not, Christie knew changes had occurred and felt the necessity of incorporating them into her fiction. In the same novel, when Poirot journeys to the village of Long Basing, Christie chronicles what has happened to the supposedly unchanging village of detective fiction:

What had lately been the local grocer's had now blossomed into calling itself "a supermarket," complete with stacks of wire baskets and packaged materials of every cereal and cleaning material, all in dazzling paper boxes. And there was a small establishment with one small window with Lillah written across it in fancy letters, a fashion display of one French blouse, labeled "Latest chic," and a navy skirt and a purple-striped jumper labeled "separates." These were displayed by being flung down as by a careless hand in the window.

. . . One or two houses had had a complete face lift and showed signs of claiming to be new and proud of it. There were also some delightful and decrepit old-world cottages some pretending to be a hundred or so years older than they were, others completely genuine, any added comforts of plumbing or such being carefully hidden from any casual glance.

. . . At the end of the village there came an abrupt transition. On one side, set back from the road, was a row of newly built council houses, a strip of green in front of them and a gay note set by each house having been given a different-colored front door (27).

*The Mirror Crack'd from Side to Side* presents the same type of change in Miss Marple's St. Mary Mead.

Change even affects the investigations of murder. Normally one would think that crime-solving would be easier with modern police techniques, but not in Christie's fiction. The increased efficiency and *impersonality* of modern life makes detection more difficult. In *Funerals Are Fatal* the difficulty of tracing a parcel, as compared to former times, is stated by Inspector Morton, "If the parcel had gone through a village post office, it's ten to one the postmistress would have noticed it, but nowadays the mail is delivered by van from Market Keynes and of course the young chap does quite a round and delivers a lot of things" (124-125). Similarly, Colin Lamb wishes for the once prevalent neighborhood prying old ladies, who now "are all sitting grouped together in Old Ladies' Homes with every comfort for the aged, or crowding up hospitals where beds are needed urgently for the really sick. The lame and the halt and the old didn't live in their own houses anymore.... It was a serious setback to criminal investigation" (Clocks, 175-176). In these two passages, Christie's nostalgia, her amusement at that nostalgia, and her recognition of the social effects of change are all present.

Perhaps the best illustration of the contradictions in Christie's presentation of the social scene is her handling of World War II. She could hint at the implications for England in *Overdose of Death* or write a super-patriotic spy novel, *N or M?*, but in most of her works *written during the war*, it was not even mentioned (*Evil Under the Sun, Murder in Retrospect, Towards Zero, Remembered Death*). Apparently Christie decided to provide her readers escape from the war by ignoring it and evoking life prior to 1939.

On the other hand, the aftereffects of the war on day-to-day life is clearly presented in the novels of the late 'forties and 'fifties. Rationing, the black market, the difficulty of obtaining eggs, butter or sugar, weed-grown gardens, reduced staffs, identity cards, unemployed and restless veterans, women performing formerly masculine jobs: these are all there. The novel best showing such effects is *There is a Tide* (1948). Lynn Marchmont, the heroine, returns from the war "different"; she has a sense of just drifting after her years of active, directed life as a Wren. She finds England unhappy, and she thinks (in italics): *"But that's what's the matter everywhere. I've noticed it ever since I got home. It's the aftermath war has left. Ill will. Ill feeling. It's everywhere. On railways and buses and in shops and among workers and clerks and even agricultural laborers. And I suppose worse in mines and factories. Ill will" (44).* The austerity and inconveniences of post-war England are given as principal reasons for that ill will. One small domestic example in the same novel indicates Christie's deft touch in portraying such irritations; Superintendent Spence says, "My word, laundry's a problem nowadays. Four ruddy weeks since they've been to our place—not a clean towel left in our house, and the wife washes all my things herself now" (170). This example is typical, for Christie rarely attempted to depict large political or economic changes. Rather, she chose to present the effects of those changes on the everyday world of her characters.

As already stated, setting is not the most important element in Christie's fiction. For her, less was more in the presentation of setting. Her dislike of long explanations caused her to avoid specialized locales or environments. The physical setting was her own world, which she outlined for the reader, leaving him the task of using his experience to fill it. Unconsciously, however, she left a social history of fifty years of upper middleclass English life, recording the changes, for good or ill, which occurred. Both nostalgic toward the past—and amused by her own nostalgia—and cognizant that change must be accepted, Christie reflected the feelings of numerous people in the twentieth century about their world past and present, and the social scene she delineated, and her manner of doing so, certainly played a role in her popularity.

# Chapter III
## Characters

*...as regards the Characters, the impossible-probable is better than the improbable-possible.*

**Dorothy Sayers**

*...the Christie characters were in many ways universal—so that an Icelander, for example, had no difficulty in recognizing his particular equivalent of Miss Marple in his Icelandic neighbor.*

**Edmund Crispin**

*Tous les personnages d'Agatha Christie sont capables de tuer dans la mesure même où ils risquent d'être tués.*

**Brigitte Legars & Jean Thibaudeau**

When classic detective fiction is attacked for its lack of reality, that attack usually begins with the form's characters. Puppets, cardboard cutouts, one-dimensional stereotypes, stock figures, plot pawns and pieces of a jigsaw puzzle are just a few of the epithets that have been used to dismiss the characters. Such name-calling evades the real question: what are the requirements of characterization in detective fiction? Since classic detective fiction is ultra-Aristotelian in placing action above character, it consists not of characters who determine the action, but action which determines the characters. Rather than existing as "real human beings," the characters follow conventional lines to accomplish the action of the plot, which is the discovery of one of them as a lawbreaker and the restoring of order to a society which has been disrupted by that person. This archetypal pattern underlying all of Christie's novels and stories does not allow for extensive psychological development of characters, for it would only impede the plot action. Dorothy Sayers has well stated the problem of realistic characters in detective fiction: "At some point or other, either their emotions make hay of the detective interest, or the detective interest gets hold of them and makes their emotions look like pasteboard."[1]

The characters should behave like *reasonably normal* human beings. If they are utterly unbelievable, their actions will also be; if they are utterly dull, the reader will not care what they do. Though basically stereotypes (yes, admittedly they are), they can be made lively, fresh and amusing within the limits of the plot requirements, that is, they can be, what Auden calls, "aesthetically interesting." But the plot requirements must be the first consideration. Barzun

38

recognizes this necessity—and its difficulty—in his statement that "the writer of detection allows us to see into his actors far enough to recognize their type and judge their ostensible motives. Were we to go farther we would see too much: the writer would have given away what it is his business to keep hidden until circumstances speak. In this half-concealment lies an art which is none other than literary."[2] The writer must somehow create characters who will involve the reader to the extent that he will speculate as to their possible motivation, without identifying with them to the point of being seriously disturbed by their peril. Christie created several thousand characters—the very rare duplication of names is remarkable—and her basic method was the combination of the familiar and the eccentric within a single character or the juxtaposition of familiar and eccentric characters within a single work. On the first of these two techniques, the following statement has been made, though with a different emphasis: "the characteristics that all these stereotypes seem to share is a mixture of attractive and suspicious traits: tyrannical but kindly, weak but handsome, dubious but elegant, rich but unhappy. Because of this basic and simple mixture of qualities, the Christie character interests the reader but does not draw him into the sort of deep and disturbing involvement where he might begin to care more about the individual person than the plot."[3]

On the familiar-eccentric basis, some of Christie's characters are developed almost completely upon a single trait, as in the humors character of early comedy. Captain Hastings' stupidity, Raymond West's modernity and Mr. Satterthwaite's snobbery are of this sort. A more common technique is to give the characters traits which are in conflict with the accepted stereotype. This addition of contradictory traits is similar to the topsyturvy characterization of the Gilbert and Sullivan comic operas. Gilbertian topsyturviness creates comic surprise, for the character is defying the audience's expectations of the stereotype to which he belongs; the conflict may be the result of his violating the norms of class, profession, age or sex. Christie uses the same technique, both for enlivening her stereotypes and to create false impressions of them. Since the writer of detective fiction may not—or, at least, should not—overtly state false information, such reversal of expectations is one of the three major ways of misleading the reader about characters, the other two being deliberate lying by a character and misleading statements made about one character by another. The latter may or may not be deliberate lying; it may involve perfectly innocent misunderstandings, inaccurate assumptions, etc. The many pairs of lovers, each of whom is afraid the other is guilty and, therefore, conceals evidence, are obvious illustrations of this technique. A few examples from many of the traits in conflict with the expected include, first and foremost, Miss Jane Marple, but also such diverse characters as Michael Rogers of *Endless Night*, Hilary Craven of *So Many Steps to Death*, Superintendent Sugden of *Hercule Poirot's Christmas*, Miss Gilchrist of *Funerals are Fatal*, and Marie Van Schuyler and Salome Otterbourne of *Death on the Nile*. Miss Van Schuyler and Mrs. Otterbourne are also evidence of how this technique is employed in conjunction with Christie's often ignored sense of humor, which she uses as misdirection to fool the reader; humor becomes another mode of reversal by which things are not always what they seem.

A final general technique of characterization is Christie's use of recurrent characters. The effect of coming upon one of Poirot's or Miss Marple's old friends for the second or third time is, again, a sense of familiarity. They supply another element of continuity, the creation of a known world for the reader, for they are defined on their first appearance, and their personalities do not change in any of their returns—though some do age. Most of them are acquainted with only one of the principal detectives, but there are exceptions. Miss Felicity Lemon is secretary to both Parker Pyne and Hercule Poirot, and Ariadne Oliver also knows both men. *The Pale Horse*, which has no series detective, includes Mrs. Oliver; Rhoda Dawes and Major Despard, who are now married, of Poirot's *Cards on the Table*; and Reverend and Mrs. Dane Calthorp, who return from *The Moving Finger*, a Miss Marple novel. Mr. Robinson, the powerful and enigmatic financier of Poirot's *Cat Among the Pigeons* and Miss Marple's *At Bertram's Hotel*, appears also in the non-series *Passenger to Frankfurt* and the Beresfords' *Postern of Fate*; in the latter two he is joined by the intelligence chief, Colonel Pikeaway. Then there are the secondary official detectives who aid the amateur protagonist, Poirot's Inspector Japp being repeated most often. Colonel Race, another intelligence officer, is Poirot's aide in *Cards on the Table* and *Death on the Nile*, but he also appears in the non-series *The Man in the Brown Suit* and *Remembered Death*. Superintendent Spence first works with Poirot in *There is a Tide* and then returns for *Mrs. McGinty's Dead, Hallowe'en Party,* and *Elephants Can Remember*. Young Inspector Dermot Craddock is Miss Marple's protege in *A Murder Is Announced* and again in *What Mrs. McGillicuddy Saw!*; he is the godson of Sir Henry Clithering, ex-commissioner of Scotland Yard and Miss Marple's friend of the early stories. Though these men act faithfully in their official capacities, they are always subordinated to the various amateur detectives with whom they work.

Therefore, it is necessary to examine in some detail Christie's principal detectives—Poirot, Miss Marple, the Beresfords, Superintendent Battle, Harley Quin and Parker Pyne—and the heroes and heroines of her non-series works, and, after them, those other two necessary figures, the victim and the murderer. The conglomeration of witnesses, suspects and bystanders also deserve study, for though not absolutely essential, they are significant in Christie's construction of a distinctive world of detection.

## A. Detectives

*The detective novel must have a detective in it; and a detective is not a detective unless he detects.*
**S.S. Van Dine**

*The detective is...the Fairy Godmother of the twentieth century folk-myth, his magic capabilities only modified to the requirements of a would-be scientific and rational generation.*
**Nicholas Blake**

*[Fictional detectives] are interested in, basically, only one thing, the truth. Not necessarily in justice, though that is a concomitant, but always, always, always in the truth.*
**Newgate Callendar**

According to the Oxford English Dictionary, the word *detective* first appeared in 1843 with the specific meaning of a plainclothes policeman. Within a short time, however, the meaning had widened; that dictionary's second definition includes "One whose occupation it is to discover matters artfully concealed.... *Private detective*, one not belonging to the police force, who in his private capacity, or as attached to a Detective Agency or Bureau, undertakes similar services for persons employing him." With the exception of Superintendent Battle, Christie's principal sleuths fall into the general category of the private detective, particularly of the type who works "in a private capacity," i.e., the brilliant amateur (Poirot's Belgian police experience does not exclude him). Thus, they are in the tradition of the "great detective," who acts outside the officialdom of the law, but is on the side of the law.

The great detective "is, at one and the same time, the outstanding personality of the story (though he is concerned in it only in an *ex-parte* capacity), the projection of the author, the embodiment of the reader, the *deus ex machina* of the plot, the propounder of the problem, the supplier of the clues, and the eventual solver of the mystery."[4] Since the detective serves all of these functions, it is not surprising that one speaks of a Poirot novel or a Miss Marple story; the detective is the character remembered longest. The great detective stands outside class. He often must be judge as well as crime-solver, as Poirot in *Murder on the Orient*

*Express*, Miss Marple in *The Mirror Crack'd from Side to Side*, or Harley Quin in all his stories. He is able to judge because he is given the power of distinguishing absolutely between good and evil. Having this power, he can perform his task of lifting suspicion, distrust and guilt in whatever community he may find himself. In the classic detective story, he achieves this social cleansing by recreating the crime in his mind from the evidence he obtains, a process of imaginative, intellectual reconstruction; once he has completed this reconstruction, he can then establish truth, free the innocent and condemn the guilty.

A figure of personal authority, the great detective moves untouched and incorruptible amidst the chaos of earthly existence, employing his intellect to conquer that chaos. Ian Ousby has compared him to the Duke in Shakespearean comedy: "a moral hero and a figure of power, he establishes intellectual certainties and restores the order which has previously been threatened."[5] His position as moral hero is the result of his knowledge of good and evil; his position as a figure of power is the result of his ability to reason from evidence. It is a truism that the great detective owes much to the nineteenth century's admiration of science. He has become the popular conception of scientific thought.[6] Just as the scientist wishes to know *the truth*, whatever the consequences, so does the fictional detective. The truth must be revealed, even though some will be hurt by the revelation, so that the onus of crime will be lifted from all but the guilty. It is in the detective's ability to "out-think" all others that his superiority lies. His solution is "a process of reasoning which, when he explains it, can be followed and concurred in by everyone—including, by implication, a jury, that microcosm of a democratic society. The detective's superiority cannot be rationally refuted, and therefore he is justified."[7]

In line with his intellectual and moral superiority is the detective's distinct individuality. Independent of official authority, he steps in to accomplish what the representatives of that authority have found impossible. He is free from the regulations and red tape of the police; he can create his own rules of work. However, it must be noted that Christie's amateurs generally work well with the police. Poirot may be condescending to Inspector Japp or call Giraud of the Surete "the human foxhound," Miss Marple may have to ignore the rude officiousness of Inspector Slack, or Tuppence Beresford may disobey orders from superiors in the intelligence service, but much more often there is close cooperation between the amateur and his uniformed colleagues. By combining the official investigation and the sleuthing of the amateur, Christie is able to achieve variety in the process of discovery. Not only are Christie's detectives independent of officialdom, they also possess great personal freedom. Of her principal detectives, only the comic Beresfords and the recessive Battle are married. Indeed, of her detectives' lives before their first cases, practically nothing is given, except a few random facts about Miss Marple and the Beresfords. Childhood, education, parents and all of the other determining factors of a person's life are omitted, leaving the detective unusually free of the mundane commitments of family and wage-earning and giving him a mobility denied to most people. The combined official and personal freedom of the detective is another means of setting him apart from those whom he must investigate and ultimately deliver or prove guilty.

Some critics have stated that readers do not identify with the detective because of his superiority and freedom. Such a view requires qualification. The reader does not identify with a Christie detective as he would with the protagonist of a realistic novel, but the fact that so many people buy "another Poirot" or "another Miss Marple" indicates that there is a reader response to the detective. The problem for the author is somehow to create a bond between the detective and the reader so that if the reader does not "identify," he will at least admire and wish to follow the detective's processes of discovery. One method is the amateur himself. Whereas a reader can flatter himself by imagining his solving a crime as a brilliant amateur, he is less likely to do so as a police officer—unless, of course, he happens to be one. It is easier for a reader to respond to the amateur, for he is not separated from him by an official title and the accompanying paraphernalia of an organization to which most readers do not belong. A second method of bringing the detective and reader together is the use of a "Watson," the aide or admiring friend of the detective, such as Poirot's Captain Hastings. The relationship of the detective and his Watson is that of knight and squire. The loyal, morally good, gullible, usually bumbling and generally comic Watson has a function which is double and paradoxical. He is, first, the reader's surrogate, allowing him to be in continuous and close contact with the detective's investigation (but without ever actually knowing his thoughts), and at the same time he is a character to whom the reader can feel superior. The reader does not identify with the Watson, but rather is amused by him. The reader can say to himself, "I would never have thought that! How can he be so stupid?" This self-satisfaction is, in reality, a clever delusion arranged by the author, for the reader may be as bewildered as the Watson. This double function—surrogate and comic scapegoat—serves to build the reader's ego and to place him on a closer intellectual level to the detective and certainly above the

Watson.

The third and most important method of creating reader response to a detective is to incorporate into his personality features which make his intellectual and moral superiority less formidable. If the amateur detective possesses the qualities of the scientist, he also possesses those of the entertainer. To be totally rational is to be totally dull, as Swift's Houyhnhnms proved more than two hundred years ago. Therefore the detective has eccentricities, idiosyncrasies, mannerisms or other distinctive peculiarities which offset his immense intellect. Such personality traits involve speech, physical appearance, habits or attitudes. Humor plays a large part in taking the detective "down a notch," so that he does not seem a forbidding figure. The reader admires his abilities, but can also laugh at his eccentricities. There is, however, a limit beyond which the author may not go in attempting to make his detective more "human"; as Auden has said, "The amateur detective genius may have weaknesses to give him aesthetic interest, but they must not be of a kind which outrages ethics."[8] Poirot can brag, Miss Marple can snoop, and the Beresfords can banter inane chitchat, but they always stand for justice and the innocent. The bland Pyne and the quiet Battle differ in that they are based upon ordinariness and are without eccentricity, a reverse process, and the mysterious Mr. Quin is supernatural, making him unique. The various amateurs who are drawn into detection in Christie's non-series works by purely accidental involvement in a crime or a mystery are not so much eccentric as confused, belligerent or frightened by their predicament (often comically so) or are engaging as a result of their sheer inappropriateness to the action required of them.

Enough has been said to indicate the general nature of Christie's detectives. She favors the brilliant amateur, possessing intellectual and moral superiority, who with freedom and personal authority accomplishes his seemingly impossible feats of detection, while retaining as a character the interest of the reader. It is now time to consider the detectives individually, and the obvious one with whom to begin is the little Belgian who appears most often.

## Hercule Poirot

A fifty-five year career as fictional detective is a very long one, yet that is the length of Hercule Poirot's. It is appropriately capped by the only obituary for such a character on the front page of the *New York Times* (4 August 1975). That obituary is a tribute to Poirot's fame, for—with the sole exception of Sherlock Holmes—no other literary detective is as widely known. According to Christie, his genesis was a dare by her sister and the presence of Belgian refugees in England during World War I, but her account of his creation in her autobiography does not really tell much. By the time she wrote that autobiography, she could not even remember the reason for the choice of his name.[9] Critics have suggested several possible literary antecedents, generally because of similar foreign backgrounds: Robert Barr's Eugene Valmont, Marie Belloc Lowndes' Hercules Popeau, and A.E.W. Mason's Hanaud, but on that basis one could as easily go all the way back to Poe's C. Auguste Dupin. If Poirot has a literary father, it is that single more famous detective so different in appearance and manner, but so similar in intellectual power, whom Christie enjoyed as a child: Sherlock Holmes. Holmes and Poirot are the two outstanding examples in British detective fiction of "The Great Detective," the genius solver of mysteries which baffle all others.

When he first appears in *The Mysterious Affair at Styles*, Poirot is no longer a young man. He has been retired from the Belgian police since 1904 and has come to England as a war refugee. To attempt to determine his age is a waste of time. By strict chronology, assuming retirement at sixty-five, he would be over 135 by the time of *Curtain*, the last novel. In his fifty-five years presented by Christie, he ages very slowly; the impression given is that he is in late middle age in the early works and in his late seventies at the time of his death. Whatever his age, he continues to investigate. He occasionally thinks of retiring again, and even attempts to do so a few times, but the attempts never last, for he becomes bored, and some interesting case always seems to come along. In *The ABC Murders* he admits: "I am like the prima donna who makes positively the farewell performance! That farewell performance, it repeats itself an indefinite number of times! . . . the retirement I care for not at all" (11). As a result, his career in England, and assorted other countries, is documented in thirty-three novels and fifty-two short stories.

In spite of his success, Christie at times grew tired of him and his mannerisms. The remarks of Ariadne Oliver about her Finn are comic evidence of the author's exasperation, as is the statement made by Christie in 1938:

There are moments when I have felt: "Why—Why—Why did I ever invent this detestable, bombastic, tiresome little creature? . . . eternally straightening things, eternally boasting, eternally twirling his moustache and tilting his egg-shaped head. . . ." Anyway, what *is* an egg-shaped head. . .? I am beholden to him financially. . . . On the other hand, he owes his very existence to me. In moments of irritation, I point out that by a few strokes of the pen . . . I could destroy him utterly. He replies, grandiloquently: "Impossible to get rid of Poirot like that! He is much too clever."[10]

She also regretted including Poirot in some works; one example is her remark that " 'Sad Cypress' could have been good, but it was quite ruined by having Poirot in it."[11] That such remarks, and there are other similar ones, were not idle is proven by the distribution of the Poirot works: seventeen novels and most of the short stories in the 1920s and 1930s; eleven novels and a collection of stories in the 1940s and 1950s; and only five novels in the 1960s and 1970s. Among those final five is *Curtain,* written in the early 1940s, and in it she finally "destroyed him utterly." *Curtain* was originally intended for publication after her death, for she had the example of Conan Doyle's futile effort to kill Holmes, only to have readers protest massively. Surely she knew that the same would have occurred, no matter her own wishes, if an earlier demise for Poirot had been attempted.

If Christie had mixed feelings about Poirot, others have been more definite, both for and against him. Two later mystery writers illustrate. Edmund Crispin calls Poirot, "an almost completely artificial conglomeration of trivial mannerisms," while H.R.F. Keating says that he is "a well-judged *omnium gatherum* of what the ordinary person might expect an eccentric to be."[12] Whichever view is held, Poirot is unchanging. Christie was too shrewd to alter him in any significant way after his first appearance. After reading a single work, a reader knows what to expect from Poirot and looks forward to the fulfillment of the expectation. Christie does not disappoint him. Poirot's unchanging personal characteristics, his major aides and repeated acquaintances, and his methods as investigator and dispenser of justice are the principal elements in Christie's creation of the detective at the center of her longest and most successful series of works.

Physically, Poirot is hardly heroic. The immediate impression he produces on others is surprised amusement, as is the case with Nurse Leatheran, the narrator of *Murder in Mesopotamia:* "When you saw him you just wanted to laugh! He was like something on the stage or at the pictures.... He looked like a hairdresser in a comic play!" (80). That hairdresser image is used again and again to convey his dandified appearance. He is five feet four inches, but carries himself with dignity—the usual term is "immense dignity." He is ultra-fastidious in dress, as in everything else, though often flamboyantly unconventional. He may wear a white camellia in his buttonhole or on vacation appear in "a white suit, pink shirt, large black bow tie and a white topee" (*Nile,* 103). His individuality toward dress is expressed in *Murder After Hours:* "He knew well enough the kind of clothes that were worn in the country on a Sunday in England, but he did not choose to conform to English ideas. He preferred his own standards of urban smartness. He was not an English country gentleman and he would not dress like an English country gentleman. He was Hercule Poirot!" (90). His sartorial splendor is completed by his "neat" wrist watch, his cane and his tiny Russian cigarettes. Capping the elegantly clothed little body is his most striking physical feature; the egg-shaped head always carried a little to one side, with the green eyes which twinkle at romance and become catlike when he is excited and the "stiff military" or "enormous" moustache, of which he is so proud. He carries a spirit stove and curling tongs to keep that moustache in immaculate condition, as well as glossy black dye for his greying hair. All these physical elements combine with his personality to form a comic exterior, which Poirot uses when necessary for his own purposes. At the same time, they set him apart from ordinary humanity. It is not surprising when he says to Inspector Japp in *Peril at End House* that he never uses disguise, that Japp's reply is "You couldn't. You're unique. Once seen, never forgotten" (131). (Poirot does disguise himself as a plumber in "The Chocolate Box" and as his "twin" Achille in *The Big Four*.)

Adding to Poirot's uniqueness is his speech. Despite his many years in England, much of the time he speaks the language like an inattentive second-year student. Christie plays with the typical Englishman's idea of the comic foreigner who must be stupid since he cannot speak English properly. (Conversely, when Poirot lapses into French, Christie always makes the phrases short and simple for that same typical Englishman.) Confusion of word order, an unconsciousness of contractions, and especially the ability to mangle idioms are Poirot's chief faults. In *The Big Four* he uses "red kipper" for red herring, "the trot of the fox" for foxtrot, and "The boot is not upon the right leg" (83, 157, 63). *Lord Edgware Dies* offers "You mock yourself at me, my friend" (47), while *The ABC Murders* has "It is the nest of the horse that I put my nose into there" (19). Hundreds of other examples could be cited, but the best—or worst— which cannot be omitted, is that "absolute riot of mixed metaphors" in *Mrs. McGinty's Dead*: "For somewhere ... there is in the hay a needle, and among the sleeping dogs there is one on whom I shall put my foot, and by shooting the arrows into the air, one will come down and hit a glass house!" (36).

Such use of fractured language is a comic characterizing device, but to stop with that statement is inadequate. Just as Poirot uses his appearance as an aid to his work, so he uses his language. He uses it as a kind of camouflage to cause Englishmen to underestimate him: "He was at his most foreign today. He was out to be despised but patronized" (Retrospect, 47). That he is thoroughly aware of the effect he is producing is shown by his answer to Mr. Satterthwaite's question in *Three Act Tragedy* as to why he sometimes speaks "perfectly good English and at other times not":

It is true that I can speak the exact, the idiomatic English. But, my friend, to speak the broken English is an enormous asset. It leads people to despise you. They say—a foreigner—he can't even speak English properly. It is not my policy to terrify people—instead I invite their gentle ridicule. Also I boast! An Englishman he says often, "A fellow who thinks as much of himself as that cannot be worth much." That is the English point of view. It is not at all true. And so, you see, I put people off their guard. Besides,...it has become a habit (252).

This deliberate overdoing of the comical-little-foreigner role as a ploy indicates that Poirot knows English much better than he usually pretends. He can even make jokes about his use of the language, as in *Curtain*: "I find here a gentleman, a baronet who is a friend of the employer of your daughter. (That phrase, it sounds a little like the French exercise, does it not?)" (3). Much earlier in *Poirot Loses a Client*, he tells Hastings, "I know your language well enough to realize that one does not talk of a picture being *ajar*. A door is *ajar*. A picture is *awry*" (65). If he is aware of such semantic distinctions, he obviously can speak correct English, and at one point in every work he does: the final explanation. There the comic facade drops, and he speaks without errors. The transformation is described in *Mrs. McGinty's Dead*, the same novel in which he indulges in that riot of mixed metaphors: "A new note crept into his voice. He was no longer a ridiculous little man with an absurd moustache and dyed hair, he was a hunter very close to his quarry" (170). In a sense Christie trapped herself into inconsistency by giving Poirot comic speech. It came to be expected of him, but, at the same time, it would be hardly appropriate—or even readable—for extended passages explaining the ratiocinative process. Therefore, she had to provide him with two voices: one comic and fractured and the other serious and correct.

Poirot's comment to Mr. Satterthwaite about his speech also indicates his awareness of his own vanity, a third principal element of his personality. As Hastings says, "Poirot has his virtues, but modesty is not one of them" (Four, 103). He takes himself quite seriously, and no one had better presume to ridicule him or his eccentricities—unless he so wishes. Over and over, his vanity is seen in the manner in which he introduces himself: "I am a detective. I am a King" (Nile, 110); "My name is Hercule Poirot,...and I am probably the greatest detective in the world" (Train, 141); " 'I am Hercule Poirot,' said Poirot with his usual embarrassed air of announcing a Royal Title" (McGinty, 64). A new acquaintance is thus immediately made aware of the honor bestowed in having met the infallible owner of those little grey cells. That he does consider himself infallible as a detective is evident when a witness says, "No one can always be right"; his answer is "I am. Always I am right. It is so invariable that it startles me" (Cards, 217), and he accepts Mrs. Oliver's comparison of himself to a computer, remarking that computers do make mistakes. (When he makes these statements, he has conveniently forgotten his one failure, "The Chocolate Box.") Since he believes he is the best, he has no intention of hiding that belief, perhaps most bluntly stated in "The Mystery of the Bagdad Chest":

> The talents that I possess—I would salute them in another. As it happens, in my own particular line, there is no one to touch me. *C'est dommage!* As it is, I admit freely and without the hypocrisy that I am a great man. I have the order, the method and the psychology in an unusual degree. I am, in fact, Hercule Poirot! Why should I turn red and stammer and mutter into my chin that really I am very stupid. It would not be true (33).

Though such vanity may be tiresome to some readers, most enjoy it as another example of his comic foreignness, another endearing eccentricity.

That vanity is fed by the attitudes of officialdom toward him. King Albert of Belgium sends English statesmen to him in the case of "The Kidnapped Prime Minister." Later, that case is remembered when he is needed in "The Submarine Plans"; "Your masterly deductions—and may I add, your discretion?—saved the situation" (163). He is immediately accepted by officials as a full partner in nearly every investigation. The usual reaction is that in "The Third-Floor Flat": "The inspector recognized Poirot and greeted him in an almost reverential manner" (156). Sarcastically described by Japp as "the Home Secretary's little pet" (Overdose, 161), Poirot never has any problems interviewing accused murderers; jail doors open for him at once, as in *Sad Cypress* and "The Mystery of the Spanish Chest." His vanity is inflated by such recognition of his success as a detective—whose would not be? The police have learned that in spite of his appearance and his eccentricities, or by his using them, he can be depended upon to solve what they cannot. Those who have worked with him know that, as Superintendent Battle puts it, "About as dangerous as a black mamba and a she-leopard—that's what *he* is when he starts making a mountebank of himself!" (Zero, 149).

Along with his personal appearance, his language and his vanity, other lesser elements contribute to Poirot's image. After World War I he moves to 14 Farroway Street, London, with Hastings; then in the 1930s he moves to 203 Whitehaven Mansions (telephone: Trafalgar 8137), a modern block of flats on Park Lane, which remains his home until the events of *Curtain*. His flat, like his dress, is the epitome of neatness and symmetry. Just as he corrects Hastings' ties or demands that his tie pin be exactly centered, he picks up dropped matches, aligns books and straightens ornaments. This fetish for symmetry even extends to his finding it "insupportable" that hens lay eggs of different sizes. Unless a case interrupts, his eating habits are strictly regulated: chocolate and croissants for breakfast, lunch between twelve thirty and one, no afternoon tea (he considers it a detestable English practice), and dinner at seven. Under no circumstances will he allow a case to be discussed at a meal and destroy proper digestion; though afterwards, when he is drinking hot chocolate, a *tisane*, or one of his sweet *syrops*, usually creme de cassis, the subject may be broached. The symmetrical arrangement of his flat and his orderly personal habits are illustrations of his belief that "to succeed in life every detail should be arranged well beforehand" (*Nile*, 80).

With such an attitude, it is not surprising that he dislikes nature and loathes discomfort. Though he says that he is an avid reader of Wordsworth—"I read him much" (Cypress, 131)—he does not have the English passion for nature or country life. It is too unplanned, too asymmetrical. His one attempt at gardening in *The Murder of Roger Ackroyd* fails, and he never again tries to grow vegetable marrows, or anything else. If nature is too uncivilized for him, discomfort of any kind is even more so. He is seen petrified with fear only once: in *Overdose of Death* when he must visit his dentist. His graphic description of his sufferings as a result of the inadequacies of Maureen Summerhayes' household in *Mrs. McGinty's Dead* is, besides being hilariously funny, revelatory of his desire for what he considers his proper comfort. Another sore point, in spite of numerous journeys, is the discomfort of travel. He especially despises sea travel, suffering agony from *mal de mer*; the only help is his series of special breathing exercises. Probably his worst travel experience is having to ride a camel in "The Adventure of the Egyptian Tomb." Hastings reports, "He started by groans and lamentations and ended by shrieks, gesticulations and invocations to the Virgin Mary and every Saint in the calendar. In the end, he descended ignominiously and finished the journey on a diminutive donkey" (67). It is doubtful if he enjoyed the donkey ride, for Poirot is definitely a man of the city, where his orderly existence can benefit from the comfort it offers.

"There is nothing of the Socialist about Poirot," says Hastings (Edgware, 158). Poirot is as conservative as his creator in social and political matters. He is firmly of the middle class, has respect for his social superiors, except when they break the law, and is courteous, if somewhat condescending, to those on lower levels. Though he is not particularly pleased when a young woman calls him a "bloody little bourgeois detective," he admits that the epithet *bourgeois* is appropriate: "His outlook on life was essentially bourgeois, and always had been" (Overdose, 127). His bourgeoiserie is best seen in that desire for his personal comfort, which brings up a not clearly explained aspect of his life: his source of money. One has to assume that he is paid for much of his detective work, but only rarely does a client say that he is sending Poirot a check. Apparently for Poirot and his creator, money is a necessity, but it is not a subject for discussion, except when it is disparaged. Poirot does not hesitate to say, "When a case interests me, I do not touch money" (Edgware, 149). Naturally, as a great detective his desire for justice and what Hastings calls his "artistic fervor" overcome any purely monetary considerations. But he does have the resources to live comfortably. His Flemish thrift has apparently enabled him to accumulate a healthy bank account from those cases for which he is paid.

Poirot's forms of relaxation may also be considered bourgeois and comfortable; they are certainly sedentary. He builds card houses to soothe his nerves and think, and he uses jigsaw puzzles for the same purposes. The preciseness required of the first and the analytical ability for the second may be more frustrating than soothing to many people, but such activities are appropriate pastimes for a detective. The same is true of his other major hobby: the reading of detective fiction. In *The Clocks* he is seen reading a number of detective stories, and his comments on them provide Christie an opportunity to express opinions on both the genre and specific writers (see Chapter V). Four novels later, in *Third Girl*, he has completed his *magnum opus*, an analysis of detective fiction: "He had dared to speak scathingly of Edgar Allan Poe, he had complained of the lack of method and order in the romantic outpourings of Wilkie Collins, had lauded to the skies two American authors who were practically unknown, and had in various other ways given honor where honor was due and sternly withheld it where he considered it was not" (1). It is a pity this definitive work has not been published.

Altogether Poirot's physical appearance, his language, his vanity and the other elements of his personality and life give him the image of an exceptionally different and often comic figure. Also adding to that image are his relationships with his repeated employees and friends. The principal satellites are George, his valet; Mr. Goby, his private inquiry agent; Miss Felicity Lemon, his secretary; Countess Vera Rossakoff, his only "romantic" interest; and, most important, his friends Captain Arthur Hastings and Mrs. Ariadne Oliver. (Inspector Japp, who could be included, is examined with other secondary police officers later.)

The three employees differ greatly, as does Poirot's relationship with each. George, or as Poirot always calls him *Georges,* is tall, cadaverous, unemotional and excessively snobbish. His first appearance is in *The Mystery of the Blue Train,* and there Poirot asks him why he demeaned himself by coming to work for him. His answer is "I happened to see in *Society Snippets* that you had been received at Buckingham Palace. That was just when I was looking for a new situation. His majesty, so it said, had been most generous and friendly and thought highly of your abilities" (219). George settles in with his bourgeois master and stays for nearly fifty years, until Poirot enters a guest house in *Curtain.* Though hardly the equivalent of Lord Peter Wimsey's Bunter, George does serve occasionally as confidant and advisor to Poirot. As stated in "The Apples of the Hesperides," "It was the habit of Hercule Poirot to discuss his cases with his capable valet, George. That is to say, Hercule Poirot would let drop certain observations to which George would reply with the worldly wisdom which he had acquired in the course of his career as a gentleman's gentleman" (278). In the same story Poirot tells George that a golden rule in life is "never do anything yourself that others can do for you" (279); he then lists a number of reliable detective agencies around the world which he employs for the gathering of information. Since his detection is mental, he requires information, but he has no intention of unnecessarily expending his energy in compiling it when others can perform that task for him. His attitude is expressed in *Sad Cypress:* "It is not for me to run here and there doing amateurishly the things that for a small sum someone else can do with professional skill.... I have some useful assistants—one of them a former burglar" (164). Readers do not meet that burglar, but they do meet Miss Amy Carnaby, leader of a successful dognapping ring in "The Nemean Lion," who becomes a successful spy for Poirot in "The Flock of Geryon." However, Poirot's mainstay in private acquisition of information is Mr. Goby, who appears at odd intervals from *The Mystery of the Blue Train* to *Third Girl.* Mr. Goby's exact methods of discovering secrets are not revealed. What is known is that he gets results quickly and is paid well for doing so. In appearance he is small, elderly, shabbily dressed and altogether nondescript. He never looks at the person he is addressing, and though successful in his job, he is always tentative in revealing what he has uncovered. Poirot admires his ability, is intrigued by his personality, and is curious about his methods, but the reticent Mr. Goby never satisfies that curiosity.

Mr. Goby holds no interest for Miss Lemon, who appears in four novels and four short stories—and earlier as Parker Pyne's secretary in three stories. An angular forty-eight year old spinster, Miss Lemon is efficiency personified. Though capable of thought, she only thinks when told to do so, for she is "gloriously uninterested in all human affairs" (Garden, 51). Whether typing like a machinegunner or taking hieroglyphic notes, understandable only to herself, from Poirot, she functions as a human machine. When she makes her first error in a letter, at the beginning of *Hickory Dickory Death*, Poirot is shocked and realizes that something serious has happened; it has and involves her sister. With this single exception, her mind is totally absorbed by either her work or her one recreation, the details of her proposed perfect filing system, which she intends to patent. She is unconcerned with the nature of Poirot's work and considers that he has been in England long enough to comprehend its slang. She is the only character in the series with a greater sense of order and method than Poirot, and at times he seems almost in awe of the combination of that sense and the total lack of imagination.

One of his most embarrassing moments, and the one time he arouses her otherwise dormant curiosity, occurs when she questions him about sending red roses to the Russian Countess Vera Rossakoff. When he leaves the room, Miss Lemon murmurs, "I wonder .... Really, at *his* age! .... Surely not...." (Cerberus, 320). Miss Lemon is wrong, for the Countess Vera fascinates Poirot; she is his Irene Adler. His age and the tradition of the brilliant bachelor detective—Dupin, Holmes, Carrados, etc.—do not allow for physical romance. He occasionally makes statements regretting his bachelor status, but they seem *pro forma* except when the Countess Vera is concerned. Though she appears only three times, he often thinks sentimentally of her. In her first appearance, "The Double Clue," she is a jewel thief; then she is a more or less willing participant in the villainous conspiracy of *The Big Four*, and finally she is the planned scapegoat of a narcotics gang in "The Capture of Cerberus." Poirot successively proves her guilt but lets her go, finds her lost son and again gives her her freedom, and finally prevents her being framed. The Countess is hardly young—in "The Capture of Cerberus" her son is grown and an engineer in the United States—but she is described by such adjectives as *voluptuous, lush, exotic* and *highly colored*. Obviously Poirot's taste in women is the exact opposite of that in furnishings: curves may be unsightly in chairs and tables, but they are a prime requisite in women. When he thinks of her as "A woman in a thousand—in a million!," the explanation is given that it "is the misfortune of small precise men to hanker after large and flamboyant women. Poirot had never been able to rid himself of the fatal fascination the Countess held for him.... To Hercule Poirot she still represented the sumptuous and the alluring" (Cerberus, 292). Nevertheless, after the third story the Countess disappears from Poirot's world. He has only her memory to tantalize him as he sips his chocolate, which is probably his preference, for life with the Countess might be exciting but it would surely not be comfortable.

One person with whom Poirot is comfortable is Captain Arthur Hastings. Poirot's very first words are *"Mon ami* Hastings! It is inded *mon ami* Hastings!"* (Styles, 15). Having known each other previously, they are already friends in this first work, and that friendship continues through eight novels and twenty-six stories. Little is given of Hastings' background, but he is the literary son of Dr. John H. Watson and second only to him in fame among the long line of aides, sidekicks and admiring friends of the great detectives. Like Watson, he narrates all the works in which he appears and, consequently, reveals his personality, but he is reticent, even secretive, about his private life. He attended Eton and was wounded in World War I: these are the only major facts known about his life before the first case, which occurs when he is thirty. After that case he moves in with Poirot, but then marries Dulcie Duveen, one of the Dulcibella Kids, a singing-dancing-acrobatic act, and they settle on a ranch in Argentina and eventually have four children. Hastings makes four trips back to England for long periods, but Mrs. Hastings never accompanies him. Poirot says that the success of the ranch is due to her, and he must be correct since Hastings is away so often. Sometime after the fourth trip Mrs. Hastings dies, and her husband's grief is stressed throughout *Curtain*, which recounts his final return to England. Very little else is known of Hastings away from Poirot. Nor is there any detailed physical description of him. *Curtain* provides as much as is given, when Poirot says, "Yes, just the same—the straight back, the broad shoulders, the grey of the hair—*tres distingue.* You know, my friend, you have worn well" (12). Physically, he is a contrast to Poirot, and apparently Christie thought that was enough: the reader can fill in the details to suit. Of course, Hastings' innate British reserve makes the lack of information understandable. Since he does not approve of prying into the personal lives of others, he would not want others to pry into his, and he certainly would not volunteer such matters.

His personality includes a seriousness which verges on pomposity, a comic vanity, a strong sense of propriety, a desire for action—usually without thought, and excessive gullibility. He has no sense of humor whatsoever; jokes pass over his head, and he generally distrusts those with witty or ironic temperaments, for he does not grasp their statements. This sobersided aspect of Hastings makes him seem foolish, which is Christie's intent; she is playing with the stereotype of the serious-minded Englishman, as when he is angrily chauvinistic about all things English. Though he never reaches Poirot's level, Hastings is also vain. He adores compliments to his intelligence and is irritated by any slights to it. His sense of propriety is a minor source of conflict between the two men. In spite of his streak of vanity, Hastings has "a horror of doing anything conspicuous" (Edgware, 93). Similarly his English reserve and Etonian training cause him to become upset at Poirot's willingness to read others' letters without permission and to eavesdrop. Hastings says, "At whatever school Poirot was educated, there were clearly no unwritten rules about eavesdropping. I was horrified but powerless" (Client, 107). The "unwritten rules" are, for Hastings, a code of conduct, which he finds difficult to break in even the most exigent circumstances, another example of Christie's exaggeration of the stereotyped proper Englishman so that readers can laugh at his correct, but misapplied values. Poirot, the man of thought, is balanced by Hastings, the man of action without thought. Whenever a case arises, Hastings wishes to be immediately up and about, and he is often frustrated by Poirot's seeming lack of energy in pursuing what is, to Hastings, a matter requiring rushing to the scene of the crime, finding clues, and whatever other activity will demonstrate that *something* is being done. The idea of analyzing by sheer logic what is already known does not appeal to him, for thinking simply confuses him. For Hastings, action replaces thought: the result is that his actions never succeed.

The last principal trait of his personality, and the most important, is his gullibility. Indeed, that gullibility is the basis for Hastings' role as confused reader surrogate and comic scapegoat. In *Peril at End House* Poirot bluntly tells him, "You are that wholly admirable type of man, honest, credulous, honorable, who is invariably taken in by any scoundrel. You are the type of man who invests in doubtful oil fields, and nonexistent gold mines" (35). Hastings angrily denies the accusation, but it is true. His acceptance of appearances without evaluation and his romantic imagination combine to make him the dupe of any clever deceiver. Allied with this gullible, romantic nature is his open countenance. In spite of his reserve, Hastings cannot conceal his emotions, especially when taken by surprise; he is utterly transparent. Because he cannot dissemble, Poirot rarely shares information, knowing that Hastings will be bound to reveal it, unintentional though that revelation may be. Hastings is simply not one with whom to share secrets. Another instance of his gullibility is his instant like or dislike of others on the basis of surface appearance as soon as he meets them. Christie is too clever to make him always wrong, an obvious giveaway to the reader, but he is far more often wrong than right. Related to his quick judgments of others is his susceptibility to pretty, charming women, especially those with auburn hair. Though never unfaithful to Dulcie, he can easily be entranced by any attractive woman who shows him attention. His actual knowledge of women is nil; as Poirot says, "You admire *les femmes*, Hastings; you prostrate yourself before all of them who are good-looking and have the good taste to smile upon you; but psychologically you know nothing whatever about them" (Cornish, 139). In fact, Hastings' attitudes toward women incorporate all five major aspects of his personality: seriousness, vanity, propriety, thoughtless action and gullibility.

Of necessity, a great deal has already been said of the relationship between Poirot and Hastings, for that relationship is the reason for Hastings' existence as a character. It is not always a completely harmonious relationship, for Hastings is continually forced to acknowledge his secondary position, a position recognized by other characters. Their comments are rarely flattering to him. Inspector Japp particularly enjoys flinging barbs at Hastings' thin skin. It is not surprising that others would be less than complimentary, for Poirot himself continually refers to Hastings as "my faithful dog"; during *The ABC Murders,* he says, "You know, Hastings, in many ways I regard you as my mascot" (12). In *Mrs. McGinty's Dead* Poirot remembers Hastings and says bluntly that he needed him as a "stooge" to serve as an ego-booster for himself. In spite of Hastings' resentment of the putdowns, any time Poirot congratulates him, he quickly melts. At the same time, Hastings makes many statements to the effect that he is the long suffering member of the pair. Poirot's vanity is one cause: "I am afraid that I have got into the habit of averting my attention whenever Poirot mentions his little grey cells. I have heard it all so often before" (Edgware, 16). The other principal cause is Poirot's already noted refusal to confide important matters to him. Most of their quarrels result from Hastings' sense that Poirot does not trust his judgment. But when Poirot does give him clues, Hastings cannot grasp their significance, and clues are as much as Poirot will give; not even pleadings by Hastings will change his mind. In *Poirot Loses a Client* Hastings humbly says, "You know, Poirot, I don't quite understand all this"; Poirot's reply is "If you will pardon my saying so, Hastings, you do not understand at all!" (190). Even after his death in *Curtain,* Poirot has to provide an explanation to Hastings, but, in spite of their occasional differences, it must be said that death itself does not break their friendship.

In an early short story "The Adventure of 'The Western Star'," Hastings says, "In spite of his idiosyncracies, I was deeply attached to my quaint little friend" (8). That feeling never changes, except to intensify, as is shown by Hastings' comment in the last novel summing up the relationship; there he says that Poirot is "the man whose influence over me was to shape and mould my life" (2).

As unchanging narrator and participant in thirty-four adventures of Hercule Poirot, Hastings is characteristic as reader surrogate and comic scapegoat—some might say almost too much so—of the traditional Watson figure. In fact, next to Watson himself, Hastings probably has done as much as any character to establish the stereotype of the great detective's incompetent aide. Christie apparently became tired of his inanities and dropped him from the Poirot stories in the late 1930s, just as she was later to tire of Poirot himself. Nevertheless, when she decided to write Poirot's last case, she brought Hastings back and gave him a more than usually important role in it. It was appropriate for her to do so, for though Poirot acted without Hastings on many occasions, the tall "silly-ass" Englishman is inextricably associated with the egotistical little Belgian.

With the elimination of Hastings, Mrs. Ariadne Oliver becomes increasingly prominent in the series. She first appears as a colleague of Parker Pyne and then with Poirot in *Cards on the Table*. After these works of the 'thirties, she does not reappear until *Mrs. McGinty's Dead* in 1952. Then she plays a part in five more novels, four with Poirot. Mrs. Oliver is a prolific writer of sensational detective fiction, who provides Christie the dual opportunity for self-satire and for critical comment on her genre (see Chapter V). In her role as Poirot's friend, she is a comic, at times absurd, foil, who amuses him by her appearance, manner and uncontrolled imagination. Her appearance is that of her creator exaggerated and parodied. In *Cards on the Table* she is introduced as

an agreeable woman of middle age, handsome in a rather untidy fashion with fine eyes, substantial shoulders and a large quantity of rebellious grey hair with which she was continually experimenting. One day her appearance would be highly intellectual—a brow with the hair scraped back from it and coiled in a large bun in the neck—on another Mrs. Oliver would suddenly appear with Madonna loops, or large masses of slightly untidy curls (17).

This basic description changes little—though the hair styles do. Her hair, her size and her poor choice of clothes are the repeated features. Her hair-do in *Dead Man's Folly* is a pseudo-Marquise style, with high-piled curls, but she is dressed in " 'country practical,' consisting of a violent yolk-of-egg rough tweed coat and skirt and a rather bilious-looking mustard coloured jumper" (7). Later in the same novel she is described in iron-grey satin as "looking like an obsolete battleship" (41), and when wearing "her Imperial Purple getup," as "voluminous" and "like a purple blancmange" (110 & 72). In *Third Girl* she chooses "unbecoming apple green brocade, surmounted by one of her more painstaking coiffures" (240). Though obsessively shy in public, she does not seem to be aware that her appearance is bound to attract attention.

Her flamboyance and changeableness in dress and hair styles are matched in her ideas of home decoration. When she redoes her Eaton Terrace drawing room, the wallpaper of gaudy tropical birds is replaced by one of cherries, so many cherries that Poirot feels as if he is in an orchard. The only surprise is that she does not choose a pattern of apples, for —again like her creator—she is excessively fond of them, that is, until a child is killed bobbing for them; then she switches to dates. Before that happens, she is either carrying bags of apples, eating them, or surrounded by their cores. Apples are her support while writing *The Death in the Drain Pipe, The Clue of the Candle Wax* and her other fifty-odd novels. Her detective is Sven Hjerson, a tall, thin, vegetarian Finn, who carries a little device for grating raw carrots and turnips. When asked why he is a vegetarian, Mrs. Oliver's irritated answer is, "How do I know?" (McGinty, 109). She also regrets having made him a Finn: "I don't really know anything about Finns and I'm always getting letters from Finland pointing out something impossible that he's said or done. They seem to read detective stories a good deal in Finland. I suppose it's the long winters with no daylight. In Bulgaria and Roumania they don't seem to read at all. I'd have done better to have made him a Bulgar" (Cards, 71-72). Hjerson is, of course, a parody of Poirot, just as—in appearance, taste, public shyness and abundance of books—Mrs. Oliver is a self-caricature of Christie.

In personality Mrs. Oliver is restlessly excitable, intuitive and wildly over-imaginative. When excited, like Hastings, she wishes to be up and doing. With pins and swatches of hair falling, she wants to be on the chase. In *Third Girl*, as a result, she is coshed. When visited by Poirot afterwards, she tells him that just before the incident she felt something evil present. Poirot is thoughtful: "Mrs. Oliver in her opinion was famous for her intuition. One intuition succeeded another with remarkable rapidity, and Mrs. Oliver always claimed the right to justify the particular intuition which turned out to be right" (145). *Cards on the Table* provides one of the best examples. Partnered with Poirot, Superintendent Battle, and Colonel Race, she warns them not to laugh at her intuition. She quite early hits upon the murderer and says, "My instincts never lie" (36), but later she suspects someone else, then goes back to her original choice, then rejects him utterly, but when he is proven guilty, she triumphantly states, "I always *said* he did it" (248). Whatever the men may think, as an avowed feminist, Mrs. Oliver takes pride in her feminine intuition, believing that this power is foolishly ignored by men. She repeatedly makes the unfinished statement, "Now if a woman were the head of Scotland Yard...," the ellipsis implying that feminine intuition would work wonders of detection. At times she does drop a phrase that serves as a clue for Poirot; after all, she is named for the Ariadne who gave Theseus the clue of thread to find his way out of the labyrinth, thus supplying the word for anything that leads to the solution of a mystery. But her restless changeability of mind usually negates the effectiveness of her intuitive insights. The most notable element in her personality—and in her success as a novelist—is her imagination. However, when involved in one of Poirot's cases, her imagination often becomes bizarre and overwrought. She continually provides lists of possible motives: she gives five, including the correct one, for Mr. Shaitana's murder in *Cards on the Table* and seven, one being a basic clue, for Marlene Tucker's in *Dead Man's Folly*. The possibilities tumble out, and the truth is hidden in the mass. As Poirot puts it, "Mrs. Oliver...can easily come up with about twelve different solutions to everything, most of them not very probable but all of them faintly possible" (Hallowe'en, 42). Even she is aware of her propensity to over-elaborate: "It is never difficult to think of things. The trouble is that you think of too many, and then it all becomes too complicated, and so you have to relinquish some of them and that is rather agony" (Folly, 13). Whereas Hastings cannot think, Mrs. Oliver perhaps thinks too much, but though smarter than Hastings, her appearance, idiosyncracies, intuition and imagination make her another comic foil for Poirot.

His comic image and relationships balance his activities as detective. They are Christie's principal means of preventing his infallible intellect and moral superiority from separating him totally from the humble reader. But what kind of detective is Poirot? Settling in London after World War I, Poirot sets himself up as a professional investigator, but as time passes he becomes more and more an independent crime-solver, choosing cases that interest him and placing him much nearer the brilliant amateur than the official detective, nearer Lord Peter Wimsey than Roderick Alleyn. Just as Christie does not essentially change his personality in the course of the series, neither does she change what he continually proclaims to be his methods of detection: "the psychology" and "order and method."

Since one of Poirot's first axioms is *"Le crime, il est partout"* (Market Basing, 106), he believes that its pervasiveness requires him to suspect everyone. He also believes that man is basically unoriginal, acting according to character patterns; therefore, he must determine the psychology of those involved in a case in order to find the pattern which will point to the guilty person. His position is stated explicitly in *Lord Edgware Dies*: "One cannot be interested in crime without being interested in psychology. It is not the mere act of killing, it is what lies *behind* it that appeals to the expert" (15). The detective is not concerned with just the motive, but with the kind of person who would commit the crime. Corollaries are the personal relations of the people involved, especially the true relationship between the victim and the murderer. These are the psychological issues with which Poirot deals. Since Christie's knowledge of psychology was elementary, the answers Poirot finds are hardly complex, but Christie covers the absence of depth by Poirot's statement about man's unoriginality and his repeated belief that the simplest explanation is always the most likely. To determine "the psychology," Poirot listens—to gossip, to ordinary conversations, to quarrels, to any type of speech that may give him a clue as to how the speaker's mind works. (Always alert, Poirot sometimes finds a major clue in a chance remark; *Lord Edgware Dies* provides the outstanding example.) He knows that if a person is hiding something, he or she will either say too much or make a slip in the attempt to prevaricate. Poirot's attitude is that though a person may be able to tell a few lies convincingly, no one can lie all the time, and whether he is lying or not, sooner or later his words will tell what he really is, to what pattern he belongs. Once Poirot knows that, he can deduce that person's guilt or innocence.

Poirot's emphasis on the psychology of a case causes him to be disdainful of tangible clues as the key to the solving of a mystery. He has been supported by the distinguished historian Robin G. Collingwood:

Scientific historians study problems: they ask questions which they see their way to answering. It was a correct understanding of the same truth that led Monsieur Hercule Poirot to pour scorn on the "human bloodhound" who crawls about the floor trying to collect everything, no matter what, which might conceivably turn out to be a clue; and to insist that the secret of detection was to use what, with possibly wearisome iteration, he called "the little grey cells." You can't collect your evidence before you begin thinking, he meant: because thinking means asking questions . . . and nothing is evidence except in relation to some definite question. The difference between Poirot and Holmes in this respect is deeply significant of the change that has taken place in the understanding of historical method in the last forty years.[13]

Poirot is less a human bloodhound than almost any other major fictional detective; rather, as Collingwood indicates, he formulates questions which must be answered. Indeed, he solves two cases without ever leaving his flat: "The Disappearance of Mr. Davenheim" and *The Clocks*. The "eyes of the mind" are his tools of detection. He says to Hastings in "The King of Clubs," "How often must I tell you that clues come from *within*? In the little gray cells of the brain lies the solution of every mystery" (149).

Poirot is aware of the one great danger of depending solely on the mind, that is, the development of a theory and the attempt to force the facts to fit it, discarding those which do not. He is cautious not to fall into this logical snare, for he knows that the facts that do not fit may turn out to be the most important: "If the fact will not fit the theory—let the theory go" (Styles, 60). Everything matters, however insignificant it may seem. Therefore, though he spends little time running about looking for fingerprints, shreds of torn cloth, or other such things, he does not ignore what is discovered. On the contrary, he says, "One never knows what may help and what may not. One has to clear out of the way so many things that do not matter and that confuse the issue" (Hickory, 118). Until the extraneous matter is eliminated, the truth cannot be found. His winnowing of the possibilities eventually leads to what has appeared to be an unrelated fact, but which, in reality, is the necessary piece to complete the whole and provide a clear, coherent pattern of persons and events. The process includes mentally classifying the gathered information, placing it in its proper sequence, and analyzing its relationships and significance. When Poirot has accomplished these three steps, he has his pattern, knows the murderer and can explain "everything." Among his many descriptions of the process is that in *Evil Under the Sun*:

One assembles the pieces. It is like a mosaic—many colours and patterns—and every strange-shaped little piece must be fitted into its own place.

\* \* \*

   . . . One arranges very methodically the pieces of the puzzle—one sorts the colours—and then perhaps a piece of one colour that should fit in with—say, the fur rug, fits in instead in a black cat's tail (144).

As his explanation indicates—whatever the nature of the evidence, psychological or tangible—it is the mind's ability to interpret the meaning of that evidence which brings him to the moment when he can say, "I know."

However, the necessity of not revealing too much too soon to the reader leads Christie to have Poirot make cryptic comments or fail to tell all he knows until he is ready. He copies Holmes' curious incident of the dog in the night in such exchanges as

"There is the matter of the footprints in the flower bed."

\*\*\*

"But I see no footprints."
"No," said Poirot, straightening a little pile of books on a table. "There are none" (Links, 82).

On a similar occasion in *Cards on the Table* he admits, "Ah, well, I am not above stealing the tricks of others" (93). Another habit is to make lists which mean nothing to anyone but himself, thus thoroughly confusing both companions and readers. Besides a list of ten questions needing explanation, *Murder on the Orient Express* presents this example: "Then there are some minor points that strike me as suggestive—for instance, the position of Mrs. Hubbard's sponge-bag, the name of Mrs. Armstrong's mother, the detective methods of M. Hardman, the suggestion of M. MacQueen that Ratchett himself destroyed the charred note we found, Princess Dragomiroff's Christian name, and a grease spot on a Hungarian passport" (205). Among many others are the timetable of events and the list of significant facts in *Appointment with Death*, the unaccounted-for evidence in "Dead Man's Mirror," and the "pieces of his jig-saw" in *Evil Under the Sun*. The lengthiest instance occurs in *Death in the Clouds*, where four pages list the items carried aboard the *Prometheus* by its passengers, only two of which items are significant to the solution. Poirot's refusal to tell all is also seen after he knows the identity of the murderer. Even though he says, "I know," "I am sure," or "It is all clear," he still does not say "who" until he is ready. His usual excuse is either that he may be wrong or that he does not have needed proof, but since he is continually stating that he is never wrong, these are Christie's subterfuges to hold off the final explanation.

Another of Poirot's statements that cannot be accepted completely is "Of facts, I keep nothing to myself. But to everyone his own interpretation of them" (Ackroyd, 241). The following demonstrate that that statement is less than the whole truth:

That little fact remains up my sleeve until the right moment (Client, 194).

You know—it is my weakness—I like to keep my little secrets till the end (Double, 21).

...the sixth point I will keep to myself for the present (Styles, 32).

"Until the last moment I keep everything here." He tapped his forehead. "At the right moment—I make the spring—like the panther—and, *mon Dieu!* The Consternation!" (Mesopotamia, 143).

Similar incidents of his refusal to tell until that right moment occur in nearly all his works. One can understand the exasperated Jane Olivera in *An Overdose of Death* saying, "I believe you just *like* making things difficult!" Poirot's calm reply to that is "It has been said of me" (151). Christie uses Poirot's vanity as a means of preventing his having to give too much away. He wishes, as he says in *Evil Under the Sun*, to "reserve the explanation for the last chapter" (145). Though a reader may have determined the murderer, very rarely will he have been able to tie up all the loose ends. In a Poirot work that task is left for him and that final chapter. Most often it takes place at what he calls a "little *reunion* in the *salon*" (Styles, 136). He admits that these gatherings are in large part for his ego: "I like an audience, I must confess. I am vain, you see.... I like to say, 'See how clever is Hercule Poirot!' " (*Nile*, 295). When he has all the suspects together, he begins to use what Hastings calls his "lecture" voice. He is very much like a schoolmaster explicating a knotty problem for his students. He enjoys stretching out the explanation as long as possible. He threatens or accuses those present in turn, waiting to confront the guilty person at what he—and only he—decides is the right moment. He has the ability to make plausible cases against almost everyone involved. He may appear during the explanations to ignore the guilty person altogether, as in *Cat Among the Pigeons*; he may seem to exonerate the guilty person early on, only to return to him or her at the end, as in *Funerals are Fatal*; or he may even present two complete explanations and allow the authorities to make a choice, as in *Murder on the Orient Express*. Poirot enjoys these gatherings, for they are his most obvious way of showing his brilliance. The analogy to a schoolmaster has been used; another perhaps even more appropriate is to an omniscient stage director manipulating the actors at first reading of a play. He is in control and can experiment with their emotions, for only he knows the end of the plot.

In order to arrive at conclusive proof to substantiate that climactic revelation, Poirot is not averse to employing tricks which no policeman would dare use. He makes illegal entry into houses in "The Chocolate Box," "The Adventure of the Cheap Flat," and "The Veiled Lady"—in the last by using false police identification. As already noted, he has no scruples about eavesdropping, and the same is true of deliberate lying. Of the latter, he says that "it does not trouble me at all," only adding that "*if* one is going to tell a lie at all, it might as well be an artistic lie, a romantic lie, a convincing lie' " (Client, 71). As unlikely as it may seem, in *The Mystery of the Blue Train* he arranges for another person's mail to be diverted to himself. *Three Act Tragedy* presents his reconstructing a murder with the person he knows guilty playing the victim. In fact, most of his tricks are used *after* he knows the guilty person. They are traps to furnish the necessary absolute proof of the guilt. He threatens a young woman in "Dead Man's Mirror" to force her mother to confess, he hires an actor in *Cards on the Table* to pretend to be a window-washer who has seen a murder committed, and he even sets up a potential victim for the murderer in *Murder on the Links*—and almost brings about that victim's death. He goads the murderer of *Death in the Clouds*, by saying that there are fingerprints, into losing control with "You lie. I wore—." Triumphantly, Poirot says, "Ah, you wore gloves...? I think, Monsieur, that little admission cooks your gander" (253). A nearly identical incident occurs in *The ABC Murders;* after the murderer has been taken away, the following dialogue takes place:

> "That fingerprint clinched things, Poirot," Hastings said thoughtfully. "He went all to pieces when you mentioned that."
> \*\*\*
> "I put that in to please you, my friend."
> "But, Poirot," I cried, "wasn't it true?"
> "Not in the least, *mon ami,*" said Hercule Poirot. (249-50).

Not being an official representative of the law, Poirot is free to employ whatever means he deems fit to serve the ends of justice, even when those means may not be strictly legal. They are accepted because he is *always* for ultimate justice and truth.

Poirot often makes such remarks as "I do not approve of murder" (Appointment, 102) or "I have a thoroughly *bourgeois* attitude to murder" (Cards, 13). His belief that justice must be done and his suspicion of too much mercy, which he believes only results in further deaths, is a significant aspect—despite his ability to lie— of his passion for the truth. In *Murder After Hours* the comment is made that for him "there was only one thing more fascinating than the study of human beings, and that was the pursuit of truth" (167). He likes to think of himself as totally objective: "I do not take sides. I am on the side only of the truth" (Overdose, 156). Since truth is his goal, he is disdainful of the falsification which is caused by sentimentality. He exclaims in *Overdose of Death*: "It is not I who am sentimental! That is an English failing! It is in England that they weep over young sweethearts and dying mothers and devoted children. Me, I am logical" (162). However, this outburst is not always supported by his actions. On the one hand, the death of a ten-year-old blackmailer in *Hallowe'en Party* leaves him unmoved, and the story in *Mrs. McGinty's Dead* of a twelve-year-old who kills her aunt with a meat chopper elicits the opinion that his sympathies are with the aunt. At the same time, he is always sympathetic to motherhood, he is gallant to young women and he loves to play matchmaker. He is seen at his most sentimental in the love story

"The Arcadian Deer." There is no crime in the central plot; rather, the story presents Poirot as miracle-worker, reviving a ballet dancer dying of consumption by reuniting her with the young mechanic, "handsome as a god," who loves her. Not as miraculous, but just as unbelievable, is his allowing a man to be tried for murder in order to reconcile him with his wife; the only excuse for this silliness is that it occurs in Christie's first novel. Whatever one thinks of these lapses from sheer logicality, they are basically another Christie method of making Poirot human.

Once the murderer has been revealed by Poirot, the expectation is that he will be turned over to the law. Though usually the case, it does not always happen. In *Murder on the Orient Express* he allows the murder to go unpunished, in *Murder in Retrospect* the murderer simply walks away, and the same is true of *Dead Man's Folly,* in which Poirot gives his explanation only to the murderer's mother. He is also willing on five occasions to allow the murderer to commit suicide: *The Murder of Roger Ackroyd, Peril at End House, Poirot Loses a Client, Appointment with Death,* and *Death on the Nile*—in the last also allowing one murderer to dispose of another. In *Murder After Hours* he even places a poisoned cup of tea, which the murderer intends for another character, so that it will be drunk by the murderer, who obligingly complies. The outstanding example of Poirot's deciding proper punishment is *Curtain,* the novel which provides an extraordinary close to his career as a detective. In his own words, "I, who value human life—have ended my career by committing murder" (217). Poirot kills to prevent further murders incited by a villain who cannot be convicted. In the sense that Poirot knows the villain from the beginning, the novel is unusual for Christie. Knowing that the villain has caused five deaths, Poirot's task is to prevent his causing another; however, the lack of evidence and his plan forbid his revealing the villain's identity. Thus, there are two mysteries for the reader: who is X? and how will Poirot stop him? The two mysteries are compounded of elements which Christie had in mind long before writing the novel. There are joking comments about Poirot's committing murder in "Murder in the Mews" (1937) and "The Dream" (1939). He scoffs at the idea, but says that if he should, he would be able to get away with it. Another germ appears in a passage of dialogue in *The ABC Murders* (1935):

"Shouldn't wonder if you ended by detecting your own death," said Japp, laughing heartily. "That's an idea, that is. Ought to be put in a book."
"It will be Hastings who will have to do that," said Poirot, twinkling at me (18).

Of course, Hastings does not solve Poirot's death; Poirot has to do it for him by leaving a written account, so Japp is correct. Still a third element is first mentioned in *Peril at End House* (1931), when Poirot praises Iago's perfect crime "because he got others to execute it" (75). Poirot makes the analogy between Iago and X explicit in *Curtain,* and it is to prevent X's secret instigation of others to murder that he makes the decision to be not only detective, but judge, jury, and executioner. He willingly accepts his own death as the price, but he dies unsure of the rightness of that decision. It is ironic that almost his last words should be

> By committing murder, I have saved other lives—innocent lives. But still I do not know... It is perhaps right that I should not know. I have always been so sure—too sure... But now I am very humble and I say like a little child: "I do not know..." (237).

Much of what has been said of Hercule Poirot consciously treats him as if he were an actual person. Such criticism is generally considered old-fashioned, but it seems appropriate for dealing with a character who is a Great Detective. Appearing in nearly half of Christie's work, Poirot has joined that select group of fictional characters who take on a life of their own, independent of the works in which they actually have a role, who are not just known, but quoted, imitated, parodied, and joked about. Among Christie's other characters, only Jane Marple has any claim to this suprafictional quality, and she does not have the popular recognition of Poirot. He may irritate by his idiosyncrasies, he may be insufferably vain, he may not always follow the methods of deduction which he claims are strictly logical, he may exasperate the reader, as well as Hastings, by not revealing what he has discovered until he is ready, or he may seem ridiculously overdone as a character. He *may* cause these reactions, *but* when he is portrayed by Albert Finney on the screen, *Murder on the Orient Express* becomes the most successful of all British films; the initial paperback publication of his last case numbers 1,875,000 copies; several dozen of his cases are always in print; and uncounted numbers of readers lament when they have finished the last of the eighty-five works that there will be no more mysteries for the dapper, egotistical, little Belgian with his grey cells to solve and, in his doing so, to provide them the entertainment of the gentle art of murder.

## Jane Marple

Miss Jane Marple is the most famous of female fictional detectives. This little old lady, this tabby, this snoop, is an utter contrast to Poirot. Whereas he is the outsider, she is most definitely the insider: the village spinster who sees all and knows all. Her village has been her experience, and it has provided her with knowledge of human nature and human actions. She has antecedents in Miss Amelia Viner, another spinster of St. Mary Mead, who is the employer of Katherine Grey, the heroine of *The Mystery of the Blue Train,* and even more in Caroline Sheppard of *The Murder of Roger Ackroyd;* as Christie stated, "I think it is possible that Miss Marple arose from the pleasure I had taken in portraying Dr. Sheppard's sister.... She had been my favourite character in the book—an acidulated spinster, full of curiosity, knowing everything, hearing everything: the complete detective service in the home."[14] Going beyond Christie's works, there is another antecedent: "Miss Marple has some affinity with my own grandmother, also a pink and white old lady who, although having led the most sheltered and Victorian of lives, nevertheless always appeared to be intimately acquainted with the depths of depravity. One could be made to feel incredibly naive and credulous by her reproachful remark: 'But did you believe what they said to you? I never do.' "[15] Also, one of the first detective novels Christie read was Anna Katharine Green's *The Leavenworth Case* (1878), which introduced Amelia Butterworth, the first elderly female detective. Whatever her origin, the Miss Marple of twelve novels and twenty short stories is most certainly not the character portrayed in films by Dame Margaret Rutherford. She is not short, squat, clumsy, and comic; rather she is a tall, slender, dignified late-Victorian of great shrewdness who solves twentieth century crimes.

Her first appearance is in "The Tuesday Night Club" (1928), in which she is described thusly:

she sat erect in the big grandfather chair. Miss Marple wore a black brocade dress, very much pinched in round the waist. Mechlin lace was arranged in a cascade down the front of the bodice. She had on black lace mittens, and a black lace cap surmounted the piled up masses of her snowy hair. She was knitting—something white and soft and fleecy. Her faded blue eyes benignant and kindly, surveyed her nephew and her nephew's guests with gentle pleasure (7).

(Christie purposely overdoes the Victorian image in order to "play with it" later.) Already Miss Marple is an elderly woman, though Christie leaves her age indefinite. In *They Do It With Mirrors,* she is in her mid-sixties. *Nemesis,* the last written Marple novel, states, "Seventy if she is a day—nearer eighty perhaps" (18); earlier in *What Mrs. McGillicuddy Saw!,* Miss Marple says, "I shall be ninety next year" (99)—though this statement is probably part of the act she is playing. In both *The Mirror Crack'd from Side to Side* and *Nemesis,* emphasis is laid in the early chapters upon her becoming more aged, feeble, and forgetful, but in both her powers of detection are undiminished. The only conclusion is that she is somewhere between her mid-sixties and early eighties.

Of her past, little is given. As a child, she had a German governess, was taught to use a back-board for proper posture, and was a student at a *pensionnat* in Florence, where she was "the pink and white English girl from a Cathedral Close" who planned to nurse lepers (Mirrors, 8 & 10). She had two uncles who were canons, of Ely and Chichester Cathedrals, a great-uncle who was an admiral, and a distant cousin in the nobility, Lady Ethel Merridew. Only one beau is mentioned, and she found him dull. These few scattered facts establish her upper middle-class background, and that apparently is their sole purpose. She inherited a small fixed income, and she has to be careful with her money, though her nephew Raymond West is very generous to her.

Also in the first story, she is already living at "Danemead," her house in St. Mary Mead, "that English Garden of Eden."[16] If it is a garden of Eden, the serpent is present. Four of the novels and five of the short stories include murders in St. Mary Mead or the country houses close by. As she continually says, "Very painful and distressing things happen in villages sometimes" (Tuesday, 10). When Raymond West says that he regards St. Mary Mead as "a stagnant pool," Miss Marple replies. "That is really not a very good simile, dear Raymond. Nothing, I believe, is so full of life under the microscope as a drop of water from a stagnant pool" (Vicarage, 166).

Though St. Mary Mead is idyllic on the surface, it undergoes great change in the course of the works. It is twenty-five miles southeast of London and twelve miles from the coast. As London expands, St. Mary Mead is affected by change. For example, by the time of *What Mrs. McGillicuddy Saw!*, jets fly over the village from a nearby airfield. In *A Murder Is Announced*, Miss Marple notes the changes: "Every village and small country place is full of people who've just come and settled there without any ties to bring them. The big houses have been sold, and the cottages have been converted and changed"; this statement seems to be one of regret, especially of the fact that people no longer know those living around them: "that's really the particular way the world has changed since the war" (127). However, in *The Mirror Crack'd from Side to Side*, she comes to terms with the changes—a supermarket; Gossington Hall being bought by a film star; modern plumbing, electric cookers, and dishwashers; The Development, a housing project which she is curious to see; and new people, such as Cherry Baker and her husband, whom she likes—"And why not? Miss Marple asked herself sternly. These things had to be.... Times change. That is a thing which has to be accepted!" (10 & 44). At the same time, she recognizes that human nature does not change: "The new world was the same as the old. The houses were different, the streets were called Closes, the clothes were different, the voices were different, but the human beings were the same as they always had been" (16). Her dual perspective, and her refusal to live in the past, is evidence of Miss Marple's clear-mindedness. Her one deliberate exercise in nostalgia, her visit to Bertram's Hotel, results in her very quick realization that it is foolish to try to recapture the past: the hotel "didn't seem real to her because she was now acclimatized in this present year of Our Lord," and her conclusion is "I learned (what I suppose I really knew already) that one can never go back, that one should not ever try to go back—that the essence of life is going forward" (45 & 195).

The effect of St. Mary Mead as a locus for most of Miss Marple's cases is to provide a repertory company of characters who appear and reappear. Her nephew Raymond West visits her and arranges vacations for her. He is a "modern" writer, whose poems have no capital letters and whose novels are "about unpleasant people leading lives of surpassing dullness" (Vicarage, 166). Besides providing vacations, his major function is to be the butt of Miss Marple's gentle raillery for his ignorance of people, as in "Ingots of Gold: "You are so credulous, my dear, so easily gulled" (49). Though West is her only close relative, she has a wide circle of acquaintances. There are her maids over the years, such as Faithful Florence, "that grenadier of a parlourmaid," who aids her in *What Mrs. McGillicuddy Saw!;* the abominable Miss Knight, her nurse in *The Mirror Crack'd from Side to Side;* Cherry and Jim Baker, who take over the chores in the same novel and continue in *A Caribbean Mystery* and *Nemesis;* and the unfortunate Gladys of *A Pocketfull of Rye,* who is one of a line of "nice little maids," with names such as Amy, Clara, Edna, and Alice, whom Miss Marple takes from St. Faith's Orphanage and trains and then sends on to better positions.

Among her own class in and around St. Mary Mead are the Rev. Leonard Clement and his wife Griselda, Colonel and Mrs. Bantry, Miss Hartnell, Miss Wetherby, Mrs. Price-Ridley, and Doctor Haydock, who pop in and out, either actually or by allusion. The Chief Constable, Colonel Melchett, becomes an admirer of Miss Marple's ability in the first novel and reappears later. Sir Henry Clithering, ex-Commissioner of Scotland Yard, is her champion in the early short stories and *The Body in the Library;* he is joined by his godson Dermot Craddock in *A Murder Is Announced,* and then Craddock appears without him in *What Mrs. McGillicuddy Saw!* and *The Mirror Crack'd from Side to Side.* Miss Marple "gets along" with the police, with one exception, once the surprise of a little old lady as detective has passed. Sometimes her reputation precedes her; Inspector Last of *Sleeping Murder* knows of her work in *Murder at the Vicarage* and *The Moving Finger*. He and such others as Inspectors Neele and Curry (*A Pocketfull of Rye* and *They Do It With Mirrors)* and Superintendents Harper and Nash *(The Body in the Library* and *The Moving Finger)* are distinguishable only by their names. All are quiet, serious, straightforward, unassuming, careful men, with unimaginative exteriors, which often cause them to be underrated, a tendency they encourage. Essentially, they are brothers of Christie's principal policeman, Superintendent Battle. The one exception is Inspector Slack of *Murder at the Vicarage, The Body in the Library* and a few early short stories. He is Christie's most satiric presentation of the stupid policeman. He is disliked by his superior Colonel Melchett and even by the Vicar of the first novel: "I had taken such a dislike to Inspector Slack that the prospect of his success failed to appeal to me. A successful Slack would, I thought, be even more odious than a baffled one" (98). His rudeness and overbearing manner are the result of his apparent determination to contradict his name; he is anything but slack, having great energy, but little else to commend him as an investigator. He is, of course, contemptuous of Miss Marple's suggestions. Her view of him is expressed to the Vicar: "poor Inspector Slack—well, he's exactly like the young lady in the boot shop who wants to sell you patent leather because she's got it in your size, and doesn't take any notice of the fact that you want brown calf." The Vicar's response is that that "is a very good description of Slack" (217). However, Miss Marple does allow him to take the public credit for the solution of the vicarage murder.

The initial reactions, whether scorn or amazement, of the various policemen to Miss Marple as detective are readily understandable. Her white hair, gentle manner, and apparent frailty make her appear to be just another spinster aunt. Her entrance in *A Pocket Full of Rye* illustrates a typical, and deceptive, first impression: "Crump [the butler] saw a tall, elderly lady wearing an old fashioned tweed coat and skirt, a couple of scarves and a small felt hat with a bird's wing. The old lady carried a capacious handbag, and an aged but good quality suitcase reposed by her feet" (75). Her gardening and birdwatching, both at least partly screens for detection—or just snooping, add to her spinster image. (In *Sleeping Murder* she prevents an attempted murder by squirting soapy water in the killer's eyes and says, "So fortunate... that I was just syringing the greenfly off your roses" [231]!) Her likes also contribute to the image. When she contemplates receiving £ 20,000 in *Nemesis,* she thinks of buying partridges and *marrons glacés* and taking a trip to the opera—all "lady-like" desires. Though abstemious, she is not a teetotaler, believing that strong drink should always be handy in case of a shock or accident *or* a gentleman caller. Her frequent offers of whiskey to her male visitors is typical of her attitude toward men, which is both old-fashioned and a shade patronizing: " 'The gentlemen' were, in Miss Marple's mind, in a totally different category from her own sex. They required two eggs plus bacon for breakfast, three good nourishing meals a day, and were never to be contradicted or argued with before dinner" (Rye, 136). She is a firm believer in the psychology of dress, and though it is a somewhat snobbish concept, it is also often accurate. Of the victim in *The Body in the Library,* she says, "to put it bluntly, Ruby wasn't a lady. She belonged to the class that wear their best clothes, however unsuitable to the occasion" (119). Consciously or unconsciously on her part, her image as elderly spinster effectively camouflages from strangers her detectival activities. Even her fondness for the hard-boiled fiction of Dashiell Hammett is presented as just another spinsterish eccentricity.

Much is made of Miss Marple's Victorian attitude toward sex in the novels and stories, particularly the early ones, but her Victorianism is not ignorance. She may blush when sex enters the conversation, but she knows what it is.

"Sex" as a word had not been much mentioned in Miss Marple's young days, but there had been plenty of it—not talked about so much—but enjoyed far more than nowadays, or so it seemed to her.... she knew [the forms of sex]. Plenty of sex, natural and unnatural. Rape, incest, perversions of all kinds. (Some kinds, indeed, that even the clever young men from Oxford who wrote books didn't seem to have heard about.) (Caribbean, 2)

When she has to read movie fan magazines for a case, she is not shocked by the activities described; in fact, her remark is "*most natural*"—"A lot of gossip. A lot of scandal. A great preoccupation with who is in love with whom, and all the rest of it. Really, you know, practically exactly the same sort of thing that goes on in St. Mary Mead" (Crack'd, 166). As any "Victorian" would be, she is well aware of the double standard: " 'Only,' added Miss Marple cynically, 'it's easier for gentlemen, of course' " (Library, 110). Her major objection to sex in the modern world is the sense that one must participate: "To have sex experience urged on you exactly as though it was an iron tonic! Poor young things..." (Caribbean, 3). If one cannot say that Miss Marple is sexually liberated, neither can one say that she is a prude or naive.

Though her manner and appearance may seem to place Miss Marple as just another charming and helpless old lady, those with whom she comes in close contact soon learn differently. In *What*

*Mrs. McGillicuddy Saw!,* the comment is made that "Everybody in St. Mary Mead knew Miss Marple; fluffy and dithery in appearance, but inwardly as sharp and as shrewd as they make them" (16-17). The reaction is even stronger in *Nemesis,* where one character says of her, "So gentle—and so ruthless," and another replies, "The most frightening woman I ever met" (264). When she is described by Miss Blacklock in *A Murder is Announced* as "a very harmless old creature," Inspector Craddock thinks, "Dangerous as a rattlesnake if you only knew" (195). Such adjectives as *sharp, shrewd, ruthless, frightening,* and *dangerous* are appropriate for her when she is on a case.

Though as an accomplished liar as Poirot—always, again, for the ends of justice—she can immediately spot someone else's lies. The reason she can is that she does not trust people. In *Murder at the Vicarage* she says, "I'm afraid that observing human nature for as long as I have done, one gets not to expect very much from it" (19). She makes such statements over and over:

It really is dangerous to believe people. *I* never have for years (Sleeping, 239).

There's nothing that you can tell me about people's minds that would astonish or surprise me (St. Peter, 79).

"As Uncle Mathew grew older, he got more and more suspicious. He didn't trust anybody."
    "Very wise of him," said Miss Marple. "The depravity of human nature is unbelievable" (Jest, 22).

You simply cannot afford to believe everything that people tell you. When there's anything fishy about, I never believe anyone at all. You see, I know human nature so well (Library, 126).

Her innate distrust and her belief that human nature does not change are primary components of her ruthlessness. Only in the last-written novel does she come to a realization of that ruthlessness: " 'D'you know,' said Miss Marple to herself, 'it's extraordinary I never thought about it before. I believe, you know, I *could* be ruthless" (Nemesis, 9). This ruthlessness takes various forms. She is pitiless to criminals, saying "I do not like evil beings who do evil things" (Nemesis, 129). She says of the murderer in *The Body in the Library,* "Really, I feel quite pleased to think of him hanging" (157), and she can accept with equanimity the deliberate killing of the murderer in *The Mirror Crack'd from Side to Side.* Another evidence of this quality is her willingness to use others for her own purpose, either by taking advantage of their images of her, by risking their lives, or by sheer deception. Though her purposes are without fail honorable, the means employed display a self-assurance and a sense of her rightness that borders on the egoistic.

Not that she shirks danger to herself; she says, "One cannot go through life without attracting certain risks if they are necessary" (*Nemesis*, 249). However, because of her age, she sometimes requires an assistant. It is noteworthy that she usually chooses another woman: Megan Hunter in *The Moving Finger*, Lucy Eyelesbarrow in *What Mrs. McGillicuddy Saw!*, and Mitzi the cook in *A Murder Is Announced*. Whatever the risk to herself or others, she is determined to see justice done; therefore, she hires Lucy and goes herself to Brackhampton, or she goes on her own to Yewtree Lodge to avenge her Gladys in *A Pocket Full of Rye*. Her attitude toward personal danger is forcefully expressed at the end of *The Moving Finger:* "I needed someone to help me, someone of high courage and good brains. I found the person I needed [Megan Hunter]...it was dangerous, but we are not put into this world, Mr. Burton, to avoid danger when an innocent fellow-creature's life is at stake" (253). Rafiel's designation of her as nemesis in *A Caribbean Mystery* and her acceptance of that designation in the novel of the same name is more than justified.

Related to her ruthlessness is her independence. She does not like sacrifices made for her. Her dislike of Miss Knight in *The Mirror Crack'd from Side to Side* is the result of that nurse's attempt to coddle her; Miss Marple's remark is "I, although I may be old, am *not* a mentally afflicted child" (12). She continually asserts her ability to run her own life, even in the presence of danger. In *A Murder Is Announced,* she tells Inspector Craddock, "I assure you, Inspector, that I can take care of myself" (130), and she is displeased in *Nemesis* when she finds that Rafiel has asked Professor Wanstead to keep a watchful eye on her. She does take care of herself; not once does she have to be rescued by a male; in fact, her one rescue from likely death is by two *female* detectives in *Nemesis*.

Her independence and toughness have an element of pride in them; that is, she is self-confident enough to glory in her own successes. After she solves the murders in *A Pocket Full of Rye,* "there came a surge of triumph—the triumph some specialist might feel who has successfully reconstructed an extinct animal from a fragment of jawbone and a couple of teeth" (182). Miss Marple is a specialist, and though often afflicted with false modesty, she knows that she is good at her specialty of crime-solving.

In *Murder at the Vicarage,* Reverend Leonard Clement states, "There is no detective in England equal to a spinster lady of uncertain age with plenty of time on her hands" (31). What makes Miss Marple perhaps a meddlesome nuisance to her neighbors also makes her a superb detective. She may enter a case out of outrage, as in *A Pocket Full of Rye* or *What Mrs. McGillicuddy Saw!* or become involved through a request for help, as in *They Do It with Mirrors* or *The Moving Finger,* or simply intrude because she is in the vicinity and curious, as in *A Caribbean Mystery* and *A Murder Is Announced.* What attracts her are "really interesting people": in *A Caribbean Mystery* she indicates that sensational society murders, with lovers, drugs, and alcohol, are "not her cup of tea" (8). Like her creator, she prefers domestic murders, and her first assumption is that if the victim is married, the spouse is the logical suspect. This view coincides with her belief that "it is always the *obvious* person who has done the crime" (Crack'd, 165). Though Christie is known for her frequent use of the "least-likely suspect," in most of the Marple works the murderer is the obvious suspect. The trick is that usually it seems impossible for that obvious suspect to have committed the crime because of the circumstances of the deed, that is, there is some form of alibi.

To solve her cases, Miss Marple uses analogy, role-playing, careful observation, and, to use Poirot's phrase, order and method. Combined with her basic distrust of others' statements, her ability to see through those statements, and her ruthless determination to see justice prevail, these abilities are the essentials of her skill as a detective.

Miss Marple has often been criticized for depending too much on intuition, but intuition, as used by her, is not just guesswork. It has a firm foundation in analogical reasoning. In the first novel Miss Marple herself answers the charge of intuition, after explaining her use of analogy: "But, after all, that is a very sound way of arriving at the truth. It's really what people call intuition and make such a fuss about. Intuition is like reading a word without having to spell it out. A child can't do that, because it has had so little experience. But a grown-up person knows the word because he's seen it often before" (85). And so her "intuition" is actually the result of close observation of human types. Later in the same novel, she presents an extended analysis of the method which becomes the basis of her detection:

One begins to class people, quite definitely, just as though they were birds or flowers, group so and so, genus this, species that. Sometimes, of course, one makes mistakes, but less and less, as time goes on. And then, too, one tests oneself.... I have always wondered whether, if some day a really big mystery came along, I should be able to do the same thing. I mean—just solve it correctly. Logically it ought to be exactly the same thing.... In fact, the only way is to compare people with other people you have known or come across. You'd be surprised if you knew how very few distinct types there are in all (216).

Such a method of classification and comparison can hardly be called intuition; rather, it is a process of observing repeated patterns of action, finding similarities between externally different circumstances, and foreseeing the likely outcome. Mr. Harbottle and the maidservant, Mrs. Carruthers and her two gills of pickled shrimp, Mrs. Pusey's nephew, Nurse Ellerton, and numerous other inhabitants of St. Mary Mead provide Miss Marple with an index system for her encounters with crime, a system for evaluating the actions of everyone involved.

Another charge that has been made against her is that she often depends upon social chit-chat and gossip. She stoutly defends the practice: *"How often is tittle tattle, as you call it, true!. . .* if [people] really examined the facts they would find that it was true nine times out of ten! That's really just what makes people so annoyed about it" ("Christmas," 149). In fact, as she says in *A Caribbean Mystery,* social conversation is her "one weapon." She realizes that people expect old women to gossip and snoop; it would be noticeable if they did not. People may be bored by an old lady's rambling conversation, but they do not suspect her of an ulterior motive. Her use of social conversation requires her to be a consummate actress, and she is. It is her success in playing the expected spinster role which enables her to gather needed information. She may often pretend to be flustered or flighty, but behind that facade is " 'What a fool I sound,' thought Miss Marple" (Caribbean, 54). That she is thoroughly conscious of the effect she presents and the advantage to herself in using it is expressed in *Nemesis:* "Yes, I can see I'm quite recognizable as an old tabby. There are so many old tabbies, and they're all so much alike. And, of course, yes, I'm very ordinary. An ordinary rather scatterbrained old lady. And that of course is very good camouflage" (49). In other words, she will accept others' opinions of her, but only to use them for her own purposes.

Miss Marple is also a person of order and method. Whether she is planning excursions around London or systematically evaluating a group of tour passengers, she proceeds logically. In *Nemesis,* when she must solve a case about which she does not even know the nature, she sensibly begins with her only contact to the man, now dead, who has challenged her to it, his former nurse. The statement in *They Do It with Mirrors* that "Miss Marple, in a precise and businesslike fashion, collected certain data" (19) is just one example of Christie's emphasis upon this quality of Miss Marple. Perhaps the best illustration of such emphasis is *What Mrs. McGillicuddy Saw!.* The reader is informed that "Miss Marple set about her plan of campaign methodically" and "Dispassionately, like a general planning a campaign, or an accountant assessing a business, Miss Marple weighed up and set down in her mind the facts for and against further enterprise" (24 & 22). More evidence in the same novel is her use of friends and friends' children who have expertise in maps and train schedules. Though Miss Marple does not talk about order and method as Poirot does, she certainly possesses those necessary traits of a successful detective.

Another element of Miss Marple's success as a detective is her power of observation. When everyone in *They Do It with Mirrors* thinks that someone is trying to kill Carrie Louise Serrocord, Miss Marple says, "That's where the misdirection comes in" (212). She has arrived at the correct deduction, that the Great Hall of Stonygates has been used as a stage setting for murder and that the "backstage" area is what is important, and so she solves another baffling case. She is not misdirected by what she calls "a conjuring trick," for she observes closely and uses her accumulated knowledge to deduce the true circumstances. The major clue in *What Mrs. McGillucddy Saw!* is the meaning of *tontine;* Miss Marple is on to that less than halfway through the novel. Likewise, in *A Murder Is Announced* she quickly realizes that no one in Miss Blacklock's parlor could have seen the murder take place, for they were in a dark room blinded by a glaring flashlight: a deduction that staggers Dermot Craddock. And in *Sleeping Murder* it is Miss Marple who realizes the significance of a quotation from *The Duchess of Malfi.*

Perhaps the stories of *Thirteen Problems* best demonstrate Miss Marple's close observation of detail, usually of a domestic nature and easily ignored. These stories are told by members of the Tuesday Night Club or by guests of the Bantrys. Everyone present is asked to provide the correct solutions to the mysteries; Miss Marple always does. In "Motive v. Opportunity" she recognizes from her childhood the use of disappearing ink on a will to determine an inheritance. Also from her childhood is the knowledge of the language of flowers, taught to her and her sister by their German governess, which helps to explain a murder in "The Four Suspects." Her knowledge that gardeners do not work on Whit Monday is the source of her solution to "Ingots of Gold," and the properties of litmus paper are the basis for her solving "The Blue Geranium." She solves a poisoning in "The Tuesday Night Club" because she knows what "hundreds and thousands" are: candy decorations for desserts. These stories solved after the fact and from a distance are studies in pure ratiocination, and they present Miss Marple as an acute observer and reasoner.

In *Murder at the Vicarage* two suspects confess to the murder very early, confessions which are palpably false even to the egregious Inspector Slack. Of this incident, Joseph M. Levine has recently commented that Slack "sees that [the early confessions] cannot be right and rejects them; Miss Marple sees that they must neither be accepted nor rejected but understood, by which means they can be made to serve after all in the reconstruction of the murder."[17] Levine is correct, for Miss Marple considers everything significant; her view is expressed in the same novel: "The point is that one must provide an explanation for everything. Each thing has got to be explained away satisfactorily. If you have a theory that fits every fact—well, then it must be the right one. But that's extremely difficult" (219). For this reason, she often says quite early that she *knows* the murderer's identity, but refuses to divulge the name because she has no proof. As she says in *The Body in the Library*, "I know who did do it. But it's not going to be easy to prove" (145); a few pages later, she adds that "it is so important, isn't it, to be quite sure—to 'make assurance doubly sure,' as Shakespeare has it?" (150). A significant result of her tendency to be close-mouthed because of lack of evidence is that, particularly in some of the short stories, there is no indication of *how* she came to *know*; three examples are "Death by Drowning," "A Christmas Tragedy," and "The Affair at the Bungalow." Apparently, her knowledge of people is the method, but no statements to that effect are given. In the novels, there is more indication, as in her occasional mystifying and Poirotesque lists of clues, such as the one in *A Murder Is Announced:* "Lamps. Violets. Where is bottle of aspirin? Delicious Death. Making enquiries. Severe affliction bravely borne. Iodine. Pearls. Letty. Berne. Old Age Pension" (240). Another result of her not having proof is that she often lays traps for the persons she knows are guilty, as in *Murder at the Vicarage, The Moving Finger, A Murder Is Announced,* and *What Mrs. McGillicuddy Saw!* traps which involve danger to herself or others, but which always succeed. In her last two cases her reticence seems to be an effort on her part to shield others from knowledge of what she considers unwholesome sexual desires: lesbianism in *Nemesis* and incest in *Sleeping Murder.* Of the latter she says, "It seems so horribly plain to me. But perhaps it's better that you shouldn't understand" (171). The only novel in which lack of proof prevents Miss Marple from bringing the murderer to justice before the final word is *At Bertram's Hotel.* She is teamed there with Chief Inspector Fred Davy, the most distinctive of her police colleagues; he is described as vaguely like a large bumblebee with a perfect photographic memory. He solves a series of baffling robberies, with some help from Miss Marple, but at the end while both know the identity of a murderer, they have no evidence. They vow to continue the case, and the reader is left to assume that guilt will be established. How can only be conjectured, but with her record of success, one can have confidence in Miss Marple's tenacity and ability as a detective.

Of the Marple works, Michael Holquist has said, "The message of the stories in which she appears is always the same: the great heart of darkness beats under the quaint surface rhythms of a village church social no less ineluctably than at the headwaters of jungle rivers."[18] Though Holquist may seem to be pressing his Conradian analogy, he makes a valid judgment, for Miss Marple is always conscious of evil lurking behind the facade of ordinary existence. She is committed to uncovering it and eliminating it from her world. Whether in St. Mary Mead, Brackhampton, London, or the Caribbean, her careful observation of human nature and her distrust of mere surface appearance, her orderly approach to her cases, her independence and fearlessness, her ability and willingness to use the images which others have of her, her consciousness of her own worth both as an individual and as a detective, and her essential ruthlessness on behalf of the innocent—expressed in her self-confidence and determination—make her a formidable adversary of evil. In Miss Marple, Christie has taken the traditional spinster of literature and added qualities which contrast with or transcend the convention and in so doing has created one of the most famous women of twentieth century fiction.

## Tuppence & Tommy Beresford

Christie's second novel, *The Secret Adversary,* introduced her husband-and-wife team of Tuppence and Tommy Beresford, and the last novel she wrote, *Postern of Fate,* also involved them. In the fifty-one year interim, there were three other Tuppence and Tommy works: *Partners in Crime, N or M?,* and *By the Pricking of My Thumbs.* These five works take Tommy from the age of twenty-five to seventy-six and Tuppence from twenty to seventy-one. There are some inconsistencies in assigned times and ages, particularly in the last two novels, and one major reason is that Christie never changes the Beresfords' personalities and their ability to act; rather, they remain essentially the same young-at-heart couple of the first novel, even when in their seventies. Tuppence and Tommy's adventures are those of a comic "dynamic duo," and, as a result, some critics of detective fiction have found them "inane," "insufferable," and "intolerable." These critics have refused to accept their works as comic adventure stories within the detective mode, rather than straight detective fiction. Tuppence and Tommy begin as, and remain, comic versions of the amateur detective. Their most serious case of detection, *N or M?,* is an exaggerated form of the spy thriller. *The Secret Adversary* is a self-parody of the young-people-catching-the-master-criminal type, *Partners in Crime* is a collection of parodies of other fictional detectives, and both *By the Pricking of*

*My Thumbs* and *Postern of Fate* consist of the relatively unimportant solving of mysteries about long past events. Christie's sense of humor and playfulness is generally ignored in discussions of her work, but Tuppence and Tommy cannot even be considered without realizing that Christie's works about them are overt comedy.

In recounting how she came to write their first book, Christie said that her first title was *The Joyful Venture*, then *The Young Adventurers*, and only finally *The Secret Adversary*.[19] This comic thriller, dedicated "To all those who lead monotonous lives in the hope that they may experience at second hand the delights and dangers of adventure," is indeed a "Joyful Venture" for its two young protagonists. Concerned with a Bolshevist conspiracy—as is the frame of *Partners in Crime; N or M?* and *Postern of Fate* shift to the Fascists—it contains sensational chapter endings; much coincidence, which is deliberately emphasized; and, altogether, the atmosphere of a P.G. Wodehouse novel. This first work not only introduces the pair, but also establishes their relationship. Christie seems to have set the pattern for husband-and-wife detective teams, with the wife as the more active comrade-in-arms and the love interest less passionate than comic, but still sincere and deeply felt. The pair are childhood friends, who after meeting during World War I in a military hospital where Tuppence is a nurse and Tommy is recovering from a wound received in France, meet again accidentally four years later at the beginning of *The Secret Adversary*. In the first novel, they meet Albert, aged nine, who is to be their lifelong servant. The novel ends with Tommy becoming the heir of a rich uncle and with their plans to marry. Six years later, at the end of *Partners in Crime*, Tuppence announces that she is going to have a baby, and in *N or M?*, the reader discovers that she has had twins, Deborah and Derek. Deborah has a war job and Derek is in the RAF—chronologically, they are approximately thirteen years old. By the time of *Postern of Fate*, Deborah is nearly forty and has provided the Beresfords with three grandchildren. As can be seen, unlike the Poirot and Miss Marple works, these of Tuppence and Tommy do indicate chronological aging of the characters, but in personality the two protagonists remain "The Young Adventurers" of *The Secret Adversary*.

*Partners in Crime* differs from the other four works in that it is not really a novel, but a collection of fourteen connected stories: the first of which serves as an introduction to the others, which are parodies of the methods and eccentricities of various fictional detectives. The detectives parodied are, in order, Dr. Thorndyke, Desmond and Francis Oakwood, McCarty and Riordan, Sherlock

Holmes, Thornley Colton: the Blind Problemist, Father Brown, the "Busies" of Lew Wallace, the Old Man in the Corner, Hanaud and Mr. Ricardo, Inspector French, Roger Sheringham, Dr. Fortune and Superintendent Bell, and Hercule Poirot. Many years after writing this book, Christie said, "Some of them by now I cannot even recognize.... They all seemed to me at the time to write well and entertainingly in their different fashions."[20] The format for presenting these spoofs is for Tuppence and Tommy's becoming the International Detective Agency at 118 Haleham Street, London—slogan: Blunt's Brilliant Detectives. They are recruited for the job by the mysterious Mr. Carter of the Secret Service in the hope that they will capture a Russian agent, known as No. 16, who communicates by blue letters from "a ham merchant anxious to find his wife" (14) with "16" written beneath the stamp. Before this agent is finally caught—in female disguise—in the last story (honors to Poirot!), Tuppence and Tommy pass the time by pretending to be the various detectives when other cases appear.

Of the fourteen cases, together they solve two, Tommy solves seven, and Tuppence solves five (one of her own devising). They treat most of the cases as contests between themselves, and there is much banter between them. A few examples will illustrate:

"I don't know that I should be at my best dealing with a gang," said Tommy. "The amateur crime, the crime of quiet family life—that is where I flatter myself that I shine. Drama of strong domestic interest. That's the thing—with Tuppence at hand to supply all those little feminine details which are so important, and so apt to be ignored by the denser male."

His eloquence was arrested abruptly, as Tuppence threw a cushion at him and requested him not to talk nonsense. (114)

"If you must be Sherlock Holmes," she observed, "I'll get you a nice little syringe and bottle labelled Cocaine, but for God's sake leave that violin alone." (77)

"You are the great Hercule Poirot."

"Exactly. No moustaches, but lots of grey cells."

"I've a feeling," said Tuppence, "that this particular adventure will be called the 'Triumph of Hastings.'"

"Never," said Tommy. "It isn't done. Once the idiot friend, always the idiot friend. There's an etiquette in these matters." (213)

Their role playing comes from their reading; when Tuppence says, "Well, I have read every detective novel that has been published in the last ten years," Tommy replies, "So have I" (18). Later he complains, "It is a pity that real life is so different from fiction" (164). He does not apparently recognize how his words apply to his and Tuppence's own adventures, for all of them are determined by the types of cases of those whom they are imitating. Christie allows them to play at being their literary idols, and she allows them to succeed at their play, while making jokes at the expense of her peers, and herself. When Tuppence tabulates their successes, one can only lament with Tommy that, indeed, it *is* a pity that crime-solving in real life is not the entertaining, exciting, and clever fun of the world of Tuppence and Tommy—the world of comedy.

With the exception of not having the parodic element, the four novels present a world which varies little from that of *Partners in Crime*. It is a world in which there are master criminals and spies and traitors; where there are secret drawers in desks and secret entrances to hidden rooms, manipulated by china birds attached to mantelpieces; where a coded message may be found in an old copy of Stevenson's *The Black Arrow* or important documents be hidden in swan-stools, called Oxford and Cambridge; where an unemployed couple decide to run an advertisement "Two young adventurers for hire. Willing to do anything, go anywhere. Pay must be good. No unreasonable offer refused." (Adversary, 9) and refer to each other as "old thing" and "old bean"; where both criminals and detectives use disguises; and where dolls full of jewels fall from chimneys and lists of spies are contained in a child's nursery book. In other words, it is a world of improbability and exaggeration, of comic adventures.

Such paraphenalia are not the only elements contributing to the purposely ludicrous atmosphere of the novels. Coincidence plays a large part in the novels, although Tommy calls it "luck." For example, "sheer accident"—he slips on a cake of soap—leads Tommy to the identity of the German agent N; no detection is involved. In *Postern of Fate* the Beresfords just happen to buy a house where a murder once took place, they just happen to find a coded message about the murder while sorting books, and there just happens to have been a census on the day of the murder, listing those present in the house. Many other examples could be given. Another element is the presentation of other characters. The criminals, especially the minions of "Mr. Brown," "the master criminal of this age," in *The Secret Adversary*, are caricatures. They range from the evilly beautiful Rita Vandemeyer, whose "eyes, of a piercingly electric blue, seemed to possess a faculty of boring into the very soul of the person she was looking at" (62) and "the well-bred Irish gentleman, the pale Russian, and the efficient German" (50) to Number Fourteen, who gloats, "The Streets is going to run with blood, so they say. . . . Dreams of it, sometimes, I does. And diamonds and pearls rolling about in the gutter for anyone to pick up!" (54). As opponents to such villains, there are the mysterious Mr. Carter of the first two works and the omniscient Mr. Robinson and Colonel Pikeaway, who says, "We know everything here," of the last. But such figures behind the scenes need aid in their fight against crime. Mr. Carter recruits Tuppence and Tommy, when they are "stony" broke, gives them £300 a year each, plus an expense account, and allows them to live at the Ritz; perhaps the mystery surrounding him is that he is a fairy godfather. Finally, one cannot omit the faithful servant Albert, who is present from the ages of nine to sixty and who is the perfect servant for Tuppence and Tommy, for even when "in his middle years, running somewhat to fat, Albert had still the romantic boy's heart which had first led him into association with Tuppence and Tommy in their young and adventurous days" (N or M?, 144).

Tuppence is the more active member of the team. Tuppence Beresford, née Prudence Cowley, is described on her first appearance as having "no claim to beauty," but possessing "character and charm in the elfin lines of her little face, with its determined chin and large, wide apart eyes that looked out from under straight, black brows" (4). The key word is *determined,* for, from youth to old age, Tuppence is a person with a mind of her own. Perhaps this quality is the reason that the imagery most often used for her is that of a terrier; for example, "If she goes after things, she's like a terrier on the trail" (Pricking, 182). Other factors in this image are her curly black hair, her "brisk trot," and her characteristic "impatient terrier shake."

Another significant image is that expressed by General Penn in *By the Pricking of My Thumbs:* "Used to make me think of a dragonfly sometimes. Always darting off after some apparently absurd idea of her own, and then we'd find it wasn't absurd. Good fun!" (140). Good fun is what Tuppence wants. Her reading of "threepenny works of lurid fiction," such as *Garnaby Williams, the Boy Detective,* leads her to think of mystery-solving as a lark, and so she is always ready to plunge "boldly into the breach with a reminiscence culled from detective fiction" (Adversary, 60 and 35). When she plays the part of Patricia Blenkensop, the husband-hunting widow with two former husbands and three sons, in *N or M?,* she says, "I'm in this to enjoy myself and I'm going to enjoy myself" (25). Though she may claim to have "the heartiest contempt for Mrs. Blenkensop" as a person (86), she can later call her "One of my best creations" and add longingly, "What fun it was, wasn't it?"; immediately afterwards, she says, "It'll be rather boring to have only one role to play" (Pricking, 45).

Tuppence is easily bored and always eager for adventure. When she is sixty-six, her daughter Deborah worries, "What's Mother been doing? She's been up to something, hasn't she? I wish at her age she'd learn to sit quiet and not do things.... I suppose she's been getting bored. That's at the bottom of it all" (Pricking, 202 & 203).

This craving for excitement includes even personal danger: " 'Do you think,' said Tuppence with a voice that was more hopeful than despondent, 'that somebody was trying to put an end to me.... I would like to feel that I had had a great escape...it's sort of fun just to *think* of things like that' " (Postern, 110 & 111). This imprudence of Prudence—a Christie joke?—is present in spite of many close calls; however, as she asks scornfully during one of them, "Did you really think I was the kind of girl to roll about on the floor and whine for mercy?" (Adversary, 88). The answer, of course, is not our Tuppence! She fully believes herself capable of handling any situation and repeatedly says so: "little Tuppence can look after herself, thank you!"; " 'I shall be all right,' snapped Tuppence with her usual resentment of any kind of pity"; and, when Tommy says that he will look after her, " 'And I'll look after *you*!' retorted Tuppence, resenting the manly assertion" (Adversary, 12, 109, & 30). Such statements are evidence of Tuppence's excessive pride, and Christie makes that explicit in the same novel: "The young lady had far too much confidence in herself to pay any heed to warnings" (60). Naturally her self-confidence and impetuosity lead her into difficult situations, but though they may be difficult or dangerous, they are thrilling, and Tuppence adores thrills.

Though she is described as being "quick-witted," she has little of the order and method of Poirot or the analogical deductions of Miss Marple. She can use logic to discover Mrs. Bandemeyer in *The Secret Adversary,* and she does uncover M in *N or M?,* but these instants are exceptions. She exhibits a *complete* ignorance of systematic research in *Postern of Fate* when age seventy-one, asking Tommy the most elementary questions about the process. Then the following conversation ensues:

"Our methods aren't the same," said Tommy. "I think yours are just as good as mine.... You have a kind of feeling for success. It seems to happen to you."

\*\*\*

"You're very unexpected sometimes," said Tommy.
"*You're* more often right than *I* am," said Tuppence. "*That's* very annoying sometimes." (90-91)

Such comments are the reason that some feminist critics have attacked the works as sexist, for Tuppence's only investigative tools are her pluck and her intuition.

Sexist or not, all of the works present Tuppence as being deeply in love with Tommy. It is true that Tuppence easily becomes bored by uneventful married life, as when she says at the beginning of

*Partners in Crime,* "Twenty minutes' work after breakfast every morning keeps the flat going to perfection" (10). She may even facetiously comment, "So Tommy and Tuppence were married and lived happily ever afterwards. And six years later they were still living together happily ever afterwards" (Partners, 9), but she always misses Tommy when he is away. When he attends a meeting for a few days, she laments, "Never, she said to herself, had she felt more miserable.... During the long course of their married life they had hardly ever been separated for any length of time" (Pricking, 61). Their only arguments are over her rash action. At the end of the same novel, Tommy says, "Don't ever do it again." She says, "I won't," but he responds, "That's what you say now, but you will" (274-275). And she does. This contrast of personalities is the basis of much of the comedy in the works, it and their ever-youthfulness.

Tommy Beresford is a simpler character than Tuppence. He continually says, "I'm not a very brainy sort of chap" (N or M?, 15), adding that whatever success he has had is the result of "pure luck." His presentation in *The Secret Adversary* is fully developed. His physical appearance matches his rather ordinary personality: "His face was pleasantly ugly—nondescript, yet unmistakeably the face of a gentleman and a sportsman" (4). The fact that he is a gentleman is reflected in his selfless courage. "Tommy Beresford was one of those young Englishmen not distinguished by any special intellectual ability, but who are emphatically at their best in what is known as a 'tight place.' Their natural diffidence and caution fall from them then like a glove" (114). Aside from his courage, his sturdy perseverance in whatever he undertakes is his major quality. "There was a certain bulldog tenacity about Tommy that made him slow to admit defeat" (52). When Mr. Carter describes him to the Prime Minister, he presents a complete analysis of him as he appears in all of the works: "Outwardly, he's an ordinary clean-limbed, rather block-headed young Englishman. Slow in his mental processes. On the other hand, it's quite impossible to lead him astray through his imagination. He hasn't got any—so he's difficult to deceive. He worries things out slowly, and once he's got hold of anything he doesn't let go" (167). "Old Carrot Top," as Tommy is called by his son Derek, does get into some tight places; for example, he is captured by Mr. Brown's gang in *The Secret Adversary* and by N in *N or M?,* but he tells Mr. Carter in the former, "I take a lot of killing, sir" (133). His capture in *The Secret Adversary* is the result of his losing his head and entering the gang's headquarters: "What he did do was entirely foreign to the sober common sense which was, as a rule, his leading characteristic. Something, as he expressed it, seemed to snap in his brain" (47). But once captured, he coolly outtalks his enemies and finally escapes in "a hail of bullets." As a friend comments afterwards, his experience "Reads like a dime novel!" (135)—of which it is essentially a burlesque.

Besides his bravery, tenaciousness, and his usual common sense—all of which are used for comic purposes, the only other major element in his personality is his love for Tuppence, which matches hers for him. Whenever she is missing, "Tommy had the depressed feeling that a faithful dog might have had" (*Pricking*, 145). As already noted, he is continually worried that Tuppence will get herself into trouble by rash action, and over and over he warns her to be careful—without success. At the same time, he enjoys bantering with her; he says, "I never can resist ragging you, Tuppence" (*Partners*, 182). However, his quips at her expense are always in fun (and returned by her), for his true feelings are reflected in his statement that "what his life with Tuppence had been and would always be [was] a Joint Venture" (*N or M?*, 51).

Throughout the series, he remains the likeable fellow who would just as soon not become engaged in mystery-solving, but who, when asked to aid his country or when he is involved by Tuppence, unflinchingly does his duty. Basically, he falls into "the silly ass" convention, which allows him to be both sympathetic and comic. Another reason for emphasizing his role in *The Secret Adversary* is that in the later novels he becomes more and more recessive, functioning principally as a scold to Tuppence, while she takes the active role. This situation is particularly true of *By the Pricking of My Thumbs* and *Postern of Fate*.

It would be less than honest to end a discussion of Tuppence and Tommy without admitting the weaknesses of the last two novels. These weaknesses are the result of inconsistencies in the times of past events and in the lack of correspondence between the ages of the Beresfords and their actions. The first is, I believe, the result of Christie's being seventy-eight when she wrote *By the Pricking of My Thumbs* and eighty-three when she wrote *Postern of Fate;* she apparently could no longer completely control the complexities of the detective form. In *By the Pricking of My Thumbs,* which seems to be Christie's treatise on age and aging, Tuppence investigates the disappearance from a nursing home of Mrs. Lancaster, a patient in her seventies. It is learned that twenty years earlier Mrs. Lancaster was married to Sir Phillip Starke at the time several children were murdered. Also, Mrs. Lancaster was a ballet dancer and involved with a group of gangsters as a young girl. Yet the gang is supposed to be still active after some fifty years, and still yet the leader of it is a man in his forties. The child murders and the gang are tenuously linked, and the chronological inconsistencies are never explained.

As Tuppence thinks, "All such a muddle—the chronology all mixed up—one can't be sure what happened when" (121). It is impossible to work out a satisfactory sequence of events.

The same is true of *Postern of Fate*. [21] Discussions of favorite books and house decorating and the anthropomorphizing of the Beresfords' dog Hannibal are padding to cover the thin and confused mystery of the novel. The plot concerns a murder just before World War I in the Parkinson home, now the Beresfords', but people in their eighties and nineties who are questioned remember it as having occurred before their time. Mrs. Griffin, a major character, is said to be the godmother of Alexander Parkinson, yet she seems barely acquainted with her god-son. A birthday book with names of Mrs. Griffin's childhood friends causes her to say that the book "was after the Parkinsons' time" (161). She also says that "my grandmother knew the Parkinson's" (181), as if they were not present in her lifetime. Other people in the village of Hollowquay make similar meaningless statements in the context of the novel. In fact, the chronology of the past events is so confused as to make the novel unintelligible as a mystery—and the weakest of all Christie's novels.

The lack of correspondence between ages and actions in the last two novels is more notable in Tuppence than in Tommy, but even he "runs up" to London almost daily in *Postern of Fate* at the age of seventy-six. Both are actively involved in the restoration of The Laurels, their new home. In *By the Pricking of My Thumbs,* while Tommy attends the International Union of Associated Security, Tuppence at sixty-six drives around the country alone to find a house which is in a painting, is coshed on the head, but quickly recovers, and generally has the energy of someone at least twenty years younger. She is over seventy in *Postern of Fate* and walks with "a slight arthritic limp," but she still climbs into a cart without controls at the top of a hill and rides to the bottom using her feet as brakes, she actively investigates a past mystery, and when she is shot, she is hardly bothered. The entire ambience of Tuppence is not that of a woman of seventy, but of someone much younger. As stated earlier, Christie does not change the personalities or the ability to act of the couple as they age, for if she had, they would not be the expected Tuppence and Tommy. As her dedication to *By the Pricking of My Thumbs* says, she presents them "again, years older, but with spirit unquenched!"

The works about Tuppence and Tommy will never have the popularity of those about Hercule Poirot or Jane Marple, for so much overt comedy and crime will always be in an uneasy relationship, one which will seem to many tactless or vulgar. But there is no other way to read these five works except as the comic adventures of two amateur detectives, who are themselves burlesques of true detectives. Tuppence says that she has "a wild secret yearning for romance—adventure—life" (Partners, 10), and Christie permits her and Tommy to find it and enjoy it, for with their persiflage, their Hannibal, their Albert, their contrasting personalities, and their love for each other, Tuppence and Tommy are Christie's dynamic duo: a comic pair of—whatever their ages—ever-young adventurers.

## Superintendent Battle

Of Christie's series detectives, Superintendent Battle, who is without a first name, is the only policeman. He appears in five novels, but is the major detective in only three of them: *The Secret of Chimneys, The Seven Dials Mystery,* and *Towards Zero.* In *Cards on the Table* he takes second place to Poirot, and in *Easy to Kill* he does not appear until the last eleven pages. Christie's fear of making technical mistakes in police procedure is probably the reason for his not being more active. She may also have felt that it would be inappropriate to give eccentricities to a policeman, for Battle is, with the possible exception of Parker Pyne, the most ordinary of her detectives. He is, however, given the personal freedom of the amateurs. Though married and the father of five children, his wife Mary and his youngest daughter Sylvia, whom Battle has to extricate from a pilfering charage at school, are the only ones who appear, and then only in *Towards Zero.* (Christie did once say of the pseudonymous Colin Lamb of *The Clocks,* "I rather think that he is Superintendent Battle's son."[22])

Battle is described on his very first entrance in *The Secret of Chimneys* as having "a face so singularly devoid of expression as to be quite remarkable" (81). Throughout the five books, this impassivity is the dominant note of his appearance and personality, though he does occasionally have a twinkle in his eyes. The word most often used to characterize his appearance is *wooden,* as in *Cards on the Table:* "A big square, wooden-faced man moved forward. Not only did an onlooker feel that Superintendent Battle was carved out of wood—he also managed to convey the impression that the wood in question was the timber out of a battleship." To this description is added the comment, "He always looked stolid and rather stupid" (17). The appearance of stupidity is false. The statement is made in *Towards Zero* that "he was, definitely, not a brilliant man, but he had some other quality, difficult to define, that was nevertheless forceful" (21), but Luke Fitzwilliam's thoughts when Battle finally arrives in *Easy to Kill* are more explicit:

He was a solid comfortable-looking man with a broad red face and a large handsome mustache.

He did not exactly express brilliance at first glance, but a second glance was apt to make an observant person thoughtful, for Superintendent Battle's eye was unusually shrewd. Luke did not make the mistake of underestimating him. He had met men of Battle's type before. He knew that they could be trusted, and that they invariably got results. He could not have wished for a better man to be put in charge of the case (163).

Poirot also recognizes his ability; he says that Battle "may look wooden, but he is not wooden in the head—not at all," and his companion Major Despard agrees, "That stolidity is a pose. He's a very clever and able officer" (Cards, 130). That they are correct is evidenced by Battle's remark in *The Secret of Chimneys:* " 'Never display emotion.' That was a rule that was given to me once, and I've found it very useful" (152). Like Poirot's foreignness and Miss Marple's tabbiness, his impassivity is a pose which he uses to his advantage. In a conversation with Poirot, he explains his "style":

"Well, every man to his taste. I don't deal much in these fancy approaches. They don't suit my style."
"What is your style, superintendent?"
The superintendent met the twinkle in Poirot's eye with an answering twinkle in his own.
"A straightforward, honest, zealous officer doing his duty in the most laborious manner—that's my style. No frills. No fancy work. Just honest perspiration. Stolid and a bit stupid—that's my ticket" (Cards, 87).

Using his style, he can appear unpolicemanlike, hide his thoughts, and even, when necessary, lie quite effectively. In spite of his "extraordinary knack of appearing out of space without the least warning" (Chimneys, 161), his pose gives him the ability to soothe those in distress. Luke Fitzwilliam feels comforted after meeting him, and Christie adds, "Many people had had that feeling after an interview with Superintendent Battle" (Easy, 165).

As detective, Battle is cautious, methodical, and infinitely suspicious, but also at times audacious. He says, "I'm a simple man. Like to believe the things I see with my eyes" (Zero, 129). His view is that anyone may be a criminal, and, therefore, his reserve partially results from his innate suspicion of everyone. This aspect of his nature is evident as he observes the characters of *Toward Zero:* "His view of them might have surprised them had they known it. It was a sternly biased view. No matter what the law pretends as to regarding people as innocent until they are proven guilty, Superintendent Battle always regarded everyone connected with a murder case as a potential murderer" (132). In dealing with suspects, he keeps quiet and lets them do the talking, believing with Poirot that they will unwittingly reveal more than they intend. His whole attitude as detective is to be as recessive as possible, letting those involved underestimate his abilities. He comments in *The Secret of Chimneys* that detective fiction is "mostly bunkum," but sometimes useful, for it encourages "the universal idea that the police are stupid" (154). He fosters this idea to provide himself freedom of action and to trap the unwary into telling him what he requires to solve his cases. On the other hand, when he feels it necessary, he can be audacious. At one point, he says, "I never have thought much of the motto 'Safety First.' In my opinion half the people who spend their lives avoiding being run over by buses had much better be run over and put safely out of the way. They're no good" (Dials, 56). His leadership of a secret crime-fighting organization in the same novel, his upending a suspect out of a boat to make sure he cannot swin in *Towards Zero,* and his forcing the murderer in that novel to collapse utterly into his insanity are just three examples of his unexpected and daring actions. Of the last, his laconic apology is "I'm sorry, but I had to push him over the edge.... There was precious little evidence, you know" (209).

The first two novels in which Battle appears are extravagant comic thrillers. Both take place at Chimneys, the ancestral home of Clement Edward Alistair Brent, ninth Marquis of Caterham, who is the ludicrous aristocrat of English stage comedy. His daughter, Lady Eileen "Bundle" Brent is, on the one hand, a reckless-driving, harum-scarum member of the bright young people, whose wild ways shatter even Battle's impassivity, while on the other, she is "the real Bundle, cool, efficient and logical" (Dials, 32). Bundle Brent is an extreme and improbable example of Christie's combining antithetical elements within one character. She and her friends are continually using such terms as "thingummy bob" or giving each other such nicknames as "Pongo" or "Socks"; the young woman known as Socks is characterized solely by her repeated use of the word *subtle,* which she interjects into every conversation. *The Secret of Chimneys* contains such other fantastic characters as Count Stylptich and Baron Lolopretjzyl of Herzoslovakia; Bundle's sisters Dulcie and Daisy, known as Guggle and Winkle; King Victor, the world's most notorious jewel thief; and Victor's partner, a former Queen of Herzoslovakia now in disguise as a governess. The hero is Anthony Cade, in reality Nicholas Sergius Alexander Ferdinand Obolovitch, heir to the Herzoslovakian throne. The convoluted plot is concerned with the memoirs of the late Herzoslovakian prime minister and with the theft years earlier of the Kohinoor diamond, which is hidden somewhere at Chimneys. It was stolen by King Victor and his accomplice, when she was Queen. Later her husband and supposedly she as well were murdered in a coup d'etat. (King Nicholas Obolovitch and Queen Varaga of Herzoslovakia are obviously based upon King Alexander Obrenovitch and Queen Draga of Serbia, who were brutally murdered in 1903). This extravagant novel also contains coded messages, two triple disguises, the Comrades of the Red Hand, and all sorts of international intrigue.

*The Seven Dials Mystery* is only slightly less extravagant. Occurring four years after the first novel, it concerns two mysteries: who is the master criminal who wishes to steal the plans of a new invention, and what is the Seven Dials? The assumption is that the Seven Dials is an organization led by the master criminal, but this is typical Christie misdirection, for it is actually a secret crimefighting group led by Battle. This topsyturvy reversal of the criminal gang has its headquarters in a secret room of a nightclub. If that were not enough to strain credulity, there are also a fake Hungarian countess, Battle in disguise as a footman, much running around the countryside in Bundle's Hispano, and all of that facetious chatter of the bright young people. The feature of the novel most difficult to accept is that one of those young people turns out to be a master criminal, and Battle says of him: "a more utterly depraved and callous criminal I never met" (183). But he is an impossible villain. Introduced in the first three words of the novel as "That amiable youth," he remains an amiable and "silly ass" young man through his final appearance. To imagine him a mastermind of crime and a coldblooded murderer of his friends requires acceptance of the novel as sheer extravaganza, in which the stolid Battle provides the only contrast to the improbable actions of his fellow characters.

The two novels contain another element that is also extravagant, but far less amusing. In *The Secret of Chimneys* Battle says, "I've always found the upper classes the same—fearless, truthful, and sometimes extraordinarily foolish" (154). He could also have added that in this novel and its sequel, they are also extraordinarily arrogant and unconsciously snobbish, more so than in any other of Christie's works. One of the heroines of the first novel remarks of a governess (Queen Varaga in disguise), "I certainly know her face quite well—in that vague way one does know governesses and companions and people one sits opposite to in trains. It's awful, but I never really look at them properly" (170). Even with the hint of apology, her statement reeks of class prejudice. At the end of the same novel, Anthony Cade delivers a long speech on the necessity of ramming democracy down people's throats, a view so arrogant as to be dictatorial. *The Seven Dials Mystery* offers a plethora of similar examples. Bundle Brent quickly achieves complete domination of an ex-footman; he is totally in awe of this young woman, for she has "a simple autocratic method of dealing with retainers" (70). Her father's aristocratic delicacy is contrasted with the crassness of the self-made Sir Oswald Coote: "A hundred delicate appreciations of life which Lord Caterham could and did enjoy were a sealed book to Sir Oswald" (90), but the reader is never given the chance to see that delicacy. Rather Lord

Caterham is both ineffectual and snobbish. In conversation with his daughter, he says that "then the coroner asked questions at the inquest, and you know how difficult it is to explain things to people of that class." Bundle agrees, "Perfectly foul" (25). Her reply can serve as a commentary on their own attitudes. Even the mild-mannered Bill Eversleigh can dismiss the Seven Dials nightclub as "Not a posh affair. Artists, you know, and all sorts of odd women and a sprinking of our lot" (60). It is "our lot" that matters to these people; all others are to be given orders, ignored, or withstood with exasperation. Christie may have been satirizing upper class snobbery in these two novels, but by giving such views to basically sympathetic characters, she diluted that satire to the point that one can only wonder to what extent she agreed with them. Fortunately, she rarely repeated such blatant class consciousness, except among her deliberately unpleasant characters.

The last two novels are quite different from the first two in that murder is treated "seriously" in them. *Easy to Kill* is among Christie's best murder-in-the-village novels. Since Battle arrives only at the end, the investigation of a series of murders in Wychwood Under Ashe is carried on by Luke Fitzwilliam and Bridget Conway, one of Christie's most effective pairs of young lovers. Both are intelligent, unsentimental, and attractive. Luke identifies himself as "that well-known character in fiction, the private investigator" (92), but it is Bridget who first discovers the identity of the murderer. Battle's only function is to assist in the final explanation. In *Towards Zero* he is the principal detective. He is on vacation, staying with his nephew, a police inspector on the Devon coast, when murder occurs. The plot premise is identical to that of *Easy to Kill:* a thwarted lover kills with the purpose of framing the person who has rejected him/her. The murderer's plan is so arranged that the reader views everything in reverse; the person who is being framed appears to be framing the actual murderer. The novel is a tour de force in misdirection and Battle's most outstanding performance. However, he has little actual evidence with which to solve the case. He also realizes that a supposed eyewitness could not have seen what he says because of rain, but he recognizes that the witness's deduction is correct, and so he forces the murderer to crack under pressure.

Battle says of this case, "If there's such a thing as murder for pure hate, this is it" (182). Christie's plot construction emphasizes that hate by allowing the reader to follow the unknown killer's plans for the crime. Thus the murder does not occur until the end of page 123. Christie is here placing much more emphasis than is usual in her fiction on the first plot that leads to murder. As Battle says, "When you read the account of a murder—or say, a fiction story based on murder, you usually begin with the murder itself. That's all wrong. The murder begins a *long time beforehand*. A murder is the culmination of a lot of different circumstances, all converging at a given moment at a given point" (204). It is the presentation of that convergence on "zero hour" which gives this novel its special place in Christie's fiction.

Each of the five novels in which Superintendent Battle appears contains elements which prevent him from being as memorable as Christie's other detectives. The extravagant action of the first two, his subordination to Poirot in the third, his very brief appearance in the fourth, and the emphasis on the murderer's stage-managing the action in the last do not allow him the scope of the brilliant amateurs. Christie's only series policeman is her most constrained detective.

## Harley Quin

Christie's only completely omniscient detective is Harley Quin, who appears in fourteen short stories. Quin's omniscience results from his being supernatural, and the stories about him are a combination of fantasy and detection. He is partially based upon the harlequin of the English pantomime, which is a descendent of the sixteenth-century *commedia dell'arte*. (Christie also uses the figures of the harlequinade in a non-Quin story, "The Affair at the Victory Ball," as well as in an early collection of poems.) Harlequin was not originally a supernatural character, but by the nineteenth century, he and Columbine, as presented on the English stage, had become fairy-like creatures not bound by time and space. Christie's memories of seeing as a child Harlequin flying in spangles through Christmas pantomimes are obviously Quin's genesis. That he is the harlequin of stage tradition is made evident in numerous ways. His first appearance is on New Year's Eve, and pantomimes generally opened during the week between Christmas and New Year's Day. On that occasion, Quin says with a double meaning to Mr. Satterthwaite, who will become his human aide, "I must recommend the harlequinade to your attention.... Its symbolism is a little difficult to follow—but the immortals are always immortal, you know" (Quin, 22). Quin's favorite restaurant in London is the Arlecchino. He appears at a performance of *Pagliacci* and says, "There are reasons why I am attracted to it" (Helen, 140). He meets Satterthwaite on Midsummer's Eve at an inn "The Bells and Motley," and he is in Monte Carlo at Carnival time. In the course of the stories, there are references to cues and speeches, people "staging acts," the Columbine-like enchantment of the victim in "The Bird with the Broken Wing," and an actual performance of a pantomime, with Quin as Harlequin, in "Harlequin's Lane." It is not surprising that several times, "when in the company of Mr. Quin, Mr. Satterthwaite had had the feeling of taking part in a play" (World's End, 115).

Quin's physical appearance is that of a tall, slender, dark young man. A British colonel's reaction on meeting him is "The fellow looked all right—quite a normal young chap. Rather dark, but not at all foreign-looking" (Love, 216). But his un-normal nature is expressed through apparent tricks of light. When he holds a bottle of wine between himself and the light, he becomes enveloped in a red glow. He can appear, "by some curious effect of the stained glass above the door, to be dressed in every color of the rainbow" (Quin, 10), or "a play of color from a stained window" can turn "his sober garb to a kind of riotous motley" (Sign, 65). In "The Shadow on the Glass," he sits and a "red-shaded lamp throws a broad band of colored light over the checked pattern of his overcoat, and leaves his face in shadow almost as though he wore a mask" (40). The resemblance to motley and the eerie effect of light on his appearance conjoin the elements of the stage harlequin and the supernatural being within Quin.

Other characteristics of the supernatural are also included in his presentation. The most obvious are his sudden appearances and disappearances (also a feature of the stage harlequin). All that Quin himself will say is "I come and go, you know. I come and go" (Voice, 124). That is an understatement. In "The World's End," he is discovered sitting on a boulder on a deadend mountain in Corsica: "They had not seen him till this moment, and his appearance had the suddenness of a conjuring trick. He might have sprung from the surrounding landscape" (109); he disappears from the scene in the same inexplicable manner. Similarly, in "The Man from the Sea," he appears suddenly on a high cliff overlooking the sea and leaves "walking to the edge of the cliff"—"the way I came" (232). The following dialogue occurs at the end of "The Dead Harlequin" and shows the lack of awareness of Quin's true nature by most of those with whom he comes in contact:

"He goes and comes very suddenly," said Mr. Satterthwaite. "That is one of his characteristics. One doesn't always see him come and go."
"Like Harlequin," said Frank Bristow, "he is invisible," and laughed heartily at his own joke. (181-82)

Bristow makes his "joke," even though he should be puzzled by Quin's face appearing in a painting he has done without his having met Quin at the time. A few characters do become aware of his powers; in "The World's End," a young woman asks Satterthwaite, "He knows things. How does he know?," but Satterthwaite has no answer (11). Nor can Quin's summoning Satterthwaite from a distance by the movement of letters on a ouija board in "The Bird with the Broken Wing" be explained rationally. Quin's sardonic, knowing comments, in such stories as "The Love Detectives," and his "pulling the strings" of other people to achieve his ends in "The Soul of the Croupier" are still other examples of his uncanny abilities.

In the last two stories of *The Mysterious Mr. Quin* and the late "The Harlequin Tea-Set," there is the suggestion that Quin is a personification of death, an idea that is absent from all other stories. In "The Man from the Sea," Quin says that he has a mission to be "an advocate for the dead." In this case, it is to bring together a man and a woman as atonement for the cruelty of the woman's now dead husband. He says to Satterthwaite, "You believe in a life after death, do you not? And who are you to say that the same wishes, the same desires, may not operate in that other life? If the desire is strong enough—a messenger may be found" (231-32). Quin is the owner of Harlequin's Lane, in the story of that name. The local name for it is "Lover's Lane." Quin takes the Russian ballerina Kharsanova dancing down the lane, and she is found dead in the rubbish pit at its end. Her death is presented as a kind of ultimate fulfillment, rather than a tragedy, and she seems to have a premonition of it. Her dream of being the partner of an ideal harlequin comes true, and she is correct in interpreting him as death: "Always one looks for one thing—the lover, the perfect, the eternal lover. It is the music of Harlequin one hears. No lover ever satisfies one, for all lovers are mortal. And Harlequin is only a myth, an invisible presence—unless—...his name is—Death!" (235). "Harlequin's Lane" is a disturbing story, for in it the shadowy, all-knowing Quin most exhibits a fearsome aspect of his supernaturalism. "The Harlequin Tea-Set" is a weak story—there is really no motive for an attempted murder—but Quin is at his most supernatural in it.

As must be evident by now, one cannot discuss Quin without including his mortal partner, Mr. Satterthwaite (he is never given a first name). In the course of the stories, he ages from sixty-two to sixty-nine, but the essential features of his appearance and personality, which are presented in much more detail than those of the shadowy Quin, do not change. He is "a little dried-up wizened old fogey of a man" (Love, 235), who is a wealthy bachelor, having had in his life only one "tepid" romance. He has a large house on Chelsea Embankment, a valet, a Rolls Royce with chauffeur, a valuable art collection, and a box at the opera. He is an epicure and "an appreciator and a connoisseur of all the arts" (Helen, 139), as well as being "an authority on French cooking, on ladies' dress, and on all the latest scandals" (Love, 200). He follows the traveling pattern of the social season, and he knows everybody and everybody knows him. A cosmopolite, he deplores an insular attitude toward life, but he is something of a snob, a fact illustrated by his being "the proud author of a book, *Homes of My Friends*. The friends in question were all rather exalted" (Harlequin, 163). He is invariably polite, but has "reactionary views about *nouveaux riches*" (Love, 200). In fact, in "The Shadow on the Glass," it is stated that "if Mr. Satterthwaite was found at the houses of those rich who had newly arrived, it was a sign either that the cooking was unusually good, or that a drama of human life was to be enacted there" (23), and in the same story, he is described as "a little old-fashioned, so much so that he seldom made fun of his host and hostess until after he had left their house" (25).

Satterthwaite's willingness to put up with even *nouveaux riches* to watch "a drama of human life" is central to an understanding of him. On his very first appearance in "The Coming of Mr. Quin," his curiosity about the actions of others and his own noninvolvement are described: "All his life, so to speak, he had sat in the front row of the stalls watching various dramas of human nature unfold before him. His role had always been that of the onlooker. Only now, with old age holding him in its clutch, he found himself increasingly critical of the drama submitted to him. He demanded now something a little out of the common" (5). He is "an earnest student of the drama called Life," but one who likes it "highly colored" (Croupier, 83). He can be sympathetic to those in difficulties, even sentimental over the romances of others, but until he meets Harley Quin, he is, as is repeatedly stated, an onlooker. At times, the realization of this fact makes him unhappy: "I am sixty-nine.... Everything I know of life I know at second hand. Sometimes that is very bitter to me. And yet, because of it, I know a good deal" (Sea, 219). That his passive watchfulness has taught him a great deal is confirmed by Quin in "At The Bells and Motley":

"You have seen much of life," said Mr. Quin gravely. "More than most people."
"Life has passed me by," said Mr. Satterthwaite bitterly.
"But in so doing has sharpened your vision. Where others are blind you can see."
"It is true," said Mr. Satterthwaite. "I am a great observer" (57).

He has trained his eyes and ears to pick up the revealing nuances of life, and, though he may be a snob, he has a shrewd and critical mind, seeing people as they are, not as they wish to appear to him.

Quin's entrance into Satterthwaite's life gives him the chance to act, and he is delighted by the change. His delight can be seen in his reaction to meeting Quin in "The Sign in the Sky": "At once Mr. Satterthwaite felt excited—pleasurably excited. His role was that of the looker on, and he knew it, but sometimes, when in the company of Mr. Quin, he had the illusion of being an actor—and the principal actor at that" (66). It is not really an illusion; in this story, for instance, Satterthwaite travels to Canada to collect evidence to free a condemned man. Over and over, Quin uses him to make the active moves of their detection, while he stays in the background. Soon the man of the audience is an actor on the stage of life, and he craves the experience.

> "You have changed since I first knew you," said Mr. Quin....
> "In what way?"
> "You were content then to look on at the dramas that life offered. Now—you want to take part—to act."
> "It is true," confessed Mr. Satterthwaite (Croupier, 91).

However, his desire for life has definite limits. In "Harlequin's Lane," Quin asks him if he regrets never having passed down Quin's lane—the lane of love, life, and death. Satterthwaite's answer is no, for he has a vision of "something at once menacing and terrifying. Joy, Sorrow, Despair" (256). And so he steps back from the fullness of life, with this defense: "I may have been only a looker on at Life—but I see things that other people do not. You said so yourself, Mr. Quin" (256).

As already indicated, the detection of Quin and Satterthwaite is a joint—almost symbiotic—affair, with Quin working through his human friend. In "The Shadow on the Glass," Satterthwaite says that Quin gives him "inspiration," for "he has a power—an almost uncanny power—of showing you what you have seen with your own eyes, of making clear to you what you have heard with your own ears" (39). This power of showing one what is already there is Quin's contribution to the pair's mystery-solving. Quin wishes Satterthwaite to have the credit, but the latter knows that he would be incapable of correctly interpreting what he sees without Quin. He says that Quin is a catalyst: "His presence is a sign that things are going to happen; because he is there strange revelations come to light, discoveries are made. And yet—he himself takes no part in the proceedings" (Sea, 210). Their adventures usually begin with a meeting, at which Satterthwaite lays out the known facts in what Quin calls "one of those wonderful descriptive portraits of yours" (Voice, 125). Of course, such a presentation is not needed by Quin, who already knows all, but it causes Satterthwaite to marshal whatever information is known into a coherent pattern. Then, with prompting from Quin, he is able to fill in the missing pieces of that pattern. Quin never gives him the answers; at one point in "The Face of Helen" Satterthwaite thinks, "It was never any use asking Mr. Quin anything. 'The threads are all in you hands'—that was the kind of thing Mr. Quin would say" (153). Quin's theory is that "one sees things better afterward than at the time" of their happening:

"The longer the time has elapsed, the more things fall into proportion. One sees them in their true relationship to one another" (Motley, 50). Quin prods Satterthwaite's memory and his views of people and events, and then Satterthwaite, by finding that true relationship, is able to solve the mystery.

Quin and Satterthwaite are a team, a matching of the supernatural and the human—surely one of the most unusual detective teams in fiction. In "Harlequin's Lane," a significant conversation takes place between them:

"You have done a lot for lovers, Mr. Quin."
***
"You are speaking of yourself—of what *you* have done—not of me."
"It is the same thing," said Mr. Satterthwaite. "You know it is.... You have acted—through me. For some reason or other you do not act directly—yourself."
"Sometimes I do," said Mr. Quin. (236-237).

It is only in "Harlequin's Lane" that Quin acts directly. To repeat, in the other stories he acts through little Mr. Satterthwaite to help lovers and to solve mysteries, criminal and otherwise. Christie has written that the Quin stories were her favorites and that she only wrote one "when I felt like it."[23] She never saw her way to extend this material to the length of a novel, but her pairing of the stage-derived, supernatural Quin with the elderly man of society Satterthwaite has a unique though small place in her works—one that deserves to be better known, for their stories are significant examples of Christie's experimentation in adding additional narrative interest to the detective genre by employing elements not generally considered compatible with it.

## Parker Pyne

Like Harley Quin, Mr. C. Parker Pyne appears in only fourteen short stories. Of these seven can hardly be called detective stories; rather they are cases in which Pyne manipulates people to give them the happiness they desire—the mystery element is how he accomplishes the task. The other seven involve detection by Pyne when he is asked to help an unhappy person. Supposedly, Christie invented him and his unusual profession "just by looking at a man at the next table in a Lyons' Corner House in London."[24] If so, one wonders what there was about the man which attracted her attention, for Pyne is not a colorful character; in fact, the adjective most often applied to him is *bland.* "He was large, not to say fat; he had a bald head of noble proportions, strong glasses, and little twinkling eyes," with "a cheerful, matter-of-fact voice" and large well-cared-for hands (Wife, 8). Such are the few physical features given. More important is his aura of trust and dependability: "Undoubtedly one of Mr. Parker Pyne's greatest assets was his sympathetic manner. It was a manner that invited confidence" (Husband, 61). As one client says, "Without knowing anything about you! I'm *sure* I can trust you" (Distressed, 48). Pyne's personal image is summed up in the statement that "He seemed very bland, very benevolent, and in some way impossible to explain, delightfully reassuring" (Everything, 121).

The "atmosphere of British solidity" which surrounds him is necessary in his work. The nature of that work is expressed in the advertisement which he runs on the front page of the London *Times:* "ARE YOU HAPPY? IF NOT, CONSULT MR. PARKER PYNE, 17 Richmond Street" (Wife, 7). Such a presumptuous advertisement would seem to be that of a charlatan, but the curious and the unhappy who answer it are quickly confiding in Pyne. They have to trust him since he almost always demands payment in advance. His fees vary according to the case and the wealth of the client; it may be five pounds, one thousand pounds, or some amount between; he says that sometimes he loses money "if it is a deserving case" (Clerk, 95). For their money the first thing clients receive is Pyne's assurance of success; he goes so far as to say, "Failure is a word not tolerated in this establishment. If I do not think I can succeed, I refuse to undertake a case. If I do take a case, its success is practically a foregone conclusion" (Distressed, 56). Nevertheless, he does have a failure, "The Case of the Discontented Husband," which he says is the result of "natural causes" that "should have been foreseen" (77). His other cases are successful, and his reputation is such that his holiday is continually interrupted by people desiring his aid; even his use of an incognito cannot prevent his being importuned, for, as "a gushing lady" says, "There's just nothing he can't do. Husbands and wives flying at each other's throats and he brings 'em together—if you've lost interest in life he gives you the most thrilling adventures. As I say the man's just a wizard!" (Pollensa, 80).

Pyne's wizardry is the result of his being "a specialist in unhappiness" (Regatta, 21). He says, "I *know* what causes unhappiness, and consequently I have a clear idea of how to produce the opposite condition" (Rich, 101-02). He knows because he classifies, his principal method of deduction. What he does is to decide the class of unhappiness and then prepare a cure. As he says, "I stand in the place of a doctor. The doctor first diagnoses the patient's disorder, then he recommends a course of treatment. There are cases where no treatment can be of any avail. If that is so, I say quite frankly that I can do nothing about it. But if I undertake a case, the cure is practically guaranteed" (Soldier, 25). He can diagnose the problems of a neglected wife or husband, "The Case of the Middle-Aged Wife" and "The Case of the Discontented Husband," the desire of a middle-aged clerk or a retired colonel for excitement, "The Case of the City Clerk" and "The Case of the Discontented Soldier," the boredom of a wealthy woman, "The Case of the Rich Woman," or the sense of entrapment of a young Englishwoman in far-off Persia, "The House at Shiraz," and he can plan means of alleviating their emotional suffering.

His basic cure is to manipulate his clients' views of their world—or the view of someone close to them. At one point, he states, "When you think of ten people you meet, at least nine of them can be induced to act in any way you please by applying the right stimulus" (Price, 177). That he has to create a world that is often false does not bother Pyne: " 'What is truth?' said Mr. Parker Pyne. 'In my experience it is usually the thing that upsets the apple cart!' " (Everything, 135). Pyne creates elaborate charades to "trick" others into accepting a reality different from that of their actual lives. To achieve these charades, he often requires his assistants. Mrs. Ariadne Oliver works for Pyne. She concocts thriller-plots when needed that are "real-life" versions of her "forty-six successful works of fiction, all best sellers in England and America, and freely translated into French, German, Italian, Hungarian, Finnish, Japanese, and Abyssinian" (Soldier, 45)—a typical piece of Christie self-mockery. More often, Pyne uses the services of his two "children": Claude Luttrell, "one of the handsomest specimens of lounge lizard to be found in England," and Madeleine de Sara, "the most seductive of vamps" (Distressed, 54). Luttrell is used in "The Case of the Middle-Aged Wife" and "The Case of the Distressed Lady" to romance middle-aged women. In the former he has some scruples about his activities, and after giving him a stern lecture, Pyne starts a new file: *"Interesting vestiges of a conscience noticeable in hardened gigolo. Note: Study developments"* (23). Madeleine de Sara is quite different from Luttrell. Though she can play such roles as Dolores Ramona in "Problem at Pollensa Bay" or The Grand Duchess Olga in "The Case of the City Clerk," she is actually, as stated in the latter, "Maggie Sayers, fourth daughter of an honest, hard-working family" (94). To her, her job is just that—a job; to the male clients, however, she is something else. Pyne says to her at the end of "Problem at Pollensa Bay" that a young man has the "usual slight attack of Madeleinitis. He'll get over it in a day or two, but you *are* rather distracting" (94). Her beauty and sex appeal are the cause of the failure of "The Case of the Discontented Husband." A final employee of Pyne is his "forbidding-looking" secretary, Miss Lemon, the same Miss Lemon who later works for Poirot.

The complexity of some of the schemes Pyne concocts may be

illustrated by "The Case of the Rich Woman." He has the bored Mrs. Abner Rymer drugged, shipped to a Cornish farm, and made to believe that she has been psychically changed into another woman's body. A newspaper and a photograph are faked, the connivance of two doctors and a farm wife are obtained, and Madeleine de Sara acts as a nurse. All of this is contrived for a fee of one thousand pounds to bring Mrs. Rymer happiness, and it works, for she finds after a year that she prefers farm life to her empty existence as a rich, out-of-place widow.

As already indicated, such successful schemes are the consequence of Pyne's ability to classify unhappiness. He tells a young woman, "I don't guess.... I observe—and I classify" (Shiraz, 167). He classifies by racial types, emotional types, and criminal types. He can even classify by posture: "That back was horribly expressive. In his time he had classified many such backs. Its rigidity—the tenseness of its poise—without seeing her face he knew...that the woman was keeping herself in hand by a rigid effort" (Pollensa, 76). This extraordinary ability has developed from Pyne's work as a statistician: "You see, for thirty-five years of my life I have been engaged in the compiling of statistics in a government office. Now I have retired, and it has occurred to me to use the experience I have gained in a novel fashion. It is all so simple. Unhappiness can be classified under five main heads—no more, I assure you. Once you know the cause of a malady, the remedy should not be impossible" (Wife, 8). And so by classification and statistics, he can diagnose his clients' unhappiness and devise the means, however complex, to end it.

On two occasions Pyne denies that he is a detective. In "Have You Got Everything You Want?" he says, "But, my dear lady, you must remember I am not a detective. Theft and crime are not in my line at all. The human heart is my province" (128). Likewise, in "Death on the Nile" he says, "You must remember I am not a detective. I am, if you like to put it that way, a heart specialist—" (198). However, Pyne does solve crimes: a kidnapping, two murders, two robberies, and he prevents two other of the latter. His ability to classify enables him to solve "The Regatta Mystery," for he recognizes the methods and appearance of the gang at work. He is also an expert at finding the one detail which does not fit, such as the reason for a supposed robbery taking place when a train is passing over water in "Have You Got Everything You Want?" He continues to manipulate people as a method of discovery, as when he describes the current scene in London to determine which features of that scene affect an Englishwoman in Persia in "The House at Shiraz," or when he deliberately traps a killer in "The Gate at Baghdad" by leading him to incriminate himself. He also bluffs another killer into a confession: "I deduced the whole story and tried it on him. It worked" ("Nile", 207). All of his cases, whether providing happiness or crime-solving, demonstrate Pyne's control over any situation and those who are a part of it.

As a result of Pyne's omnipotence, Christie's stories about him are rather improbable. His ingenious schemes to provide people happiness by manipulating their views of their world, his astounding ability at classification, and his insight into human character based upon that classification are far beyond the powers of most people. The improbability is lessened, however, by the nature of most of his cases. They are human interest stories, dealing with problems that face the average person: problems of love, boredom, and money. Also, Pyne is without eccentricity; rather, he is presented as an "ordinary," elderly English middleclass man in his tastes and personal life. The blending of improbable action and ordinary characters is the hallmark of the Pyne stories.

## Others

The thirteen novels and seventeen short stories of mystery which Christie wrote without her six series detectives fall into four groups: comic thrillers, tales of international intrigue, works of straight detection, and novels and stories which are unique in some way. This non-series fiction indicates Christie's range, while, at the same time, bearing resemblances to various works having a series detective. However, many of these works do not have a detective as such, being mysteries rather than detective fiction.

The largest number of short stories are comic thrillers, including among others, "Mr. Eastwood's Adventure," "The Rajah's Emerald," "The Mystery of the Blue Jar," "The Girl in the Train," "Jane in Search of a Job," and "The Manhood of Edward Robinson," but there are only two novels: *The Man in the Brown Suit* and *Why Didn't They Ask Evans?* The comic thriller may be briefly defined as a story in which there is a mystery and generally peril for the central character or characters, but which is treated as if the entire affair is a lark. In the short stories detectives play little or no part; rather someone unwittingly becomes involved in or is tricked into a mysterious situation. Three stories can illustrate the type. "The Rajah's Emerald" concerns young James Bond at a seaside resort. He accidentally finds a stolen emerald in a bathing hut, where it has been hidden by the thief, who then poses as a detective to get it back. Bond has both of them arrested, and the truth is then revealed. Much of the story is taken up by Bond's being rejected by the snooty Grace for his rival Claud Sopworth; he gets his revenge in the end when he is invited to have lunch with the rajah. In "Jane in Search of a Job," Jane Cleveland is selected to impersonate the Grand Duchess Pauline, who is touring England; actually the "Grand Duchess" is an American girl bandit and the leader of a gang of thieves, who are masking their activities under the guise of international intrigue. Jane undergoes difficulties, but emerges with a boyfriend. The most amusing of these slight works is "Mr. Eastwood's Adventure," which is both a burlesque of the thriller and a satire on mystery writing. Eastwood is a mystery writer who is attempting to fulfill a contract for a novel. He says, "The two essentials for a story were a title and a plot—the rest was mere spadework" (132). He has his title, "The Mystery of the Second Cucumber," but is stuck for a plot. He laments,

The kind of story [his editor] wanted, and insisted on having (and incidentally paid handsomely for getting), was all about mysterious dark women, stabbed to the heart, a young hero unjustly suspected, and the sudden unraveling of the mystery and fixing of the guilt on the least likely person, by the means of wholly inadequate clues—in fact, 'THE MYSTERY OF THE SECOND CUCUMBER'.

'Although,' reflected Anthony, 'ten to one, he'll alter the title and call it something rotten, like "Murder Most Foul" without so much as asking me!' (133)

Eastwood is tricked by a gang of thieves and robbed; their plot is a farrago of mysterious phone calls, a sinister glass shop, a girl in distress, and two thieves posing as detectives. However, at the end he is happy, for he has his plot—that is, theirs—and a new title, "The Mystery of the Spanish Shawl."

*The Man in the Brown Suit* is another of Christie's extravaganzas of the 1920s. It resembles such other novels as *The Big Four* and *The Secret of Chimneys*. It introduces Colonel John Race, who is an erect, bronzed, close-cropped empire-builder and intelligence officer, but the true protagonist is Anne Beddingfeld. She is one of Christie's spunky young women on their own. She calls herself "Anna the Adventuress," and she certainly has adventures: in England, on board an ocean liner, and in South Africa and Rhodesia. Among the novel's extravagant elements are theft of the DeBeer diamonds, which are hidden in a pack of film; a subway murder; a crook in triple disguise as a Russian count, Anglican clergyman, and middle-aged Englishwoman; an exotic Eden on an island in the Zambezi River; an attack on that island and escape by swimming the crocodile-infested river; a South African revolution; and two attempts on Anne's life, including her being pushed over the Zambezi Falls. Anne also meets John Eardsley, an ultra-virile young man, who enters her ship's cabin wounded and who produces the following violently romantic reaction in her: "I love him. I want him. I'll walk all over Africa barefoot till I find him, and I'll make him care for me. I'll die for him. I'd work for him, slave for him, steal for him, even beg or borrow for him! There—now you know!" (89). At the end of the novel, he takes her back to that river isle for what appears to be a kind of Tarzan-Jane existence. Adding to these adventures is the villain, who is by far the most amusing and likeable of all Christie's villains. He is the aesthete as criminal, ever ready with a clever story or a witty quip, and significantly Christie allows him to escape to Bolivia, from where he writes Anne an audacious letter of apology. Earlier, when they confront each other openly, after his attempts to kill her, he proposes marriage to Anne. Though she turns him down, she bears no malice: "I could not think of him as other than our amusing, genial traveling companion" (201). Such are the extravagant characters and actions of this comic thriller.

Similar to Anne Beddingfeld is Lady Frances "Frankie" Derwent, the heroine of *Why Didn't They Ask Evans?* The same adjectives can be used for her as for all of Christie's active young women heroines: vivacious, peppy, energetic, pert, courageous, brisk, brimming with life, for—whenever the works in which they appear were written—they are of a type: the "modern" young woman of the 1920s. Anne and Frankie are sisters of Tuppence Beresford, Bundle Brent, Emily Trefusis of *Murder at Hazelwood,* Victoria Jones of *They Came to Baghdad,* Hilary Craven of *So Many Steps to Death,* and Ginger Corrigan of *The Pale Horse.* When Bobby Jones says to Frankie, "You were simply splendid! So frightfully plucky" (287), he is summing up both the nature and function of these heroines. Frankie is described as being "distinctly attractive," "despite a certain resemblance to an organ grinder's monkey" (19); these heroines are never conventionally beautiful. More intelligent than her male partner, Frankie often allows her enthusiasm to overcome her sense, still another general characteristic. She can also sound as snobbish as Bundle Brent: "Nobody looks at a chauffeur in the way they look at a *person*" (82). Her partner Bobby Jones is a twenty-eight year old boy, with a friendly, unhandsome face. He is continually feuding with his father, the Vicar of Marchbolt, for he desires action, his mind being "nourished on *The Third Bloodstain, The Case of the Murdered Archduke,* and *The Strange Adventure of the Florentine Dagger"* (57). The result of his reading can be seen in his comment on invading the grounds of a doctor's rest home: "No tame pythons. No cheetahs, no electrically-charged wires—the man is shamefully behind the times" (218). When he feels that he is not being allowed an important enough role in the investigation, he feels injured, "This, he felt, was his own particular crime, and now he was being ousted" (81). At one point Bobby impersonates a staid lawyer to obtain information; when the lawyer discovers the impersonation, he is led to believe that Bobby is a Duke, and he exclaims, "Oh! you

Bright Young People—You Bright Young People" (209). That is exactly what Frankie and Bobby are—bright young people on a lark, having a great time playing at being sleuths.

Other elements of comic extravaganza include four disguises by the pair, references to fictional detectives, Bobby's miraculous recovery after being drugged with eight grains of morphia, another affable villain who escapes to South America and sends a letter signed, "Your affectionate enemy, the bold, bad villain of the piece" (284), and a villainess, whose "haunting, wistful face" is transformed to "demonic rage" when caught: "That beautiful mouth opened and a stream of foul and hideous curses poured out" (276). (Since she already has £700,000, one wonders why she is still trying to obtain more.) The action, as in all of Christie's comic thrillers, is a ludicrous exaggeration of the crimes and detective investigations of her more sedate novels and short stories of straight detection.

Three novels make up the non-series tales of international intrigue: *They Came to Baghdad, So Many Steps to Death,* and *Passenger to Frankfurt.* They are among her weakest novels, for Christie had to deal with matters (if the pun may be pardoned) foreign to her experience. The domestic crime was her forte, not the world of international conspiracy. Perhaps the fact that she used three almost identical basic plots for these novels is evidence of her lack of surety. Each is concerned with a "superman" who wishes to enlist young men and women, especially scientists, in his cause either to create world anarchy or to obtain a monopoly on science in order to control the world (for the thematic element of these works, see Chapter VI). The first two also have in common typical examples of Christie's young heroine.

*They Came to Baghdad* is another of Christie's archaeological novels in that it takes place in Iraq, both in the city of the title and at a dig in the countryside. It has an extremely complicated plot, concerned with a plan to foment dissension between the United States and the Soviet Union by disrupting a conference the two countries are holding in Baghdad. Without realizing it, Victoria Jones is recruited to play a vital part in the plans of the novel's "superman." She is both "a young woman of optimism and force of character" and "an amiable nitwit with a lot of common sense" (28 & 158). She has great self-assurance: "Victoria had no inhibitions about making friends with strange young men in public places. She considered herself an excellent judge of character and well able to check any manifestations of freshness on the part of unattached males" (22). She needs this self-assurance; an orphan and without a job, she goes to Baghdad and is quickly embroiled with spies and murder, when a dying man enters her hotel room (as the wounded

Eardsley entered Anne Beddingfeld's stateroom). However, though her trials are many, with the aid of British intelligence, she prevents the outbreak of world chaos.

Hilary Craven, her fellow heroine of *So Many Steps to Death,* is also recruited, but knowingly. Her husband has left her, her daughter has died, and she is suicidal, when a super-secret intelligence official named Jessop persuades her to impersonate the dead wife of a missing scientist in order to discover his whereabouts. She embarks on a journey which takes her to a secret scientific complex hidden in the mountains of North Africa, disguised as a leper colony. She is aided by a young American agent called Peters, whose real name is Boris Andrei Pavlov Glydr! What they discover is that Mr. Aristides, one of the world's richest men, is "buying" young scientists to corner the market in scientific discovery. Mr. Aristides is a financial variant on the megalomaniac scientist of sensational fiction. When he explains his grandiose plan to Hilary, she exclaims, "It's like a typists' pool! You've got a pool here of brains" (141). His pool of brains is drained by Hilary and Peters, but not before its impossible accommodations are described—there is even a ballet corps to entertain the sequestered scientists! When all is revealed, Mr. Aristides escapes punishment; he simply says, "I wash my hands of this affair," and that is that: "Mr. Aristides was unperturbed by failure.... He had always accepted it philosophically and gone on to the next *coup*" (160). After this unsatisfactory conclusion, Christie then announces four pages from the end of the novel that Peters has been tracking a murderer—the possibility of murder has not previously been mentioned—and finds him at the complex, even though he has undergone plastic surgery, by a Z-shaped scar in the crook of his right elbow! In spite of its intended sensations, the novel is one of Christie's dullest, for disbelief in its improbabilities destroys reader interest.

The title page of the third novel reads *Passenger to Frankfurt,* "An Extravaganza," but it is not one of the comic extravaganzas. Rather it is Christie's attempt to present a view of the world condition in the late 1960s; unfortunately, at times it becomes quite preachy. It contains her only extended authorial introduction, indicating the seriousness with which she approached the work, and its caustic view of politicans is emphasized by the epigraph from Jan Smuts at the beginning: "Leadership, besides being a great creative force, can be diabolical." Again, there is a plot to use the young to create world chaos. This time there are five leaders, making up "The Ring," and representing finance, armaments, drugs—"to finish off the weaklings among the young" (176)—science, and assassination. Using a combination of Wagnerian motifs and the theory that Adolf Hitler had a son, they set up an actor as "the Young Siegfried" to front for their world takeover. Opposed to The Ring are the enigmatic Mr. Robinson, the all-knowing Colonel Pikeaway—who is described as "a cross between an ancient Buddha and a large blue frog" with "a touch of a bar sinister from a hippopotamus in his ancestry" (44-45), Sir Stafford Nye, his aunt Lady Matilda Cleckheaton—an aristocratic Miss Marple, and "Mary Ann," also known as Countess Renata Zerkowski. Sir Stafford and Mary Ann are the active world-savers. He is a middle-aged, unstuffy, Buchanesque aristocrat, and she is a beautiful woman of mystery. Their active opponents are Milly Jean Cortman, the wife of the American Ambassador, whom she murders, and Grafin Charlotte von Waldsausen, née Krapp, known as "the Old Woman of the Mountain." The Grafin, apparently derived from Christie's ideas of the Krupp family, is enormously wealthy and monstrously fat. Her gross appearance is an obvious symbol of her greedy, corrupt nature. The final confrontation between these forces of good and evil comes with the murder of Lord Altamount, who seems to be based on Prime Minister Harold Macmillan, though the purpose of The Ring's killing him is never made clear. The shock of his death, however, miraculously restores the invalid scientist Shoreham, who promises to provide the formula for Benvo, his discovery which creates permanent benevolence in people, thus ending violence in the world. The similarity of purpose of Benvo to the Ludovico technique of Anthony Burgess's *A Clockwork Orange* is striking and unintentionally raises the same question: is the cure worse than the disease?

Turning from these novels of international conspiracy to the non-series works of straight detection is to reenter the world of Christie's classic British detectives. This group contains the largest number of novels, but only three short stories. In "S.O.S." Mortimer Cleveland prevents a planned poisoning by sheer deduction. By careful observation Sir Edward Palliser, K.C., solves a murder in "Sing a Song of Sixpence," a story based on the device of the absent clue: something which should be present is not. In this case, the absence of a sixpence piece from the victim's handbag provides the beginning of Sir Edward's correct hypothesis. "Philomel Cottage" is one of Christie's two or three most famous short stories and the source for a play and two films. It deserves its fame, for it is a superb story of peril. Alix Martin realizes from analysis of various clues that her husband of a month is a notorious wife-murderer and that she is his next victim. Though not even an amateur detective, she makes the obvious deductions and finds a most effective way of thwarting his plans and preventing her death.

The five novels of detection are *Murder at Hazelmoor, Remembered Death, Crooked House, Ordeal by Innocence,* and *The*

*Pale Horse.* Each has both official and amateur detectives; however, the emphases in the pairings vary. In *Murder at Hazelmoor* Inspector Narracott of Exeter and Emily Trefusis are the pair. He is a tall Devonshire man with faraway gray eyes; an efficient officer, he has "a quiet persistence, a logical mind, and a keen attention to detail" (26). But he is surpassed by his amateur female colleague, who has "a face that having once seen you could not forget. There was about her an atmosphere of common sense, *savior faire*, invincible determination, and a most tantalizing fascination" (74). Though she spends much time in the company of Charles Enderby, a comic young newspaper man, she enters the case because her fiance has been accused of the murder and she intends to prove his innocence. When she has determined the murderer, she says that she cannot think of his motive. It is not surprising, for the motive is an extremely weak one. In fact, the novel is based solely upon a gimmick: the perfect alibi, involving time, distance, and snow. The gimmick is that the murderer uses skis. But on that simple device is loaded an excessive amount of elaboration and obfuscation. The major clue, the pair of skis, is hidden in a list of the contents of a cupboard, a favorite Christie ploy for concealing the importance of objects relevant to a case. The weakness here is that the victim's valet does not notice the extra pair of skis when closing up his former employer's home, but is aware that the victim's ski boots are missing. Altogether, though at times amusing, *Murder at Hazelmoor* is one of Christie's more strained novels of detection.

The same can be said of *Remembered Death*. One has first to accept that two strangers would meet and within four days fall so deeply in love that they would plan a deliberate murder for profit. Then one must assume that because of the misplacement of one purse on the table of a restaurant the members of a dinner-party, on returning from dancing, would simply sit at one remove from their former seats. What about the purses of the other two women present? Could the contents of the plates and glasses be identical? No one in the novel is bothered by such matters; they simply accept that people would be so unaware of their surroundings and that someone has been poisoned. To solve this improbable murder at a "party" on the anniversary of what turns out to have been an identical murder, but with the proper victim, are three detectives. Colonel John Race returns again, to be joined by Chief-Inspector Kemp of Scotland Yard and Anthony Browne. Race is now over sixty and no longer heads the Counter-Espionage Department, but he is still "a tall, erect, military figure, with sunburned face, closely cropped iron-grey hair, and shrewd dark eyes," who could easily serve as "the model of a strong silent man so beloved by an earlier generation of novelists" (81). Inspector Kemp is a former subordinate of "that grand old veteran, Battle." Having "perhaps unconsciously" copied Battle's mannerisms, he has "the same suggestion of being carved all in one piece—but whereas Battle had suggested some wood such as Teak or Oak, Chief Inspector Kemp suggested a somewhat more showy wood—mahogany, say, or good old-fashioned rosewood" (103). Browne is the romantic hero; he is a secret agent, who has even served a term in prison "to get the goods" on criminal activity. To him go the honors, such as they are, of solving the method of the murder and realizing that the wrong person was killed at that restaurant table. Three detectives, an improbable crime, and a less than convincing novel—that is *Remembered Death.*

The third novel, *Crooked House,* was often mentioned by Christie when she was asked to name her favorites among her works. It is doubtful that many readers would place it in a list of her top ten, for though the choice of murderer is a novelty, the *detection* never really gets anywhere. Charles Hayward, the son of the Assistant Commissioner of Scotland Yard and a member of the diplomatic service is the active amateur, assisted by Chief Inspector Taverner. Hayward narrates this novel of murder in the Leonides family, which consists, according to Sophia Leonides, Hayward's fiancee, of "One brother, one sister, a mother, a father, an uncle, an aunt by marriage, a great-aunt and a step-grandmother" (8). The first victim is the patriarchal grandfather of this domestic menage, who has married a second wife from the lower classes fifty years younger than himself, and she is attracted to the tutor of her step-grandchildren. Hayward's comment is "It was, certainly, an old and familiar pattern. The mixture as before" (21). This "mixture as before" is not given any distinctive variation and, therefore, seems hackneyed. However, the major weakness of the novel is the lack of effective detection. Hayward says, "I suppose we were really incredibly stupid. But we were looking at it, of course, from the wrong angle" (106); that is certainly true of himself and Sophia. His father apparently knows the murderer's identity all along, but does nothing; the elderly nannie suspects and is murdered; the great-aunt discovers the murderer and, to prevent scandal, kills the two of them; and only then do the two lovers finally know. *Crooked House* needs Miss Marple, but perhaps not, for with her knowledge of domestic affairs, she would solve the case before the novel were half over.

A better novel of *detection* is *Ordeal by Innocence,* which is also significant as the most extended treatment of one of Christie's principal themes: the effect of suspicion on the innocent (see Chapter VI). The amateur detective is Dr. Arthur Calgary, a scientist who returns to England from an expedition to discover that

Jack Argyle was sent to prison and died there for a murder he could not have committed, for he was with Calgary at the time. With a deeply felt sense of duty and justice, he reopens a case which was satisfactorily over for everyone concerned, as the now dead Jack was the *enfant terrible* of the family and everybody's favorite suspect. Working with the melancholoy Superintendent Huish, Calgary sets out to solve the two-year-old mystery. Before he finds the killer, there is another murder and an unsuccessful attempt at a third. Being another closed circle domestic murder, the novel requires that the murderer has to be a member of the household at Sunny Point, the Argyle home. Christie varies the domestic situation by making all of the children of the family adopted, thus allowing for their quite different personalities and providing multiple motives. Mrs. Argyle, their adoptive mother, is the perfect victim; like Marina Gregg of *The Mirror Crack'd from Side to Side,* she is, with all of the best intentions, guilty of taking children out of their natural environment during World War II, lavishing attention on them, and then sending all but the five she adopts back to readjust to a bleak existence. As her lawyer says, "Everything was done for those children. They were given a luxurious home. I remonstrated with her, pointing out to her it was going to be difficult for the children, after several years of war, to return from these luxurious surroundings to their own homes" (37). Even those she adopts are not completely happy in their new state, as the novel goes to lengths to demonstrate. Eventually, however, it is proven that none of them is the murderer. The most unusual feature of the novel is that, when discovered, the murderer is allowed to walk out of the house to freedom—though the reader is informed that capture is certain. Finally, Calgary gets the youngest Argyle daughter, and the ordeal of the innocents is over.

The final novel of this group is *The Pale Horse,* in which the pairing of amateur and official detective is more nearly equal than in any of the others. Detective-Inspector LeJeune is the typical quiet, sturdy policeman; his graphic gestures are his one distinctive feature, and they betray his French Huguenot ancestry. He is one of Christie's most philosophical detectives, making such statements as "Evil is not something superhuman, it's something *less* than human. Your criminal is someone who wants to be important, but who never will be important, because he'll always be less than a man" (195). LeJeune's amateur companion is Mark Easterbrook, who describes himself as "scholar, author, man of the world" (67). Of indeterminant age, he is the widower of an unfaithful wife. While writing a study of Mogul architecture, a series of coincidences and his own curiosity bring him into the case, for most of which he is narrator. He is a friend of Ariadne Oliver and the cousin of Rhoda

Dawes, now Despard, of *Cards on the Table,* and when he visits Rhoda in Much Deeping, near Bournemouth, he meets and is greatly impressed by Mrs. Dane Calthorp of *The Moving Finger.* Though he is of help to LeJeune in determining the method of murder, it is LeJeune himself who discovers the murderer. When Easterbrook and his girlfriend Ginger Corrigan devise a plan to flush out the murderer, which involves great danger for Ginger, he has the sense to inform LeJeune of the plan before attempting it; that alone makes him an exceptional amateur. What he and LeJeune are up against is a modern assassination bureau, which has committed at least eight known deaths. The scheme of the murderer uses elaborate secrecy and a false supernatural cover to hide a very clever method of poisoning.[25] If the murderer were just willing to keep quiet, there would be nothing to connect him to the killings, but he has to interfere and assert himself and, as a result, is caught. The philosophic LeJeune says, "Killing people. It makes you feel powerful and larger than life. It makes you feel you're God Almighty" (191). But as he knows, the murderer is just another screaming little megalomaniac. *The Pale Horse* is one of the most praised of Christie's late novels, and its unusual murder plot, its pairing of LeJeune and Easterbrook, and its effective use of characters repeated from previous novels make it worthy of that praise.

The three unique novels are *And Then There Were None, Death Comes as the End,* and *Endless Night. Endless Night* will be considered in the section on murderers. Suffice it to say here that it is a longer version of the short story "The Case of the Caretaker," has the same basic murder plot as *Death on the Nile,* uses the narrative technique of *The Murder of Roger Ackroyd,* and resembles in reverse the Had-I-But-Known school of mystery fiction, but yet is absolutely unique among Christie's works. Before examining the other two novels, the four unique short stories require some comment. "Accident" is a chilling story of the murder of Inspector Evans by a woman whom he rightfully suspects of having already murdered two others. What makes the story so superbly ironic is that Evans mistakenly assumes that the woman's husband is her intended victim, and in trying to prevent that husband's death, he causes his own. The story gives every indication that the murderess has succeeded for the third time. Another successful murderer is Charles Ridgeway of "Where There's a Will," but his success in not being detected is spoiled by his not receiving the expected reward of his crime. He uses a rigged radio to produce "a voice from the dead" and frighten to death his wealthy aunt, but the accidental destruction of her will deprives him of the money. Then his disappointment is doubled when he learns that if he had waited a few months, she would have died of natural causes, and he would have had the money without having committed murder. From the pun in the title to the final sentences, this story is an ironic black comedy, a type of fiction not associated with Christie. "Swan Song" is her only story involving music, which is surprising as she studied both piano and voice when young and retained a love of music throughout her life. It is a tale of the operatic world: a famous prima donna arranges to have a baritone who once betrayed her play Scarpia to her Tosca and then uses a real dagger in the second act. There is little mystery, for she quietly surrenders to the police after the murder, but it is a well-executed story of revenge, paralleling the plot of Puccini's *Tosca*. "The Witness for the Prosecution" is better known in its stage and film versions than as a short story. It contains no detective, but the determination of the guilt or innocence of Leonard Vole in the death of Emily French, the part Romaine Vole plays in her husband's trial, and the final plot twist in the last three words of the story combine to create a singular mystery.

Also singular is the novel *And Then There Were None*. To Indian Island, a mile off the Devon coast, come ten people. They have either been invited or hired by "U. N. Owen" (*unknown*). Before the weekend passes, they are *all* dead. This novel is really the ultimate in whodunits, requiring an epilogue to explain who and how. Nine victims are executed, after being "indicted" for having escaped the proper penalty for causing the deaths of others; in other words, they are murdered for being murderers. Since Indian Island is *completely* isolated, the murderer has to be one of the ten present, but the last one whose death the reader observes is obviously not the murderer. The major clue to the puzzle is in the British nursery rime "Ten Little Indians," an alternate title along with *Ten Little Niggers*. (The clue seems to be a Christie in-joke, for it is "a red herring," a common term for misdirection in detective fiction.) The most effective things in the novel are the guilt of their past actions working in various ways upon the members of the group and the continual shifting and gradual tightening of suspicion, both of which are heightened by the cinematic effect of the point of view moving from character to character. The success of the novel led Christie to dramatize it, and it has been filmed three times—in 1945, 1965 and 1975—more than any other Christie work. The first version, directed by Rene Clair, is the most admired, but with its semi-comic approach, Christie's revised happy ending (two lovers survive), and its rather Gothic setting, it is quite different from the original novel. There the house on Indian Island is the opposite of that in Clair's film and a reversal of what might be expected: "this house was the essence of modernity. There were no dark corners—no possible sliding panels—it was flooded with electric light—

everything was new and bright and shining. There was nothing hidden in the house, nothing concealed. It had no atmosphere about it. Somehow, that was the most frightening thing of all" (49-50). In this almost antiseptic modernity, a mad killer carries out his plan to murder nine people, and though he has to become the tenth victim, he succeeds.

The most unusual setting of any Christie novel is that of *Death Comes as the End:* ancient Egypt circa 2000 B.C. The protagonist is Renisenb, a young widow who returns to her family's home after her husband's death. In the course of nine months, eight members of the household are murdered. The murderer is discovered by Hori, the family's scribe; he is not presented as a detective, but rather as a young man who is just an intelligent observer of others. His belief is that "The only clue to what is in people's minds is in their behavior"; therefore, he becomes suspicious of the one person who does not show any change of personality during the period of the murders, for it is not natural to be unaffected by such a chain of events. Hori realizes that deceit is at work: "A man whose mind is evil and whose intentions are evil is conscious of the fact and he knows that he must conceal it at all costs" (122). Despite the uniqueness of ancient Egypt as the setting for murder, the novel is still a closed domestic mystery. The estate on the Nile, the family's closing ranks against the father's new concubine Nofret, and the motivations for the murders are equivalent to the country house, the despised second wife, and the desire for inheritance of so many of the novels set in England. That the cause of the murders is within the closed family circle is stated explicitly by Hori: "There is an evil that comes from outside, and attacks so that all the world can see, but there is another kind of rottenness that breeds from within—that shows no outward sign" (9). Another resemblance to less exotic works is Christie's use of that favorite plot device; the apparent look over another's shoulder of a victim, in this case immediately before a murder. The uniqueness of this novel lies in its combination of Christie's typical techniques and the carefully researched historical setting; it illustrates her ability to work changes on her formulas.

These four groups of non-series short stories and novels are varied in quality as well as in subject-matter. Some can only be considered slight efforts, while others equal the best of her series works. Each reader will have his own favorites. Nevertheless, as a body of work, they do illustrate Christie's prodigious ability at original plot invention. Whether employing a detective or not to unravel the mystery, she was never at a loss in finding new ways to commit murder.

# B. Victims

*Murder, in ordinary cases, where the sympathy is wholly directed to the case of the murdered person, is an incident of coarse and vulgar horror.*

**Thomas DeQuincey**

*Victims, then, are killed out of greed, lust, revenge, meanness, hubris and insensitivity. None of which makes them interesting. It makes their killers interesting.*

**Rosamund Bryce**

*The victim is always important. The victim, you see, is so often the cause of the crime.*

**Hercule Poirot.**

One of Hercule Poirot's repeated dicta is that the victim is the cause of or the clue to the mystery of his or her own death. In *Evil Under the Sun* he says, "Murder springs, nine times out of ten, out of the character and circumstances of the murdered person. *Because* the victim was the kind of person he or she was, *therefore* was he or she murdered!" (68), and in *Mrs. McGinty's Dead,* he expresses the same idea: "Usually it is in the personality of the murdered person that the crux of the situation lies" (17). He makes such statements so often that one must assume that Christie agrees with him. However, the works rarely prove those statements, for generally her victims are uninteresting, unsympathetic, or essentially unknown. It is within the conventions of classic detective fiction that an answer can be found for the conflict between Poirot's stated view and the actual presentation of victims within Christie's works. There is one overriding convention regarding victims in classic detective fiction: the reader must not be unduly disturbed by the victim's death. The concept was stated many years ago by Carolyn Wells: "the victim must be of the greatest importance generally, yet not specifically in the sympathy of the reader."[26] The usual methods of preventing the reader from becoming emotionally involved are to give the victim traits which make him or her objectionable, or worse, or to deny the reader any but minimal access to the victim before the murder. Christie's constant employment of these two methods to fulfill the convention makes, in spite of Poirot's assertions, the victims in her works less significant than the murderers and the detectives.

The advantage of an unsympathetic first victim (subsequent victims will be discussed later) is that his or her personality can provide multiple motives for the crime. If the victim is faultless, there can be few reasons for desiring his or her death. The greater the number of motives, the more puzzling the case and the greater display of the detective's ability. If the victim is so objectionable that everyone has a motive, not only does this intensify the mystery, but it also frees the reader from any sense of guilt in accepting the death calmly. What makes a victim unsympathetic can vary considerably, from minor irritating habits to commission of immoral or illegal acts, but all such victims, in some way, break the social code.

Among Christie's unsympathetic women victims are the obnoxious teenager Joyce Reynolds of *Hallowe'en Party,* who wishes to make herself important; Grace Springer, the malicious games mistress of *Cat Among the Pigeons;* Ruth Kettering of *The Mystery of the Blue Train* and Linnet Ridgeway of *Death on the Nile,* both of whom are willful, even tyrannical, as a result of wealth—which also separates them from most readers; the demanding hypochondriac Adeline Clapperton of "Problem at Sea"; and such "vamps" as Louise Leidner of *Murder in Mesopotamia* and Arlena Marshall of *Evil Under the Sun.* All of these, and many others, have character traits which mitigate their deaths for the reader. Another technique is to prepare the reader for the murder of an apparantly innocuous person by the comments of an authorially approved character. For example, the narrator of *The Moving Finger* says of a mother of three children who is to become a victim, "It occurred to me at that moment that I did not much care for Mrs. Symmington. That anaemic, slighted, faded prettiness concealed, I thought, a selfish and grasping nature" (49). In a Christie work, such a statement is practically a death warrant. A more complex method is the presentation of Gladys Martin of *A Pocket Full of Rye.* When Gladys is murdered, Miss Marple, who has taught her to be a maid, rushes to the scene, filled with pity and determined to avenge her death. But even Miss Marple has to admit, "She was very keen on men, poor girl. But men didn't take much notice of her, and other girls rather made use of her" (77). In her one big scene when questioned by the police, Gladys is described as "the frightened rabbit" and as an "unattractive, frightened-looking girl, who managed to look faintly sluttish in spite of being tall and smartly dressed in a claret-colored uniform" (30). Miss Marple may grieve and wish justice done, but Christie does not let the reader care.

Unsympathetic male victims are most often criminal or sexually immoral. The criminals include a large number of blackmailers, such as Mr. Shaitana of *Cards on the Table,* David Baker of *Third Girl,* and Henry Reedburn of "The King of Clubs." Murderers themselves may become victims, as Monsieur Renauld of *The Murder on the Links,* Samuel Ratchett of *Murder on the Orient Express,* and Paul Deroulard of "The Chocolate Box." The sexually immoral victims are usually unfaithful husbands, like John

Christow of *Murder After Hours* and Amyas Crale of *Murder in Retrospect*. Christie's circumspection in dealing with sex almost never allows her to go beyond this area. The major exception is the fourth Baron Edgware. In *Lord Edgware Dies* there are hints of sadism and homosexuality, the latter implied in the presentation of Edgware's handsome young butler Alton. Poirot says of Edgware, "I fancy that he is very near the border line of madness, Hastings. I should imagine he practices many curious vices, and that beneath his frigid exterior he hides a deep-rooted instinct of cruelty" (44). As might be expected, few tears are shed for any of these men.

In *A Caribbean Mystery* Mr. Rafiel says, "I'm the person who ought to be murdered.... Proper type casting. Who's the victim in murder stories? Elderly men with lots of money" (155). If *and elderly women* is added, he is defining the single largest group of Christie's unsympathetic victims: the elderly "blocking character" of either sex.[27] Prosperous, irascible, and often stupid, this character corresponds to the *senex iratus* of classical comedy. Whether negative mother or father, this person is an "expendable obstacle." Standing in the way of youth, either through denial of money or hindering of romance, this character has only to make a will or contract a marriage with a much younger person to seal his or her fate. If such a character is not definitely unsympathetic, he or she is essentially unknown, such as Aristide Leonides of *Crooked House*— who does make one of those May-December marriages, Emily Arundell of *Poirot Loses a Client,* and Amelia Barrowby of "How Does Your Garden Grow?". Obvious examples of the type are Roger Ackroyd, Rex Fortescue of *A Pocket Full of Rye,* Simeon Lee of *Hercule Poirot's Christmas,* Sir Reuben Astwell of "The Under Dog," Gervase Chevenix-Gore of "Dead Man's Mirror," Rachel Argyle of *Ordeal by Innocence,* and Mrs. Boynton of *Appointment with Death.* Gervase Chevenix-Gore can illustrate the males. Though he is seen only in death, he is described as having "a swollen idea of his own importance" because of his ancestry (12). Therefore, he is arrogant, demanding, and oblivious of the feelings of others. He is murdered because he has drafted a new will disinheriting a young woman unless she marries the man of his choice. He is domestic bully and perfect victim. The foremost example among the women is, without question, Mrs. Boynton, who is "that hulk of shapeless flesh with her evil gloating eyes" (45) and "a stupid, malignant, posturing old woman" (55). She is compared over and over to a snake or a spider, and the desire to murder her is expressed from the first page. A former prison wardress, she cruelly dominates her children for sheer pleasure. A doctor in the novel comments that *"she became a wardress because she loved tyranny.*

In my theory it was a secret desire for power over other human beings..." (34), and he later says, "I think she rejoices in the infliction of pain—mental pain..." (35). In her case, the reader is actually relieved when she is murdered, for she is a monster, and only with her death can her put-upon family have lives of their own.

Murder is the ultimate crime and can never be accepted as a permissible action. However, like most of her Golden Age colleagues, Christie does not let her readers suffer from the deaths in her fiction, and one of her principal methods of preventing any suffering on their part is the use of unpleasant, unsympathetic, even evil victims. They do not deserve the reader's grief or guilt, and they do not receive it.

If a victim is admirable in any way, he or she must be basically a stranger to the reader. The death of one unknown can be accepted with equanimity. Minimal description and little grief are the rule with such victims, and they are relegated to the background as the investigation proceeds. Stage center is for the detective and the murderer. The simplest method of keeping victim and reader apart is for the murder to have already occurred before the first page or to occur very soon thereafter. Such is Christie's novelistic practice; very few first murders occur late. Detective short stories, of course, do not allow for acquaintance. Christie's large number of murder-in-the-past novels is the ultimate instance of this method. In such novels as *Murder in Retrospect, Elephants Can Remember, Nemesis,* and *Sleeping Murder,* the first victims may have been dead years before the events of the novel begin. A second group consists of one or more murders having already occurred, but there is one early in the novel which precipitates the investigation; examples include *Easy to Kill, Hallowe'en Party, Dead Man's Folly,* and *A Caribbean Mystery.* Then there are those in which the murder has been committed shortly before the novel opens: *Poirot Loses a Client, The Body in the Library, Mrs. McGinty's Dead,* and *The Clocks.* In others, the first murder occurs very early; among many are *Why Didn't They Ask Evans?, Sad Cypress, Death in the Clouds,* and *Three Act Tragedy.* Many of the first victims in these works are innocent, decent people, but since the reader has had, at the most, only fleeting contact with them, he is not overwhelmed by their deaths. Instead, he can concentrate on the detectives' investigations of those deaths.

Occasionally, Christie conjoins the two methods: what little is known is unfavorable. *The Murder at the Vicarage* illustrates this technique. Colonel Protheroe is discovered dead on page 39. Though he has been talked about by other characters, he has appeared only once (34-35) to allow him to demonstrate his disagreeable personality. Except for that trait, the reader knows nothing about him and, therefore, is not moved by his death. Other examples of this technique are Mrs. McGinty, Madame Giselle Moriot of *Death in the Clouds,* Heather Babcock of *The Mirror Crack'd from Side to Side,* Rudi Scherz of *A Murder Is Announced,* and Marlene Tucker of *Dead Man's Folly.* The point to be emphasized is that whether using the two methods together or separately, Christie puts emotional distance between her victims and her readers. The death is secondary to its solution.

The following dialogue concerning subsequent murders occurs in *Crooked House:*

"I should say it's about time for the next murder, wouldn't you?"
"What do you mean—the next murder?"
"Well, in books there's always a second murder about now. Someone who knows something is bumped off before they can tell what they know" (150).

In nearly sixty percent of Christie's novels, there are one or more subsequent murders. (The short stories rarely have subsequent murders.) These subsequent murders are limited to one or two in the vast majority of the cases. The two novels with the most deaths are *And Then There Were None* with ten and *Death Comes as the End* with eight, though series of previous murders are part of *The Pale Horse* and *Curtain.* These four novels, plus *The ABC Murders, Easy to Kill,* and *What Mrs. McGillicuddy Saw!,* present series of intentional killings. Much more prevalent is the first murder's being intentional and the subsequent one's being the result of fear on the part of the murderer. As indicated by the passage from *Crooked House,* the most likely subsequent victim is the character who knows something about the original murder—or is thought to know something by the murderer. A character may be concealing information in order to blackmail the murderer—the most common reason—(Henet of *Death Comes as the End,* Victoria Johnson of *A Caribbean Mystery,* Guiseppe the butler of *The Mirror Crack'd from Side to Side),* because of uncertainty (Laura Upward of *Mrs. McGinty's Dead,* Agnes Waddell of *The Moving Finger,* Elizabeth Temple of *Nemesis),* or simply out of contrariness (Philip Durrant of *Ordeal by Innocence,* Joyce Reynolds of *Hallowe'en Party,* Ernie Gregg of *They Do It With Mirrors).* There are also those who do not realize what they know (Amy Murgatroyd of *A Murder Is Announced,* Edna Brent of *The Clocks,* Celia Austin of *Hickory Dickory Death)* and those who plan to reveal information but are not given the opportunity by the murderer (Donald Ross of *Lord Edgware Dies,* Salome Otterbourne of *Death on the Nile,* Lavinia Fullerton of *Easy to Kill).* Finally, there are those who have been involved, innocently or otherwise, in the original murder plan in some way and must also be killed (Gladys Martin of *A Pocket Full of Rye*, Dr. Henry Morley of *An Overdose of Death*, and Pamela Reeves of *The Body in the Library*). Whatever the subsequent victim may or may not know, in all cases the murderer decides the person is a threat great enough to risk killing again.

These subsequent victims also fulfill the convention of being either unsympathetic or unknown. Greed and stupidity are the two character traits most often used to make them less than admirable. The numerous blackmailers are obvious examples of the greed; they attempt to gain profit from another's death and instead pay with their own lives. The stupid subsequent victims receive death for their lack of thought—admittedly a high price, but logic is supreme law in classic detective fiction. The stupid victim is also nearly always basically unknown except for his or her stupidity. Seen once or twice and then removed forever are such halfwits as Gladys Martin, Edna Brent, and Agnes Waddle. Other subsequent victims are so utterly unknown that their deaths hardly seem to matter: Mr. Amberiotis of *An Overdose of Death*, Louise Bourget of *Death on the Nile*, George Earlfield of *The ABC Murders*, and Ann Moriot of *Death in the Clouds*. The principle at work seems to be that if the original victim's death, which supplies the reason for the detective's investigation, must not disturb the reader's emotions, then any subsequent deaths must be even less disturbing. Otherwise, they will not just provide a complication in that investigation, which is their purpose, but will disrupt it.

The number of exceptions to the two types of victims is very few. Though readers may differ as to the exact number, as well as to the amount of sympathy aroused, hardly ten victims whom the reader is allowed to know to any degree are basically sympathetic. Five choices are Mary Gerrard of *Sad Cypress*, Dora Bunner and Amy Murgatroyd of *A Murder Is Announced*, and Celia Austin and Patricia Lane of *Hickory Dickory Death*. The major exception is Ellie Rogers of that singular novel *Endless Night*, who is almost saintlike; even her murderer comes to a realization of her nobility and compassion. All six of these exceptions are women, and it is not surprising that they are, for Christie kills nearly twice as many women as men in her novels. What is surprising is that of her several hundred victims, so few of either sex are exceptions to the unsympathetic-unknown convention.

When Christie has Poirot assert that the victim is the key to his or her death, she is unconsciously considering the victim as plot-element, rather than character. In the investigation of a death the detective must often explore the past, personality, and personal relationships of the victim to solve the case, but the victim becomes more an object for study than a human being. Indeed, it can be said that death in classic detective fiction transforms a character into a plot device. Another illustration of this transformation is that there is usually much discussion of a victim *after* his or her death by the other characters, but those statements are part of the plot, for they reveal possible motives for the murder. In essence, in nearly all of Christie's fiction, the victim is the passive figure in the first plot which leads to death; the murderer is the active character who determines events. In the second plot, the investigation of the death, the victim is essentially only the device which creates the confrontation between detective and murderer.

## C. Murderers

*Murder is negative creation, and every murderer is therefore the rebel who claims the right to be omnipotent.... The problem for the writer is to conceal his demonic pride from the other characters and from the reader, since, if a person has this pride, it tends to appear in everything he says and does.*

**W.H. Auden**

*I suspect everybody, and if you've read any detective stories, Suzanne, you must know that it's always the most unlikely person who's the villain.*

**Anne Beddingfeld**

*One can have likely murderers anywhere, or shall I say unlikely murderers, but nevertheless murderers. Because unlikely murderers are not so prone to be suspected.*

**Hercule Poirot**

One of Christie's longest statements on the nature of murderers occurs in *Crooked House* and is spoken by Assistant Commissioner Hayward of Scotland Yard:

The brake that operates with most of us doesn't operate with [murderers]. A child, you know, translates desire into action without compunction. A child is angry with its kitten, says 'I'll kill you,' and hits it on the head with a hammer—and then breaks its heart because the kitten didn't come alive again!...[gradually most children learn to know and feel what is right and wrong.] But some people, I suspect, remain morally immature. They continue to be aware that murder is wrong, but they do not feel it.... Murderers are set apart, they are 'different'—murder is wrong—but not for *them*—for *them* it is necessary—the victim has 'asked for it,' it was 'the only way' (108).

Moral immaturity and egoism: these are the central qualities of Christie's murderers. They are people who decide to correct their personal problems at the expense of the lives of other human beings. Not only do they take the life of one or more other persons, but they are in opposition to all those around them, for they place those others in danger by making them suspect for the murderer's actions. In the murderer's attempt to conceal his crime and appear innocent, others become entrapped in suspicion as the possible murderer. In Christie's fiction this concealment is relatively easy, for rarely is the murderer a professional criminal; he is "one of us." As he is nearly always from the same class as his victims—the dead and the suspected—he can hide behind the accepted and expected social pattern of that class. If guilt, fear, or, most often, egoism cause him to deviate from that social pattern, he becomes vulnerable. The necessary course for a murderer is to act normally and keep quiet. Miss Marple's, Battle's, and Poirot's repeated statements that if people are allowed to talk they will reveal more than they intend are based upon an understanding of human egoism, which is so often present in Christie's murderers. (She has only four remorseful murderers: in *Murder in Mesopotamia*, *A Murder Is Announced*, *Nemesis*, and *Endless Night*.) Some of Christie's murderers are so sure of themselves that they brag about their cleverness. For example, the unsuspected murderer of "Three Blind Mice" says to another character, "There's just one thing I'd like to say to you. *The murderer's enjoying himself.* That's the one thing I'm quite sure of" (60). The over-confident murderers of *Three Act Tragedy*, *The ABC Murders*, and *The Pale Horse* even intrude themselves into cases where otherwise there would not be the least suspicion of them. Their overweening pride and desire to outwit the detective show both their immaturity and their egoism.

The murderer has little existence outside of his crime. In this respect, he is like his victim; the reader does not identify with him. However, because of his greater prominence in the story, the presentation of the murderer is quite different from that of the victim. Since he is concealing his true nature, the reader cannot fully know him until the detective's explanation; otherwise, there would be no mystery. Also, if the reader did understand the murderer's feelings and motivation, the probability of sympathy for him would be manifestly increased. At the same time, he must be a major figure in the story, or the reader will feel cheated. A character seen only once or twice is an unsatisfactory murderer. He must be known and not known. This paradox is resolved by the fact of his leading a double life. Until his hidden life is revealed, the reader sees only the facade he wishes to present. The success of that facade—and sometimes the entire situation—may make him *seem* one of the most sympathetic characters. In fact, seldom does a Christie murderer have a truly odious personality; it is common for him to appear more likeable than his victim. One example of many is the female killer in *Death on the Nile*, who is a much more pleasant person than the principal victim. Poirot is fond of her, and his attitude affects the reader's view. However, whether likeable or not, a murderer has committed the irreversible crime, and so when guilt is proven, whatever the reader may have previously thought of him is radically altered and the necessity of his expulsion from society is accepted. He must be removed, for he has presumed to take on the powers of God and bring death to a fellow human being.

Among Christie's greatest talents is her ability to vary her murderers so as to conceal them from the reader among the other characters. In an interview she once expressed her attitude that murderers are not necessarily obvious: "You couldn't have a *doubtful* murderer—all brakes are removed and he's certain of what he's doing. But this needn't be obvious to others. Especially as one gathers it [is] very rarely in real life. In real life, when there's a murder, everyone seems so astonished. People always say about the murderer: 'He was such a charming man. So kind, so good to children.' "[28] Certainly, murderers are not obvious in Christie's fiction. They may be young or old, male or female, proud or remorseful, rich or poor, acting alone or working with a partner. *Anyone* may be the murderer in a Christie work; the following descriptions of twelve murderers are evidence of that fact:

...might have been any age over thirty. She was a tall, thin woman with dark hair, rather prominent light "boiled gooseberry" eyes and a worried face. A fashionable hat was perched on her head at an unfashionable angle and she wore a rather depressed-looking cotton frock (Client, 120).

She was a tall, handsome woman of forty-odd, her golden hair was lightly tinged with grey, her eyes were brilliantly blue, she oozed competence from the finger tips downwards (Hallowe'en, 47).

Her dark hair was ruffled and gave her an elfin look. There was something elfin about her altogether. The small vivid face, pansy shaped, the enormous dark blue eyes, and something else—something haunting and arresting (Peril, 8).

She was...completely the country spinster. Her thin form was neatly dressed in a tweed coat and skirt, and she wore a gray silk blouse with a cairngorm brooch. Her hat, a conscientious felt, sat squarely upon her well-shaped head. Her face was pleasant and her eyes, through their pince-nez, decidedly intelligent (Easy, 38).

She was a tall, willowy girl, with long black hair, a heavily made up dead white face, and eyebrows and eyelashes slightly slanted upward—the effect heightened by mascara. She wore tight velvet pants and a heavy sweater (Girl, 24).

A flat homely face...a face like a pancake, the face of a middle-aged woman, with frizzy yellowish grey hair plastered on top of her head. She seemed to hover, waiting, like a watchful dragon.... Of course, this should have been a nun's face! (Ordeal, 5 & 6).

...a good specimen of humanity. Lean, bronzed with broad shoulders and narrow thighs, there was about him a kind of infectious enjoyment and gaiety—a native simplicity that endeared him to all women and most men (Sun, 16).

...a small, middle-aged man, with a bald domed head, a round ingenuous face, and glasses (Horse, 25).

...a tall broad-shouldered young man with very dark blue eyes, crisply curling brown hair, a square chin and a boyish appealing simple smile...(*Nile*, 26).

The man who came in did so with a kind of parody of a brisk bedside manner. He was a cheerful, highly coloured individual of middle age. Small twinkling eyes, a touch of boldness, a tendency to *embonpoint* and a general air of well-scrubbed and disinfected medical practitioner. His manner was cheerful and confident. You felt that his diagnosis would be correct and his treatment agreeable and practical...(Cards, 18).

...was the acme of calm respectabililty, the sort of man who would never give his wife a moment's anxiety. A long neck with a pronounced Adam's apple, a slightly cadaverous face and a long thin nose. A kindly man, no doubt, a good husband and father, but not one to set the pulses madly racing (Finger, 34).

...an undeniably attractive personality. He is, I suppose, about thirty years of age. He has dark hair, but his eyes are of a brilliant, almost startling blue. He is the kind of man who does everything well. He is good at games, an excellent shot, a good amateur actor, and can tell a first-rate story. He is capable of making any party go. He has, I think, Irish blood in his veins (Vicarage, 27).

Because of their variety, Christie's murderers can be classified in a number of ways. Three groups will be considered here because of their repeated use: the murderous pair, the least-likely murderer, and the most-likely murderer (a later classification will be by motive). Christie's murderous pairs always consist of male and female partners. Her fondness for this combination is evidenced by the nineteen novels and six short stories employing it. Whether the purpose of the murder is to eliminate an unwanted husband or wife or to obtain wealth—the motives in all except *N or M?*—these pairings provide the obvious advantage of greater complication for the plot. The pair can supply alibis for each other, they can divide and act separately if necessary, and through the use of disguise, particularly by the women, they can confuse the identity of the victim and the time of the death. To prevent the reader from suspecting that a duo is at work, Christie varies considerably the amount of guilt between the partners. At times, the woman is merely an accomplice (*Mystery of the Blue Train, A Pocket Full of Rye, The Seven Dials Mystery, Dead Man's Folly*): in others, she is the driving force (*The Body in the Library, The Clocks, Hallowe'en Party, Endless Night*, "The Mystery of Hunter's Lodge"). However, in most instances, guilt is evenly shared *(Why Didn't They Ask Evans?, The Murder at the Vicarage, N or M?, Death on the Nile, Remembered Death, Third Girl, Evil Under the Sun*, "Greenshaw's Folly," "The Bloodstained Pavement," "The Love Detectives"). The most interesting aspect of these duos is the misdirection created by Christie's delight in unexpected, even outlandish, pairings.[29] She joins a snivelling, unattractive maid with the handsome son of her rich employer in *A Pocket Full of Rye*, a pair in *Hallowe'en Party* described by Poirot as Lady Macbeth and Narcissus, two people who seem to dislike each other intensely in *The Mysterious Affair at Styles* and *Endless Night*, and pairs who are supposedly unknown or barely known to each other in *N or M?*, *The Clocks*, and *Remembered Death*. Such pairings are similar to the technique of the least-likely murderer, for the reader does not suspect any murderous connection between the parties of these mismatched or "unrelated" pairs. Only when the connection between them *is* made by the detective can the mystery be solved.

Though Christie did not invent the least-likely murderer, she has been criticized for overuse of the device. Her belief that murderers are not obvious allowed her to consider the device a legitimate one, though she could make jokes about it in such statements as that of Tommy Beresford in *Partners in Crime:* "I was really going on the well known principle of suspecting the most unlikely person" (182). She used the device throughout her career and became famous—or, if you will, notorious—for that use; nearly half the novels and a number of short stories include it. In the vast majority of cases, she is able to make the reader accept the revealed murderer as inevitable no matter how unlikely he may have seemed during the course of the action: no other alternative is possible. When she fails to accomplish this acceptance, the reason is either inadequate motive *(Hercule Poirot's Christmas)* or too minor a role for the murderer—and, therefore, lack of clues *(What Mrs. McGillicuddy Saw!)*. Among her variations on the least-likely device are the narrator as murderer *(The Murder of Roger Ackroyd* and *Endless Night)*, all suspects as co-murderers *(Murder on the Orient Express)*, two murderers acting independently *(Cat Among the Pigeons)*, and policemen as murderers *(Hercule Poirot's Christmas* and "The Man in the Mist").

Though there are other single variations, four large categories within the type are predominant. First is the supposed victim as murderer, whose effect is to turn the reader's view topsyturvy: if Smith is the intended victim, then the murderer *must* be someone else. The reader is led to look at all circumstances the wrong way around. Such misdirection is present in *Peril at End House, Overdose of Death, A Murder Is Announced, The Mirror Crack'd from Side to Side, At Bertram's Hotel,* and *By the Pricking of My Thumbs.* In *Peril at End House* and *The Murder on the Links* the murderers even call in Poirot for "protection" from supposed killers, prime illustrations of that egoism of Christie's murderers. Second and similar is the murderer as "aide" to the detective in his investigation. Again the reader is misdirected, not expecting someone to participate actively in the revelation of himself as a murderer. *The Murder of Roger Ackroyd* is the most famous example, but others are *Three Act Tragedy, The ABC Murders,* and *Death in the Clouds.* The murderer is in charge of the investigation in *Hercule Poirot's Christmas,* since he is the local superintendent of police; it is only Poirot's presence which counters the superintendent's manipulation of the evidence. A third group consists of murderers who fake attempts on their own lives to divert suspicion. The idea that one would deliberately endanger his own life is so foreign to most people that these murderers succeed, at least for a time, in concealing the truth. Since the characters in the works accept the attempts as genuine, the tendency is for the reader also to accept them as such. However, anyone who reads a number of Christie's works becomes aware of her fondness for these fake attempts and is rightly suspicious of any character who is almost, but not quite, killed. Occasionally, this type of murderer is also in the first group, as in *Peril at End House* and *Overdose of Death.* Other examples include *Funerals are Fatal, Crooked House, Death on the Nile, And Then There Were None,* and *Death Comes as the End.* The misdirection in the final category is created by a double bluff. The murderer is the principal suspect, then is apparently proven innocent, but is finally shown to be guilty after all. The murderer may plan to be accused, even confess, realizing that evidence is lacking or that an alibi is ready for his protection. Usually there is an accomplice to aid the murderer in his plan. Among the novels using this double bluff are *The Murder at the Vicarage, Towards Zero, The Mysterious Affair at Styles, Lord Edgware Dies,* and *Murder After Hours.* A variation occurs in *There Is a Tide,* where a man is accused of a death he did not commit, actually an accident, is jailed, then released, but in the meantime has arranged the death of another person. All of Christie's least likely murderers are devices for mystification. They upset expectations and trick the reader into looking in the wrong direction. Though some critics may be irritated by their frequency, they are a staple of Christie's fiction: her favorite murderers.

Far fewer in novels than the least likely murderers are the most likely ones, but they are still a significant group. On the other hand, because of the smaller number of suspects, the majority of the short stories use this type; in them it is more a question of how it was done than who did it. "The Under Dog" is an example of Christie's technique in using the type. Not only do the title and most of the circumstances point to Owen Trefusis as the murderer of his employer Sir Reuben Astwell, but Lady Astwell continually says that he did it. But since she is rather dotty, no one pays any attention to her statements; eventually Poirot proves her correct. The problem for an author in using the most likely murderer is to find some strategy for making the reader refuse to accept the obvious. In "The Under Dog" Lady Astwell's statements about other matters serve that function, for if she cannot be trusted about them, then she cannot be trusted to identify the murderer.

More complex strategies are necessary in novels. The most likely murderer appears in *Why Didn't They Ask Evans?*, *Murder at Hazelmoor*, *Sad Cypress*, *Sleeping Murder*, *Hickory Dickory Death*, and *The Body in the Library*. In the first four, the suspects' physical presence on the scene and their major roles make them most likely, but there is apparent lack of motive. In the last two, Christie reverses her usual method: she deliberately blackens the character of the murderer. Nigel Chapman is the most disliked and most obvious suspect in *Hickory Dickory Death*, and therefore the tendency of the reader is to assume that he cannot be a Christie murderer. Inspector Sharpe says, "The only person we've got any evidence against is young Chapman. And there we've got too much" (105). In most Christie works such a statement would automatically exclude Chapman as murderer, and so the reader, expecting an unobvious murderer, ignores nasty Nigel and looks elsewhere. Similarly, in *The Body in the Library* the obvious suspect is Mark Gaskell. Over and over, everyone suspects and/or dislikes him. Miss Marple does say that she likes him, but she qualifies the statement with "Most women would. But he can't take me in" (93). Other characters are more blunt. Both Sir Henry Clithering, an ex-policeman, and Colonel Melchett, the Chief Constable, are antagonistic to Gaskell. Colonel Melchett's thoughts on meeting him are "He didn't much care for the fellow. A bold, unscrupulous, hawklike face. One of those men who usually get their own way and whom women frequently admire. *But not the sort of fellow I'd trust....* Unscrupulous—that was the word for him. The sort of fellow who wouldn't stick at anything" (58). Gaskell himself contributes to his image as likely murderer, saying, "It's just dawned on me that I'm Favorite Suspect Number One to the police!" When the reply is that he has an alibi, he then says, "No innocent person ever has an alibi!" (110-11). Eventually, that alibi is broken, and Gaskell is proven not to be innocent.

The most likely murderer is another Christie technique of misdirection, for one does not expect her murderers to be obvious. Though most of her methods of misdirection are part of the plot structure, there are a few directly related to the presentation of the murderer which demand mention here. One of the simplest and most common is to have one or more characters—never the author—say that the murderer cannot be the person who actually is. Of course, the reader should not uncritically accept one character's statements about another, but if the character speaking seems to have authorial approval, it is likely the reader will accept the statement at face value, especially if there is an "explanation" of why that person could not have done it. A second and related technique is to have an authorially approved character evaluate the murderer in the opposite of murderous terms. The heroine of *Death Comes as the End* says of the murderer: "She had always been fond of her brother Yahmose. He was gentle and affectionate to her and had a mild and kindly disposition" (6). At times, this technique is combined with a hidden clue, as when Tuppence meets the villain in *The Secret Adversary*: "She read in his glance kindliness, and something else more difficult to fathom" (69). Giles Reed's "convincing" argument in *Sleeping Murder* (76) as to Dr. Kennedy's personality and probable actions is another instance. One of the cleverest twists on this method occurs in *Nemesis*. Miss Marple is thinking of Clotilde Bradbury-Scott:

> Clotilde...was certainly no Ophelia, but she would have made a magnificent Clytemnestra.... But since she had never had a husband, that solution wouldn't do. Miss Marple could not see her murdering anyone else but a husband—there had been no Agamemnon in this house (87).

What Miss Marple does not yet know is that Clotilde did kill the person she considered her "mate," but it was a girl rather than a man and because the girl was leaving her rather than Clotilde's wishing to be rid of her. Miss Marple has read the personality correctly, but without the facts, she seems to remove the woman from suspicion. A third technique is a romance between an innocent person—always a woman—and the murderer. The murderer as member of a novel's principal romantic couple seems to exclude him from suspicion. Usually there is another young man in the wings to salve the innocent young woman's sorrow, as in *Three Act Tragedy* and *There Is a Tide*. In *Death in the Clouds,* knowing that he is going to prove her fiance a murderer, Poirot provides a young woman with a new boyfriend, but in *A Pocket Full of Rye* the reader is not told what happens to the charming young wife of the murderer after he is discovered. Perhaps the most widely used method of misdirection in regard to murderers is their ability to lie and throw suspicion on others. They do so repeatedly, often actually describing themselves when speaking of someone else. An illustration is provided by a murderess in *Why Didn't They Ask Evans?*, who says of another woman, "She seems a very simple woman. But sometimes I fancy that she isn't so simple as she seems. I've even wondered sometimes whether she is an entirely different woman from what we all think she is . . . whether, perhaps, she isn't playing a part and playing it very well" (152). These methods of misdirection enable Christie to mystify the reader as to the identity of the murderer. Another method involves motive.

In *Hallowe'en Party* Ariadne Oliver exclaims, "I can't believe— I simply can't believe that anyone would do murder just to make a garden on a Greek isle" (242). Mrs. Oliver is wrong, for in that novel and a few others, the murders are the result of just such farfetched motives. Murder is committed to acquire a teashop in *Funerals Are Fatal*, as a rehearsal for a later murder in *Three Act Tragedy*, and from sheer hatred of a father which lasts for over thirty years before the murder is attempted in *Hercule Poirot's Christmas*. The most fantastic is that of the murderer in *They Do It with Mirrors*, who kills in order to be able "to establish an overseas colony for a co-operative experiment in which juvenile delinquents should eventually own this territory and administer it" (218). Fortunately, Christie only rarely gives way to such flights of fancy in ascribing motives, for an inadequate motive for a crime as terrible as murder leaves a reader unsatisfied. There must be a motive, and it must be believable. Apparent lack of motive is naturally one of the best means a murderer has of concealing his crime. Confronting an intended victim, the murderer in *Easy to Kill* says, "But of course I was always safe, because I never had any motive, and you can't suspect anyone of murder if there isn't a motive" (160). To prove motive or to find the correct motive among several is often a major task for the detective, and a major task for the author is to provide that motive and make it believable.

The usual motives for murder in Christie's works are money, fear, and revenge. Additionally, her women murderers are often motivated by love or passion.[30] Money is by far the most common motive for a first murder. In twenty-eight of the novels and over half of the short stories, it is the dominant motive. Christie's upper-middle class sense of the sanctity of property makes greed to possess wealth her natural favorite as a cause of social harmony being disrupted by murder. Fear of exposure for the original murder is the principal motive for any succeeding murders. However, fear of loss of position—which again may involve money and which is usually the result of some past crime—can be the cause of the first murder in a novel; examples include *A Murder Is Announced, Cards on the Table, Dead Man's Folly, Appointment with Death,* and *Overdose of*

*Death.* When revenge is the motive, it may take the form of a carefully worked out plan, as in *Murder on the Orient Express,* or it may be the result of sudden uncontrollable anger, as in *The Mirror Crack'd from Side to Side.* Revenge is often associated with insanity as in *Easy to Kill, Towards Zero, Elephants Can Remember,* "Three Blind Mice," and "Miss Marple Tells a Story." Revenge may also be related to disappointment in love, as in the three novels just mentioned. Christie's male murderers, however, rarely kill for love; the major instances are in *Murder in Mesopotamia, Sleeping Murder,* "The Herb of Death," and "The Mystery of the Baghdad Chest." Love as a motive for murder is much more prevalent among Christie's women. Besides the women in the murderous duos, who nearly always act at least partially from love of their partners, there are women who kill for love in *Murder After Hours, Murder in Retrospect, Ordeal by Innocence, Nemesis,* and "Death by Drowning." For Christie, love is more overpowering in women than in men, the traditional view of her time and class.

Money, fear, revenge, and love cover practically all of the motives of Christie's murderers, whether "one of us" or a professional criminal, but, insanity is occasionally present without the motivation of revenge ("The Lemusurier Inheritance," *By the Pricking of My Thumbs, And Then There Were None, Crooked House,* and *Endless Night*). The last two novels indicate Christie's differing methods of presenting insanity. The murderer in *Crooked House* is twelve-year-old Josephine Leonides, who kills her grandfather because he refuses to let her take ballet lessons and her nanny who suspects her. Though it is never stated explicitly that she is insane, her unbalanced mental state is evident throughout her presentation. She has a morbid curiosity, an absolute sense of her own superiority, and an utter callousness. One character says, "Sometimes I think that child isn't right in her head.... She gives me the shivers sometimes" (74). Her mental state is attributed to heredity:

> She had had an authoritarian ruthlessness of her grandmother's family, and the ruthless egoism of Magda, seeing only her own point of view. She had also presumably suffered, sensitive like Philip, from the stigma of being the unattractive—the changeling child—of the family. Finally, in her very marrow had run the essential crooked strain of old Leonides (220-21).

Thus, Christie "explains" Josephine's insanity as the coming together in the ugly little girl of two lines of instability, expressed in ruthlessness and unscrupulousness.

Christie does not attempt to explain the insanity of Michael Rogers in *Endless Night;* rather she allows him to present it himself. Using the narrative technique of *The Murder of Roger Ackroyd,* she provides her only full-scale portrait of a psychotic murderer. Rogers murders for money—the basic plot is identical to that of *Death on the Nile*—but his greed cannot be separated from his insanity. He is twenty-two, handsome, irresponsible, and unwilling to work, but in love with luxury. He has murdered twice before the opening of the novel and murders three more times during the course of the novel, as well as unintentionally causing the death of a fourth person, which is his undoing. In the first two murders of the novel, he is directed by his mistress Greta Andersen, who becomes his final victim. His comment on her death is "Yes, I was wonderfully happy when I killed Greta" (240). Their plan to marry him to Ellie Guteman, kill her, and inherit her millions is complicated by his growing attraction to Ellie, but his mania for owning "his house" compels him to kill her. Ellie realizes his nature, but does nothing to stop him, merely saying, "You're you, and I love you" (167). His greatest fear is his mother, who recognizes his dangerousness and warns him of his course, but, like Ellie, she is powerless against the promptings of Greta and his own insane greed. Within Michael Rogers Christie encapsulates many of the varied features of her other murderers: insanity and money as motives, the narrator as least-likely suspect, moral immaturity and egoism as well as later remorse, the double life including surface pleasantness, the murderer as partner in the principal romance, and, with Greta Andersen, the murderous duo. Yet with all of these similarities to other murderers, Michael Rogers is an unique murderer in a singular novel—and evidence of Christie's ability to create new surprises from typical conventions within the formulas of her genre.

It is assumed in classic detective fiction that murderers must be punished, and such usually happens in Christie's works. Though there are no executions in those works, the reader often sees a murderer arrested and, therefore, expects that he is tried, convicted, and given just punishment. When arrested Christie's murderers vary in reaction. They may be nonchalant: "I throw in my hand. You've got me!" (Cards, 247) or "I'm a gambler—but I know when I've lost the last throw" (Tide, 221). A murderer may just collapse, as in *The Moving Finger,* but more often he turns on the detective who has destroyed his clever scheme, and his ego, and releases a "low-pitched flood of invective," as in *Cat Among the Pigeons* (199); other instances include *Death in the Clouds* and *Evil Under the Sun.* In the last the murderer calls Poirot, "You damned interfering murdering lousy little worm!" (175). Aside from the arrests, the three most common ends for Christie's murderers are suicide, total insanity, or death by another. In some cases, the detective allows suicide to take place without hindrance: *The Murder of Roger*

*Ackroyd, Peril at End House, Death on the Nile, Poirot Loses a Client,* and *Appointment with Death*—all Poirot novels. In others, the suicide occurs so quickly that prevention is impossible: *The Secret Adversary, Hallowe'en Party, Nemesis.* Besides Michael Rogers, total insanity claims the murderers of "Three Blind Mice," *Three ActTragedy, Funerals Are Fatal, Easy to Kill, Towards Zero,* and *Sleeping Murder.* All go "right over the edge." Superintendent Battle explains this happening in *Easy to Kill:* "They can't face the shock of not having been so clever as they thought they were" (171). The murderer may himself be murdered, either while attempting to kill again, as in *Death Comes as the End* and *The Murder on the Links,* or by someone who thinks death the best solution for all concerned, as in *Crooked House* or *The Mirror Crack'd from Side to Side.*

Whether arrest, death, or insanity brings a murderer's criminal career to a close, it is ended. However, there are a surprising number of murderers in Christie's works who either escape or whose fate is left vague. The murderers of *Why Didn't They Ask Evans?* and *The Man in the Brown Suit* escape to South America. Poirot absolves the murderers in *Murder on the Orient Express,* gives another a twenty-four hour headstart in "The Cornish Mystery" (but says he will be caught), and allows still another to walk away in *Murder in Retrospect.* What happens to the murderers is never explained in *Murder in Mesopotamia, Evil Under the Sun, Sad Cypress, Ordeal by Innocence, Dead Man's Folly, The Clocks,* and *At Bertram's Hotel.* The reader is left to assume that since the detective has uncovered the murderer's identity, there will be no escape from justice, but the ultimate fate of the evildoer is left to the imagination of the reader.

Christie's view seems to be that revelation of the murderer is enough. If he is known, he is no longer a serious threat, for generally not being a professional criminal, he is punished in just being revealed for what he actually is. The innocent have been saved, and the guilty party can never again take his former place in society. As has been said, "Since the offender in detective fiction is...an offender against both moral and social codes, his expulsion from society reaffirms the value of both."[31] It is classic detective fiction's requirement of that affirmation which makes his removal necessary. As long as he is removed, the form of retributive justice is, for Christie, relatively unimportant. Whatever his personality and whatever his motive, he has murdered, has dueled with the detective, and has been exposed. Truth is triumphant, and guilt and suspicion have been lifted from the innocent.

## D. Bystanders, Witnesses, and Suspects

*The witnesses...comprise the chief movers of the machinery and it is in their power to make
or mar the plot. For if the plot of a detective story is the knot and its unraveling, the evidence of the
witnesses constitutes the strands of the skein.*

Carolyn Wells

*The Admirable Eccentric...The Flighty Dowager...The Dotty Duchess...The Horsy
Lady...The Tweedy Lady...The Drab Dame...*

Jeanine Larmoth

*...the other characters serve an emblematic function...*

George Grella

Though central, the victim, the murderer, and the detective
cannot alone be the cast of characters in detective fiction. There
must be those supporting players: the bystanders, witnesses, and
suspects. On these necessary characters, Max Mallowan quotes an
unnamed French critic, *"Ce ne sont pas des caractères, ce sont des
traits de caractères,"* and, as translation and comment, adds, "They
are not characters but character sketches, and the more interesting
because the reader is frequently left to make his own effort to
penetrate the surface."[32] It is doubtful if many readers feel the need
"to penetrate the surface," for these characters are functional,
serving five principal roles in Christie's works (and on a few
occasions, a specialized sixth: as narrator): to provide information
about victim and/or murderer, to provide red herrings, to provide
social commentary, to provide humor, and to provide a sense of
familiarity by recurrent appearances. In their fulfillment of these
functions, they contribute significantly to the distinctiveness of
Christie's fiction. (The fourth function is one part of the larger
matter of humor in Christie's fiction and will be considered in that
context in Chapter V. The fifth has already been examined at the
beginning of this chapter.)

The providing of needed information to the detective is the most
obvious function of secondary characters; as stated
ungrammatically by a government agent in *Cat Among the
Pigeons,* "Everybody always knows something, even if it's
something they don't know they know" (111). Many characters exist
solely to provide what they know to the detective: landladies,
railroad employees, some servants, etc. However, the second
function of providing misinformation or red herrings often crosses
the first. What the detective must do, in Poirot's words, is "to
separate the harmless lies from the vital ones" (*Christmas,* 138). He
must determine what information is true and relevant and what is
not. Since, for most of a work, the murderer appears to be just one of

the witnesses or suspects, the detective must approach all involved from the dual perspective of their being suppliers of needed evidence and deliberate deceivers.

His task of winnowing the truth or falsity of statements is complicated by several factors directly related to the nature of bystanders, witnesses, and suspects. An innocent person may have motive, means, or opportunity to commit the murder, making that person's statements suspect. Such a character is himself a red herring, for he diverts attention from the actual murderer. One of Christie's greatest skills is the spreading of motive, means, and opportunity among those involved in such a manner as to make any statement by any character suspicious or worse. Other complications may result from a character's attempt to solve the crime on his own, thus obstructing the progress of the detective's investigation, or one character's fear for another's safety may cause information to be withheld or distorted, the latter is particularly true between lovers or among family members. Poirot says disgustedly, "Loyalty, it is a pestilential thing in crime. Again and again it obscures the truth" (Mesopotamia, 137). Another difficulty is that all of the suspects may seem innocent. When Tuppence Beresford encounters the female guests at a seaside boardinghouse in N or M?, her reaction is "There's a young mother, a fussy spinster, the hypochondriac's brainless wife, and a rather fearsome-looking old Irishwoman. All seem harmless enough on the face of it" (49). All but one are harmless; the problem is which one. A related problem is that though these characters represent the norm of society which is threatened, generally present are one or more guilty of something other than murder which they wish to hide. That guilt causes them to conceal or falsify information to protect themselves, thus again impeding the murder investigation. To produce these other "guilty suspects," Christie occasionally resorts to a rather incongruous collection of individuals. The passenger-list of the Karnak in Death on the Nile is perhaps the prime example; on it are a jewel thief, a terrorist, a kleptomaniac, an alcoholic, a blackmailer, a communist nobleman, a jilted lover following her now married boyfriend, his millionairess wife, and assorted lesser characters. That list includes victims and murderers, but also those who make the solution more difficult for Poirot. These various complications indicate that the functions of providing both information and misinformation cannot be separated, for they are inextricably linked in detective fiction's structure of mystification.

In their third role, secondary characters are the principal conveyors of the social scene discussed in Chapter II. They range from the sympathetic through the satiric to the despicable, but they all have something to say about twentieth century British life. Whether they first appear in one of Christie's prefatory descriptive lists or just show up in the course of a work, they populate her England, and they determine the reader's view—and expectations— of that England. For example, among the thirty-odd law firms in the works, there are nearly always three or more members—Barkett, Markett and Applegood; Ballard, Entwhistle, Entwhistle and Ballard; Partingdale, Harris, Lockeridge and Partingdale; ffoulkes, ffoulkes, Wilbraham and ffoulkes; etc.—whereas the numerous land and house agents are always duo partnerships: Lovebody and Slicker, Gabler and Stretcher, Breather and Scuttle, etc. In this world of Stretchers and Scuttles, the reader encounters a mother going to Anatolia on a bus and another who is an alcoholic aristocrat *(Cat Among the Pigeons)*, a young man "out of one of Mr. P.G. Wodehouse's books" (Mesopotamia, 20), a duke who looks like a haberdasher and is outwardly priggish, but seethes with passion *(Lord Edgware Dies)*, a hippie artist and a new aesthete *(Third Girl)*, and a revolutionary described by Poirot as "a wolf with ideas" (Overdose, 66). One is taken behind the facade of upperclass marriage on meeting Jeremy and Frances Cloade of *There Is a Tide* and Harold and Lady Alice Crackenthorpe of *What Mrs. McGillicuddy Saw!*. In *A Caribbean Mystery* Raymond West arranges to let Miss Marple's house to a homosexual writer and says that "surely even dear old Aunt Jane must have heard of queers" (4-5). Christie obviously had; Mr. Pye of *A Moving Finger* and Johnny Jethroe of *The Mirror Crack'd from Side to Side* are two quite different types of homosexual, and lesbianism is implied in the relationship of Miss Hinchliffe and Miss Murgatroyd of *A Murder is Announced*. On a different level are the respected country squires, such as Major Phillpot of *Endless Night,* of whom Michael Rogers says, "I was getting my values now. I knew that [in spite of his battered old car] he was still God, all right, and he'd set the seal of his approval on us" (132-33). In contrast, Miss Marple recognizes in Major Palgrave, a victim, numerous other garrulous ex-officers: "In the past, it had been predominantly India. Majors, colonels, lieutenant-generals—and a familiar series of words: *Simla. Bearers. Tigers. Chota Hazri—Tiffin. Khitmagers,* and so on. With Major Palgrave the terms were slightly different. *Safari. Kikuyu. Elephants. Swahili.* But the pattern was essentially the same" (1). Among the women are met such feminists as Aimée Griffith of *The Moving Finger* and Cecilia Williams of *Murder in Retrospect.* The latter has been the governess of Angela Warren, now a famous archaeologist, in whom Poirot finds "just a sufficient nuance of the *femme formidable* ... to alarm him as a mere man" (105). Poirot's appreciation of women runs more to the likes of Bessie Burch of *Mrs. McGinty's Dead:*

> She was a big plump woman with a healthy colour and a good humoured mouth. The small house was neat and clean and smelt of furniture polish and Brasso. A faint appetizing smell came from the direction of the kitchen.
> A good wife who kept her house clean and took the trouble to cook for her man. He approved. (25-26)

Examples of the varied social types could be extended for pages; suffice it to say that widows, soldiers, actors and actresses, farmers, businessmen, doctors, photographers, teachers and many others move through the pages of Christie's fiction, forming the society whose harmony is disrupted by murder.

A sixth role, as narrator, is rarely given by Christie to secondary characters. Setting aside the Poirot novels narrated by Hastings and the two narrated by murderers, only four other novels are totally first-person accounts: *The Murder at the Vicarage, Murder in Mesopotamia, The Moving Finger,* and *Crooked House;* though, there is partial narration in other works. Reverend Leonard Clement is the narrator of *The Murder at the Vicarage.* He is a sober, middle-aged clergyman, with a much younger and most unvicarish wife, and their relationship is used for comic effect. At the same time, Clement's close knowledge and shrewd observation of the people of St. Mary Mead make him a good delineator of those involved. His being a clergyman, which effectively removes him from suspicion in a Christie work, and his not being an active investigator of the case make him a detached, though limited, recounter of events. (Some form of limitation is, of course, necessary if the solution is not to be revealed prematurely.) The same dual elements of comedy and shrewd observation are present in Nurse Amy Leatheran, the narrator of *Murder in Mesopotamia.* The comedy results from her being a kind of Hastings in reverse. Though she is eventually won over by Poirot, she is decidedly unimpressed by him for some time. She corrects his English: "Even if he *was* a great detective he'd realize he *didn't* know *everything!*" (163). When he knows the solution, but will not tell, her thought is "I saw perfectly well that he meant to make a song and dance of it" (188). Numerous other comments on his appearance, his methods not being up-to-date, and his vanity could be cited to indicate Nurse Leatheran's comic response to Poirot. Her competence as nurse is stated in the "Foreword," where she is described as "Cheerful, robust, shrewd, and matter-of-fact" (10), and the last two adjectives also apply to her as narrator. Her no-nonsense attitude reassures the reader that he is being given a truthful account. Jerry Burton, the narrator of *The Moving Finger,* is used differently. Recuperating from an accident in the village of Lymstock, he serves as the outsider who unwillingly becomes involved in local events and is the active investigator throughout the novel—even after the very late appearance of Miss Marple. He is also Prince Charming to Megan Hunter's Cinderella, and their developing romance is a large part of the novel. Much the same is true of Charles Hayward of *Crooked House.*

Partial first-person narrations include the diary of the villain of *The Man in the Brown Suit,* the accounts of the investigators in *The Clocks* and *The Pale Horse,* and the recollections of suspects in *Murder in Retrospect* and *Remembered Death.* The first is another example of misdirection; the second two, which are the most extensive, are straight-forward narratives of what happens; and the final two provide complication by the differing views of the same events. Christie apparently realized that a narrator, unless of the admiring Hastings type, generally has too great a place in a novel, thus diminishing the centrality of the detective. The omniscient approach allows the author of detective fiction greater freedom in the manipulation of plot and character, and Christie preferred, except in these few cases, to present those involved herself, rather than allow one of them to dominate the others as narrator.

Though it is impossible, and unnecessary, to examine all of Christie's secondary characters, five major groups among them deserve some comment: the large families, the ne'er-do-wells, the lovers, the police, and "the lower orders."

That Christie had a fondness for murder within large families is evidenced by such families appearing in eleven novels and two long short stories: *The Mysterious Affair at Styles, Poirot Loses a Client, Appointment with Death, Hercule Poirot's Christmas, Crooked House, Funerals Are Fatal, A Pocket Full of Rye, They Do It With Mirrors, What Mrs. McGillicuddy Saw!, Ordeal by Innocence, Murder After Hours,* "The Under Dog," and "Dead Man's Mirror." The large family gathered for some occasion or already living together provides closed circle intimacy, domestic—often comic—interplay, and, most importantly, hidden antagonisms which can erupt, thus scattering suspicion among the family members. Though variations occur, the typical large Christie family consists of a patriarchal or matriarchal tyrant (so frequently the victim); sons and daughters with suitable and unsuitable wives and husbands; a spinster aunt; and one or more poor cousins, nephews, or nieces. Surrounding the immediate family are secretaries, companions, family lawyers, butlers, and the rest of the staff. Children rarely figure prominently in these families, though there is, of course, Josephine Leonides. (The very few other major child characters are outside the large families: Miranda Butler of *Hallowe'en Party* and Julia Upjohn of *Cat Among the Pigeons.* Christie apparently felt that a murderous environment was no place for children.)

Sometimes the families are of a size and complexity to make the reader wish for a genealogical chart. The outstanding example is the Serrocord menage of *They Do It With Mirrors.* Carrie Louise Serrocord has been married three times, and the progeny of her and her husbands together and separately fill Stonygates in bewildering profusion. In fact, multiple marriages of the family head always create problems. Emily Cavendish's marriage to Alfred Inglethorpe is resented by her adult children in *The Mysterious Affair at Styles.* The same is true of Rex Fortescue's and Aristide Leonides' marriages in *A Pocket Full of Rye* and *Crooked House.* As noted previously, such marriages seem invitations to murder; certainly, they supply the family members with a definite motive—though it usually turns out not to have been acted upon.

The Abernethies, the Angkatells, the Argyles, the Astwells, the Crackenthorpes, etc. are families whose members are often as divergent as the heterogeneous groups Christie gathers at hotels or on trains and boats. The principal difference is the long past relationships among the family members. In Christie's family murders, these relationships cause the red herrings to swim in schools. A contributing element is that in most of these families there are one or more black sheep, ne'er-do-wells, or rogues. If not in the family proper, such a character appears as friend or guest of the family. There are many different sins or illegalities committed by such characters, but murder is rarely one of them. The young men who seem continually to be forging checks at Oxford, the crooked businessmen, the husband-stealing vamps or womanizing playboys, the wastrel heirs, and the bohemian "artistic" types are often suspects but seldom murderers. For instance, Michael Rafiel, son of a millionaire in *Nemesis,* is in prison for killing his fiancee, but he is such an utter black sheep that a reader of much detective fiction quickly realizes that he has to be innocent of that murder. On the other hand, Christie also uses the charming rogue who is the murderer and even allows him to escape in *The Man in the Brown Suit* and *Why Didn't They Ask Evans?*

The largest distinct sub-type within the ne'er-do-wells is what might be called the restless veteran. H.R.F. Keating has said, "A war record was a handy way of making the reader believe, as truth or red herring, that a character was a goodie or baddie."[33] Christie uses the device both ways. In two cases, a young war hero turns out to be the villain, but more often comments about past heroism and present troublemaking or fecklessness are employed for misdirection. As social commentary, they are another reflection of the changes wrought in British society by two world wars. Restless veterans appear in a number of works, either not fitting in, just drifting, or engaged in criminal activity, but *There Is a Tide* presents the most extended comments on them. There Charles Trenton is apologized for by a relative: "He's been in prison, I'm afraid, and he wasn't a scrupulous person, but he did well in the war" (182). In the same novel Superintendent Spence says of the type: "in wartime, a man like that is a hero. But in peace—well, in peace such men usually end up in prison. They like excitement and they can't run straight, and they don't give a damn for society—And finally they've no regard for human life" (149-50). Though most of them appear in post-World War II novels, it is possible that Christie's first marriage to a World War I hero who could not easily settle down afterwards accounts for the number of such characters. Perhaps the repetition of war gave her this opportunity to comment indirectly on her own relationship with this type of man who is happier in battle than in an office and, therefore, a problem for others when there are no battles to be fought.

The ne'er-do-wells occasionally provide half of the romantic couple so prevalent in Christie's fiction. Such romantic couples have frequently been the object of critical irritation. Somerset Maugham was quite stern about them: "It may be that love makes the world go round, but not the world of detective stories; it makes it go very much askew...the philandering of young women, however charming, with young gentlemen, however lantern-jawed, is a tiresome diversion from the theme."[34] The central problem is the difference between romantic suspense (Will boy get girl?) and detectival suspense (Whodunit?): between passion and intellect. The romantic element can intrude upon the investigation of the crime, dissipating the focus of the work. A romance may serve as padding for a dull or slight mystery, but Christie rarely resorts to such a strategem. She also avoids one of the most annoying forms of romance in detective fiction: the detective in love with a suspect; the only instance occurs in *The Clocks*. The principal weakness of Christie's lovers it that many of them are uninteresting in themselves. Because of this vacuity of personality, the reader does not care whether their romance succeeds or fails. A major reason for their lack of vitality is the total absence of sex. Christie's fiction supports Jeanine Larmoth's statement that "The classic English mystery may be romantic but, like the classic Western, it is sexless."[35] There are no physical couplings in Christie's works; meaningful glances and tender embraces are as close as her lovers come to expressing their emotions. Her vamps and gigolos who supposedly represent sex are usually either pathetic or ludicrous. Unfortunately, though sexual purity is an admirable moral quality, it makes for pallid fictional lovers.

Another objection to lovers in detective fiction is that two suspects are essentially eliminated; if they are to be paired off at the end, they obviously have not committed the murder. However, as already noted, Christie plays with this expectation of the reader in a few novels, such as *Three Act Tragedy* and *Death in the Clouds,* by making one of the lovers unsuitable and guilty and by having a more appropriate replacement waiting in the wings. The resulting sudden, and sometimes unbelievable, transferrals of affection may be prepared by the detective. Poirot is especially fond of playing matchmaker. In *Death on the Nile* he reforms the thief Tim Allerton for Rosalie Otterbourne, and Colonel Race comments that "the marriage has been arranged by heaven and Hercule Poirot" (291). When in *Three Act Tragedy* he proves Hermione Lytton-Gore's fiance is a murderer, he says to the ready replacement, "Be very good to her." The reply speaks for itself: "I will, sir. She's all I care about in the world—you know that. Love for her made me bitter and cynical. But I shall be different now. I'm ready to stand by. And some day, perhaps—" (251). The least believable of Poirot's matches is in *Third Girl.* On being contacted by Poirot, Dr. John Stillingfleet solves all of Norma Restarick's mental and emotional problems, the result of being on various combinations of drugs for months, in ten days and then casually proposes marriage and life in Australia— and is accepted.

Just as lovers are nearly always removed from the lists of suspects, so are they eliminated as possible victims. Though they may undergo serious danger, as stated in *Easy to Kill,* "Heroines are never killed" (71), and neither are their male counterparts. If they were, their deaths would prohibit their being the symbols of the returned harmony to society and the beginning of a new life (see Chapter VI). To bring about that symbolic harmony, some of Christie's heroines have to demean themselves. Rosamund Darnley of *Evil Under the Sun* happily agrees to give up her successful business to marry Kenneth Marshall; his comment is "If you don't, you'd be no good to me" (189). In *There Is a Tide,* Lynn Marchmont says to Rowley Cloade after he has tried to kill her, "When you caught hold of me by the throat and said if I weren't for you, no one should have me—well—I knew then that I was your woman!" (222). Rosamund and Lynn are supposedly modern young women, but Christie forces them to surrender their independence, not from their innate personalities, but merely for the sake of providing that symbol of new life: the marriage of a young couple.

The two romances of *The Moving Finger* are the most blatant examples of feminine subservience and male domination in Christie's fiction. One couple consists of Joanna Burton and Owen Griffith. Joanna is another modern young woman who is aloof toward Owen until she has to assist him at the delivery of a baby. Then she dissolves into a dreamy-eyed worshipper of him and his medical genius, losing her own personality. The second and major romance is between Jerry Burton, Joanna's brother, and Megan Hunter. It is a Cinderella story, with Jerry transforming the backward, trampled-upon Megan into a beautiful, self-assured young woman—principally by taking her to London and buying her new clothes. Before that transformation takes place, Jerry continually refers to Megan by animal imagery. His first evaluation of her is that "she would have been a very nice horse with a little grooming" (27). He says that she has "the disposition of a dog" (63), and in speaking to her he adopts "the tone one does adopt when you want to reassure a frightened animal" (82). He even greets her "affectionately" with "Hallo, catfish!" (216). Though a reader may find such comments offensive, he still has no choice but to assume that Jerry and Megan live happily ever after, for that is the convention of classic detective fiction, and Christie's lovers, whether considered chauvinistic, silly, insipid, unbelievable, or unnecessary, fit that convention.

When murder occurs, an official investigaton is required. Even the presence of the brilliant amateur cannot negate that requirement. Since the solution is left to that amateur, the inspectors, superintendents, and chief constables serve subsidiary roles. They and their sergeants and constables perform the tasks of supplying information, giving legal authority to the amateur's actions, and finally taking the criminal away. Though never having the grey cells of Poirot or the analogic powers of Miss Marple, they are honorable men. Some are comically stupid, as Inspector Japp and most of the chief constables; others are egoistic and antagonistic to the amateur, as Inspectors Giraud, Crome, Miller, and Slack; and still others are active partners of the amateur, as Colin Lamb, Inspector Craddock, Superintendent Spence, and Chief Superintendent Garroway. Of whichever type, one can be sure that they are not brutal or corrupt. Like Superintendent Battle, they are usually stolid in appearance, but their stolidity masks a capable, if unimaginative, mind. Superintendent Spence, who appears in four of the Poirot novels, is an illustration. He is described as having "a typical countryman's face, unexpressive, self-contained, with shrewd but honest eyes. It was the face of a man with definite standards who would never be bothered by doubts of himself or by doubts of what constituted right and wrong" (McGinty 6-7).

In *The Body in the Library* Sir Henry Clithering asks a child who reads detective stories, "The head of Scotland Yard is usually a complete dud in books, isn't he?" The child replies, "Oh, no; not nowadays. Making fun of the police is very old-fashioned" (93). Christie does occasionally make the official investigator a comic foil for the brilliant amateur, but just as often he is presented as a helpful, if lesser, colleague, without disparagement. When a policeman in Christie's work is treated comically, it is the person who is ridiculed, not the position. The role of the police is respected, even when it requires help. It is the individual policeman who, through arrogance or blindness, hinders the amateur who receives ridicule. Whether comic foils or straight colleagues, Christie's police represent the law, and her genre and her own temperament forbade mockery of the law.

"The Adventure of the Christmas Pudding" is weak as a detective story, but it is instructive as to the view of Christie's upper class characters towards those "beneath" them. A young woman brings home for Christmas an undesirable young man with whom she is infatuated. His invitation is instigated by her grandmother, who realizes that he will be totally out of place among the family at the historic country house of Kings Lacy. The grandmother's plan includes making such remarks to Sarah, the young woman, as "You know, I like these very tight trousers these young men wear nowadays. They look so smart—only, of course, it does accentuate knock knees" (25). Such comments achieve their purpose, as does the young man's behavior. When he wishes to take Sarah to the local pub on Christmas eve, she feels "an instinctive revulsion": "The women of Kings Lacey had never frequented the bar of the Speckled Boar. She had an obscure feeling that to go there would be to let old Colonel Lacy and his wife down" (23). The young man turns out to be a jewel thief, but even before that is revealed, Sarah has reached the position of wishing "that Desmond had not come down here at all. It was much more fun seeing Desmond in London than here at home" (26). The implicit message of the story is that there are still two Englands: one consisting of *us,* the wealthy upper class, and the other of *them,* the lower orders.

The few working class people, other than servants, who appear in Christie's fiction are types: pompous clerks, officious nurses, put-upon secretaries, scruffy radicals, giggly or adenoidal shopgirls, cantankerous gardeners, bored or surly waitresses, and so on. The reader immediately recognizes Edna, a sniffly clerk in a post office, who looks "Exactly like a skinned rabbit" (McGinty, 138), or Jim Kimble of *Sleeping Murder,* who is an inarticulate, slow working-man, characterized by his use of "Ar" as a response to almost every question. Christie was quoted in Chapter II as saying that she knew nothing miners; the statement could be extended to cover working class life in general. This lack of knowledge is a partial explanation for the often crude characterization of such people, but the prejudices of her class are also a factor. Her only major attempt to present a more balanced view of working people is Cherry and Jim Baker in three of the Miss Marple novels, and even there Cherry is presented as not quite adequate at housework, though a superb cook. Jim Baker has an unspecified job, but Cherry, like many of her peers, must also work: "Owing to the insidious snares of Hire Purchase, they were always in need of ready money, though their husbands all earned good wages; and so they came and did housework or cooking" (Crack'd, 10)—a statement containing at least a mild reproof for their living beyond their means. Nevertheless, Miss Marple likes Cherry and Jim, and so does the reader. They remain the one instance, if not totally successful, of Christie's presenting working class people as something more than stereotypes or caricatures.

By far the largest number of working people in Christie's fiction are the house servants. If they are elderly and long in service as butlers, nannies, or senior maids, they are totally devoted to their employers and generally unflappable. A family member says of the butler Tressilian in *Hercule Poirot's Christmas,* "He's like the faithful old retainers of fiction. I believe he'd lie himself blue in the face if it was necessary to protect one of the family!" (25). This statement is intended as high praise. In *Murder After House* Lady Angkatell says that "murder *is* an awkward thing—it upsets the servants and puts the general routine out" (102), but her butler Gudgeon saves the day with sandwiches and coffee. Lady Angkatell is nevertheless correct that most servants in detective fiction are, to say the least, upset by murder. Ghoulish relish or quivering terror are the common reactions of anyone below the rank of butler—and even some of them succumb. In *A Pocket Full of Rye* Inspector Neele reports on Yewtree Lodge's staff: "The butler and the parlormaid both seem nervous. There's nothing uncommon about that. Often happens. The cook's fighting mad and the housemaid was grimly pleased. In fact, all quite natural and normal" (49). Cooks are particularly susceptible to the effects of murder in the house. Mitzi, the hysterical refugee cook of *A Murder Is Announced,* is the prime illustration, but there is also "the calm and imperturable" Mrs. Cocker of *Sleeping Murder,* who is "taken queer" by the digging up of a skeleton (224). Murder produces the same reaction in Rose, the cook of *The Moving Finger:* she "rolled her eyes and clutched her heart and explained again how she'd been coming over queer all the morning" (157).

A major contributing factor to the distress of servants in a house of murder is their distrust, fear, and often contempt for the police. Mrs. Medway, the cook in *Murder After Hours*, tells a talkative kitchen maid, "It's *common* to be mixed up with the police, and don't you forget it." She then summarizes the feelings of herself, her sister cooks, and all other faithful retainers: "I don't feel as I'm going to have a light hand with my pastry. That nasty inquest tomorrow. Gives me a turn every time I think of it. A thing like that—happening to *us* " (190). Naturally, the police have a quite different view, and in the same novel Inspector Grange states it: "There's always hope where there's a kitchen maid. Heaven help us when domestic staffs are so reduced that nobody keeps a kitchen maid any more. Kitchen maids talk, kitchen maids babble. They're so kept down and in their place by the cook and the upper servants that it's only human nature to talk about what they know to someone who wants to hear it" (179). The most egregious instance of the police acting on Grange's philosophy is in *Cards on the Table,* when handsome Sergeant O'Connor, "The Maidservant's Prayer," is sent incognito to romance the young parlormaid Elsie Batt for information. He happily reflects "how fortunate it was that Elsie was being approached unofficially. On interrogation by Sergeant O'Connor of the Police, she would have virtuously protested that she had not overheard anything at all" (138). Probably he is correct, but one can understand Elsie's reticence in the face of officialdom, for, however stupid she may be, she must know that to the police and her betters she is considered imbecilic, uncooperative, inefficient, stubborn, possibly dishonest, probably promiscuous, and loquacious only when it suits her. To paraphrase W.S. Gilbert, a servant's lot in detective fiction is not a happy one.

Of all the many comments about servants in Christie's fiction, the one that most clearly sums up the gulf between employer and employee is that of Miss Amelia Viner in *The Mystery of the Blue Train*. When she is asked why she says Ellen, instead of Helen, in referring to her maid, her answer is "I can sound my h's, dear, as well as anyone; but Helen is *not* a suitable name for a servant. I don't know what mothers in the lower classes are coming to nowadays" (249). Faced with such an attitude, servants have little choice but to wear a mask of servility and keep their private lives—however dull or drab they may be—just that: private. The reader never really knows the Ednas, Annies, Agneses, and Beatrices, or the Lorrimers,

Parsons, Snells, and Lanscombes. He knows only their employers' impressions, and those are determined largely by the position, not the person.

Servants, police, lovers, ne'er-do-wells, and assorted family members: these are major groups of bystanders, witnesses, and suspects in Christie's fiction, and a varied lot they are. Though stereotypical, they are responsible for much of the works' flavor by fulfilling their roles of supplying information, causing misdirection, providing humor and social commentary, and creating a sense of familiarity. Though secondary to the victim, murderer, and detective in the structure of crime and investigation, they populate that structure to make it fiction rather than just puzzle.

* * *

A general conclusion on Christie's characters is not necessary. The three central figures and the surrounding aides, suspects, and others fulfill the formulas of classic detective fiction and the British comic thriller, the two forms to which Christie remained loyal; in other words, they serve plot.

# Chapter IV
## Plot

*...there is only one known way of getting born, there are endless ways of getting killed.*
**Dorothy Sayers**

*The whole test is,* can *the thing be done? If so, the question of whether it* would *be done does not enter into it.*
**John Dickson Carr**

*"Those chaps are certainly hard to please. If you plunge straight into murder they say the story starts well but tails off. If you keep the fireworks until the end they say it's a slow beginning. If it starts well and finishes well they say it sags in the middle. Difficult."*
*"Why not keep the tension up all the way through?"*
*"Then it's melodramatic."*
**Andrew Garve,** *The Cuckoo-Line Affair*

The Aristotelian structure of Golden Age detective fiction, so well argued by Dorothy Sayers and W.H. Auden, is the central fact of the genre's plot. That plot goes through a series of peripeties, beginning with the commission of a crime and ending with that crime's solution. The simplest plot outline of any detective story is: the murderer kills a victim; many are suspected; the detective investigates, reveals the murderer and absolves the innocent. Though this basic plot allows for seemingly infinite variety, it is always present beneath whatever external covering the author chooses to give it. Essentially, Golden Age detective fiction consists of plot as discovery. It attempts to understand a crime which has occurred. Raymond Chandler quotes Mary Roberts Rinehart as having once remarked that mystery fiction is "two stories in one: the story of what happened and the story of what appeared to have happened."[1] The difference between the two is the question which the plot discovers: what *really* happened? The answer to that question involves not only who, but where, when (opportunity), how (means), and why (motive). Each of these can be a source of deception, providing one or more peripeties.

The author of detective fiction manipulates clues and misdirection to control the plot of discovery and to outwit the reader's ability to forecast the peripeties. As Christie said, "You start with the wish to deceive, and then work backwards."[2] Since

144

most of Christie's murders— at least the first murders—occur early, the bulk of her novels is concerned with the detective's progress to the final peripety, the revelation of the murderer and the explanation of what really happened. Her short stories, not having the amplitude of the novel form, present a problem, the mystification caused by it, and the solution to it: the same basic structure, but without the extended investigation (process of discovery) and, therefore, without any peripeties except the final one.[3] In her best works, every detail of plot is subordinated to either the concealment or discovery of what really happened. The irrelevant or repetitious is banished. For example, after *The Mysterious Affair at Styles,* she avoided presenting lengthy inquests. In novel after novel statements are made that such presentation would be merely repetition of information already given. Dr. Sheppard's comment in *The Murder of Roger Ackroyd* is typical: "I do not propose to give the proceedings in detail. To do so would only be to go over the same ground again and again" (142). In contrast to this admirable economy, Christie's major weakness in plotting is the handling of exposition, initial information needed by the reader. Though it seldom descends to the parody of it in Tom Stoppard's *The Real Inspector Hound,* it can at times come close. The worst major example is the first chapter of *Sad Cypress,* but the most ludicrous—and unnecessary—occurs in *Postern of Fate* when Tommy turns to Tuppence and says, "Betty, our adopted daughter, went to East Africa.... Have you heard from her?" Tuppence's reply is "Yes, she loves it there—loves poking into African families and writing articles about them" (87). This dialogue sounds like that of the Smiths in Ionesco's *The Bald Soprano,* but unintentionally so. Much better examples of exposition are the first chapters of *Easy to Kill* and *Death on the Nile.*

Christie's brilliance in plotting can most clearly be seen in her ability to dramatize the investigation of a crime. She rarely resorts to just a series of interviews of suspects. Rather she employs various plot stratagems to enliven the often tedious parade of witnesses, while also deceiving the reader by misdirection so that her detective does not seem stupid for not having the answers at once. Since, as said, the investigation may be three-fourths or more of the novel, such dramatization is required to prevent a dully repetitive pattern. Among her methods are seven prevalent enough to merit comment here (some of them are discussed more fully elsewhere in the study). First is her typically large number of suspects, usually eight to twelve, the prefatory lists lining them up for the reader. Such a number allows for continual shifting of suspicion from one to another: any one of them *might* have done it. A suspects B, who is shielding C, who is unaware that D is deeply jealous of C's attraction to E; meanwhile, F is attempting to frame G, who hated the victim H, but is being foiled by an alibi provided by I. Christie's ability to spread effectively the possibilities throughout such a group is perhaps her most important means of avoiding tedium during an investigation. It is so common that when she chose to limit the suspects in *Cards on the Table,* she felt the need to include a "Foreword by the Author" : "There are only *four* starters and any one of them, *given the right circumstances,* might have committed the crime. That knocks out forcibly the element of surprise. Nevertheless there should be, I think, an equal interest attached to four persons, each of whom has committed murder and is capable of committing further murders" (7). A second method, the most obvious, is the later murder, which, as Hastings declares, "cheers things up" in a book. Related to it is the faked attempt by the murderer on himself to throw off suspicion. Though avid readers of the genre may have become wary of any character who survives an attempt on his life, the device can if not cheer at least confuse. The addition of thriller elements is a fourth method. Christie does not use it to a great degree, but occasionally there is what might be called a *coup de chapitre,* such as ending a chapter of *Easy to Kill* with the murderer's hands around the heroine's throat and then not returning to the scene until the end of the next chapter. Such *coups* are artificial but legitimate. Fifth is the murder-suicide-accident gambit. Very often what looks like suicide or accident is murder, but also what looks like murder may be suicide or accident. Christie's most intricate plot for a novel joins all three; in *There Is a Tide* each type of death occurs, and all three are thought to be murder until Poirot untangles the complexity. A sixth method involves the concealment of the murderer's identity. The first suspect, apparently exonerated, may prove eventually to be the actual murderer or the person thought guilty throughout the novel may prove to be innocent—or, indeed, guilty. The least likely person, not even suspected, as with a person not in the group of suspects of *Hercule Poirot's Christmas* and *What Mrs. McGillicuddy Saw!,* may have committed the crime. Needless to say, Christie's tricks with her murderers are many. Finally, though the reader may guess the identity of the murderer, he may not be able to explain how the murder was done. Can anyone, without reading the "Epilogue," fully explain *And Then There Were None?* This talent of Christie for complicating a "simple" murder and going beyond just the *who* of *what really happened* is one of her principal strengths as a writer of detective fiction. These seven methods by no means exhaust her ways of enlivening the process of discovery, of making her detective's task difficult, and of confounding the reader's expectations of its course—as will be seen in considering her repeated plots and plot devices, her types of murders, and her use of clues and misdirection.

Christie was economical with plots and plot devices. She frequently reused earlier plots, making changes of various kinds to conceal the repetition. The plot linkages among her works are many and multiple. They range from single incidents to basic premises. Two illustrations of linked incidents are representative. In *The Secret Adversary* Julius P. Hersheimmer climbs a tree to peer into a doctor's rest home and then falls; Bobby Jones does exactly the same in *Why Didn't They Ask Evans?*, and in that novel Frankie Derwent crashes a car into the wall of an estate to gain admittance as a guest, and then the incident is repeated by Oliver Manders in *Three Act Tragedy*. Second, the starting point of *By the Pricking of My Thumbs*—an old lady, a glass of milk, and talk of a dead child— is recounted very briefly and not developed in two novels written much earlier: *Sleeping Murder* and *The Pale Horse*. Dozens of other plot linkages by single repeated incidents could be cited, but more significant are the repetitions of basic plot premises and Christie's management of her favorite plot formulas.

Christie's most common form of plot repetition is to repeat a significant premise of a short story in a later novel or longer story. To explain the premise in each case would reveal too much of the plots; therefore, the following list gives only the corresponding titles:

| Short Story | Later Novel or Story |
|---|---|
| "The Mystery of the Plymouth Express" | *The Mystery of the Blue Train* |
| "How Does Your Garden Grow?" | *Poirot Loses a Client* |
| "The Companion" | *A Murder Is Announced* |
| "Greenshaw's Folly" | *Elephants Can Remember* |
| "The Ambassador's Boots" | *Hickory Dickory Death* |
| "The Herb of Death" | *Postern of Fate* |
| "The Case of the Caretaker" | *Endless Night* |
| "Yellow Iris" | *Remembered Death* |
| "Triangle at Rhodes" | *Evil Under the Sun* |
| "The Blood-Stained Pavement" | *Evil Under the Sun* |
| "The Submarine Plans" | "The Incredible Theft" |
| "The Second Gong" | "Dead Man's Mirror" |
| "The Mystery of the Baghdad Chest" | "The Mystery of the Spanish Chest" |

(This list does not include the many reversals of plot situations, one example of which is the murderess posing as the housekeeper in "The Mystery of Hunter's Lodge" and the murderess posing as the mistress of the house in "Greenshaw's Folly.")

The longer versions obviously allow for greater elaboration of the mystery-detection formula, and, with the exception of "Greenshaw's Folly," they are superior as detective fiction. The murder of "The Mystery of the Baghdad Chest" is explained better, but it is still not as interesting as the longer "The Mystery of the Spanish Chest." Because of the greater elaboration, the same basic plot situation may be quite changed in its details in the longer version. The final outcomes may differ, as they do in "The Second Gong" and "Dead Man's Mirror." In "The Companion" and *A Murder Is Announced,* a murderess assumes the identity of a dead woman; in the story that woman is the murderer's victim, in the novel she is not. "Greenshaw's Folly" uses the same premise as "The Companion," but this time the impersonation is to effect the murder, while in *Elephants Can Remember* the murderess is asked to impersonate her victim by another as an answer to that victim's dying request. *Evil Under the Sun* combines elements from two stories. It has the identical plot premise of "The Blood-Stained Pavement": a murderer assisted by his wife, romances young women, gets their money, and then kills them. The novel is also a development of the character relationships of "Triangle at Rhodes." The setting is transferred from the Mediterranean island to one off England's south coast, but the situation of two couples on holiday, one a handsome young man with a meek wife and the other a taciturn man with a seductive wife, is the same. In both cases, the seductive wife is the victim, and the meek wife is the murderer's accomplice. The taciturn husband is the murderer in the short story, but the handsome young man is in the novel. Perhaps these repetitions and permutations demonstrate Christie's skill at plotting better than her works with non-repeated plots, for even though she multiples the length by anywhere from four to fifteen times the original, there is never the sense that the novel is a reworking of an earlier and shorter concept that has been padded to achieve that length.

Not all of the repetitions are from short story to longer works. There are three Poirot stories which turn on the premise of a person's making a suicide look like murder in order to incriminate someone else. In order of publication, they are "The Market Basing Mystery," "Wasps' Nest," and "Murder in the Mews"; the last, and longest, is by far the best. Though there are no novels having such an exact correspondence with one another, there are numerous similarities between plots of novels. The most striking instance is that, though completely different in effect, the murder plans of *Death on the Nile* and *Endless Night* are the same. Another example is the identical character of the victims in *Murder in Retrospect* and *Murder After*

*Hours.* Both are married philanderers who are killed by jealous women. This parallel is deepened by both men being presented as caring much more for their work than for any woman, and that trait is directly related to their being murdered. The comment on John Christow, the victim of *Murder After Hours,* is that "he wasn't, actually, a man who thought much about woman. It wasn't *women* who mattered to him most, it was his *work!*" (156). The same view is stated repeatedly of Amyas Crale, the artist who cares only for his painting and dies completing a portrait of his murderess in *Murder in Retrospect.* Many other parallels among the novels could be mentioned, but they are not so much plots as plot devices, which are almost bound to be repeated by a writer as prolific as Christie.

Some of her favorite plots have already been discussed: the least-likely suspect plot, the obvious suspect plot, the murder in transit, the family murder, and the partnership murder, as well as— if it can be considered a plot pattern—the comic thriller. Others which are more method than type, such as disguise or impersonation and the time puzzle, will come later. Here eight frequent plot premises will be examined: the perfect alibi, the locked room, the master criminal, the crime in the past, the detective (or aide or client of the detective) as criminal, the nobody-looks-at-a-servant and the look-over-the-shoulder gambits, and multiple unrelated crimes. As Christie often combines these to prevent their being too obvious, an individual work may contain more than one. Therefore, the classification is arbitrary, but it does provide a means of seeing the variety within the plot formulas of a large portion of her fiction.

Christie does not make a specialty of the perfect alibi plot as did Freeman Wills Crofts, whom she spoofed in "The Unbreakable Alibi," nor of the locked room plot, for which John Dickson Carr is famous. However, there are a number of examples of each among her works. As will be seen shortly in the discussion of the timing of her murders, the most common alibi is established by the aid of an accomplice, as in *The Body in the Library, A Pocket Full of Rye, Lord Edgware Dies, Death on the Nile,* and *Hickory Dickory Death.* The participation of the accomplice, whether knowing or unknowing, makes a seeming impossibility of the murderer's involvement because he or she is apparently not present when the crime is committed. Similarly, the murderer of *There Is a Tide* arranges to be in jail when his murder plan succeeds. The outstanding example of the perfect alibi in Christie's fiction is *Curtain,* for the murderer is legally untouchable: he does not commit murder; he causes others to commit it for him. Though Christie likes the closed circle or sealed space murder, such as *And Then There*

*Were None, Death in the Clouds,* "Three Blind Mice," etc., she does not often attempt the intricate complexities of the murder in a locked room or its equivalent. When she does, the usual solution is that the death has occurred earlier than supposed; this is the case in *Why Didn't They Ask Evans?, Hercule Poirot's Christmas,* and "Dead Man's Mirror." Variations include "The Dream," in which the murder is committed through the windows of adjoining rooms, and "The Dead Harlequin," in which disguise is used. A reversal of the type, and also another form of perfect alibi, is the murderer's being apparently locked in a room at the time the murder occurs elsewhere; this is used in "Greenshaw's Folly" and is the basis for *They Do It with Mirrors.* Christie's most successful example of a locked room story does not actually contain a locked room. It is *Murder in Mesopotamia.* Though the room is not locked, its single entrance is under constant observation, yet its occupant is killed without anyone entering the room. Much of the novel is concerned with proving that no one entered; then Poirot has to discover how the murder was committed from outside, a seeming impossibility.

The master criminal plot is the basis of seven novels. Four are thrillers in which the villains are attempting to achieve world domination: *The Big Four, They Came to Baghdad, So Many Steps to Death,* and *Passenger to Frankfurt.* The villain of *The Secret Adversary* is less ambitious: he only wishes to rule England. The man who wears the brown suit in the novel named for him also wishes power, but of what nature or for what purpose is never clear. Finally, there is the impossible villain of *The Seven Dials Mystery,* whose aim is money. In spite of his "silly ass" manner, he is thief, murderer, and traitor—and totally unbelievable. None of these novels would be on a list of Christie's twenty best. (It is noteworthy that four are from the 1920s and three from 1951-1970—none from the 1930s and 1940s, the decades of most of her greatest successes.) Their plots are sensational, episodic or inconsistent, and often feebly comic. Her talents lay with the domestic, amateur murder, not with gigantic secret conspiracies. The thriller form does not allow for the careful interplay of mystification and detection which she could manipulate so skillfully. If she had written nothing but these works, she would be a forgotten writer.

Another plot which Christie liked, but did not always manage successfully, is the crime in the past. The late examples are the weakest because of the confusion of chronology: *By the Pricking of My Thumbs, Elephants Can Remember,* and *Postern of Fate.* Better are *Murder in Retrospect, Remembered Death, Nemesis,* and *Sleeping Murder,* as are all of the Miss Marple stories of *Thirteen Problems* and the Harley Quin stories: "The Coming of Mr. Quin,"

"The World's End," and "The Dead Harlequin." In the novels, the investigation of the crime, whether one, ten, or twenty years in the past, is the result of someone in the present—a now-grown child, a friend, or the detective—wishing to know the truth. The detective must reconstruct events long after physical evidence has disappeared. He depends exclusively upon the oral evidence of witnesses, most of whom are also suspects, and must deduce the truth from what may be lies, misconceptions, forgetfulness, or prejudice. This pattern is another way of avoiding overt violence and placing emphasis upon discovery by rational thought. Its weakness is the possible boredom from the lack of immediacy of the crime; that weakness is undoubtedly the reason that *Rememberd Death, Nemesis, Sleeping Murder,* and *Postern of Fate* also contain "present" murders resulting from the investigation of the earlier ones.

By its sheer number of appearances, Christie's favorite plot premise is some variation on the villain being a person directly concerned with investigating the crime: the official detective, a fake detective, an aide to the detective, or the client of the detective. Her fondness for the premise is easily understood, for it offers a prime method of misdirection. The detective and his associates in detection are hardly likely to be suspected of the very crime they are attempting to solve, nor is the client who brings a case to the detective's attention. In the latter instance, the client's version of events is accepted as truth and affects the reader's perception of the story, for without that client's plea for help, the investigation would not begin. The clients of "The Veiled Lady" and "The Case of the Distressed Lady" come to Poirot and Pyne respectively with false stories to enlist their aid in furthering plans for jewel theft. Similar is the attempt of the murderers in *Peril at End House* and *An Overdose of Death* to make themselves appear to Poirot as the intended victims. These people ultimately fail in their schemes, but before they do, they mislead both detective and—more importantly for Christie's purposes—the reader. Only one policeman, "The Man in the Mist," and one detective, Superintendent Sugden of *Hercule Poirot's Christmas,* are murderers in Christie's fiction, but there are several fake detectives: the insane murderer of "Three Blind Mice" (the basis of *The Mousetrap*), and the professional criminals of *The Secret of Chimneys, Partners in Crime,* and "The Erymanthean Boar." More prevalent is the murderer who assists the detective in the investigation of his own crime. *The Murder of Roger Ackroyd* is the most famous example, but there are such others as *The Man in the Brown Suit, Three Act Tragedy, The ABC Murders,* and *Death in the Clouds.* As an added plot twist, in three novels young couples unknowingly go to the villains for help in solving cases: *The Secret Adversary, Why Didn't They Ask Evans?*, and *Sleeping Murder,* and the heroine of *They Came to Baghdad* does the same. In all of these variations, the purpose is the least-likely person motif. They make the detective's discovery more surprising and enforce that principle that *everybody* must be suspected.

Two other premises which serve as distinctive keys to the solutions of Christie's plots are the look-over-the-shoulder and the nobody-looks-at-a-servant gambits. The first appears in *Appointment with Death, Death Comes as The End, The Mirror Crack'd from Side to Side,* and *A Caribbean Mystery.* In each of these, someone stares over another person's shoulder fixedly or with shock. What or who the person sees is not indicated; on the discovery of that and the reason for the starer's reaction hinges the plot. Variations occur in *Towards Zero* and *Hallowe'en Party,* but the effect is identical. Christie's ability to employ the gambit for different purposes is shown in that four of those who stare are victims and two are murderers. Also, she varies the misdirection by such "props" as a glass eye and a picture of a madonna and child, as well as by the comments of the person staring. More prevalent, and always related to disguise, is the idea that the appearance of a servant or working person does not make any impression on those of higher status. There is an element of snobbery in this gambit, but Christie neither approves nor disapproves of the attitude; she merely presents it as a social fact and uses it for mystification. The concept is stated by Poirot in italics in *Death in the Clouds:* "*Nobody notices a steward particularly*" (252), and in *Remembered Death* the statement is made that no one pays attention to "that portion of the restaurant's furnishing—the waiter!" (191). Other examples include murderers going unnoticed by posing as a butcher delivering a leg of lamb in *The Big Four* (convenient for spattered blood), as a repairman in *The Pale Horse,* as a butler in *Three Act Tragedy,* as a governess (by a former queen) in *The Secret of Chimneys,* as a housekeeper in "The Mystery of Hunter's Lodge," and as a chambermaid in "Miss Marple Tells a Story." *Funerals Are Fatal* reverses the process, but is based upon the same premise; the discovery of the imposture is again a necessary step in solving the case. These two gambits are clear instances of Christie's continual practice of making the solutions to her plots turn upon required discoveries, while finding means of concealing the nature of the discoveries which must be made.

The presence of one or more other crimes unrelated to the central murder is an obvious source of red herrings and complications. Christie is particularly fond of drug peddling *(Evil Under the Sun* and *Peril at End House,* the latter also including a forgery plot) and robbery (*The Mystery of the Blue Train, Murder in Mesopotamia, Death on the Nile* and *At Bertram's Hotel*). Such other crimes are legitimate, even if unlikely, additions as another form of misdirection. However, if the other crimes are given too much prominence, they become irritating distractions, weakening the plot structure by diffusing both the mystification and the detection. *The Clocks* consists of two separate plots, one of which is a domestic murder and the other the activity of Communist spies. The two are joined only by setting and the coincidence of a mother being in one and her daughter in the other. The reader is required to shift continually back and forth between the two. The result is loss of interest in both, since the suspects of neither are "on-stage" long enough to make a strong impression. Even less satisfactory is *Cat Among the Pigeons,* in which murders are committed by two unrelated people for different reasons: envy and jewels. If that were not enough, it also contains a gang of jewel thieves and a blackmailer, who becomes another victim of one of the murderers. The novel is a poorly structured mishmash. If incorporated skillfully, unrelated crimes can serve the mystification of a detective novel, but unrelated murders only create confusion, which is *not* the same as mystification.

Already a number of issues relating to the nature of Christie's murders have been raised. The lack of violent description, the predominance of amateur criminals, and murder by partners are three. Respectively, these provide "clean" deaths, powerful motives, and added complications. Other issues are the number of murders, the simple versus complex crime, the management of time, and favorite methods of dispatching victims.

The proper number of murders in a detective novel is hotly argued. Some readers feel that one is enough, others prefer one or two later murders but consider them the maximum, while still others believe that multiple mayhem is not only appropriate but desirable. Just as Christie introduces three murderers in the first sentence of their novels, she prefers the early or pre-opening murder. Therefore, there is a long period—and many pages—before the final solution. As already noted, other deaths are one of Christie's means of enlivening that long period of investigation. In over sixty percent of her novels, at least one or more later murders occur, but usually not more than two. The most common victim is the witness who will not tell what he knows. As a plot device, such a murder has two contradictory functions. It prevents the knowledge of the victim from being received, thus hindering an early solution to the case, while, at the same time, it provides added clues which may help to solve it. The more murders committed, the more likelihood the murderer will make a crucial mistake and incriminate himself, particularly since, as Poirot claims, murders always follow the same pattern of killing. The same is true if the murderer is carrying out a series of planned murders. The discovery of the plan will inevitably lead to the planner; *The ABC Murders* is an obvious instance. Except for such series murders, the central murders in Christie's novels are usually early, the beginning of the detective-murderer confrontation, and any succeeding murders are the desperate attempts of the murderer to protect himself from discovery by the detective.

Edgar Allan Poe was the first to state that the more complex a case appears, the easier it is to solve. The source "The Murders in the Rue Morgue" indicates that the statement is true only for fictional detectives, not for most readers. Actually, the statement has become an excuse for writers to devise extremely complex crimes to show off the brilliance of their detectives. Though Christie has her share of the apparently impossible crime, her murders are rarely as improbable as those of such colleagues as Dorothy Sayers or John Dickson Carr. Nevertheless, she allows her detectives to repeat Poe's dictum. Poirot has a firm belief that fancy touches are a killer's undoing. Miss Marple agrees; in discusssing the murder of *The Mirror Crack'd from Side to Side,* she says, "It was really a very perfect murder; because, you see, it was committed on the spur of the moment without pausing to think or reflect" (190). She is correct in so far as the perfect murder would be one committed without thought, but it would also have to be purposeless: one stranger killing another without motive. Not even Poirot, Marple, Holmes, and Wimsey together would be able to solve such a crime—unless the murderer were very careless. Such a murder would not make a detective novel. Its utter pointlessness would not provide the material necessary—suspects, clues, etc.—for the Golden Age genre. Rather, the murder in detective novels must be, if not complex, at least elaborate. Authors, including Christie, who say they write only about simple murders are saying that the solution is simple once one understands all of the elements of the case. The discovery of that solution is not—and cannot be—simple.

A principal technique of Christie for making a basically simple crime complex is the management of time, which includes both the placement of the murder in relation to the total work and tricks involving the scheduling of the murder by the murderer. The early or past murder dictates that most information about the pre-death circumstances will be brought out during the investigation, that is, after the fact. The major problem for the writer is to find ways to prevent the reconstruction of those circumstances from becoming a recital of dry facts. Christie's ability to dramatize the investigation while supplying the necessary information is of primary importance in overcoming this problem. Besides others already mentioned, devices range from the thoughts of suspects to family arguments and from amateur detection by a suspect to long flashbacks. A favorite Christie ploy for an early off-stage murder in the Poirot stories is the letter from someone in danger asking for his help, but failing to explain the nature of the problem. When Poirot answers the summons, the letter-writer has been murdered. This device first appears in *The Murder on the Links* and then is repeated in *Poirot Loses a Client*, "How Does Your Garden Grow?," "Dead Man's Mirror," and with some variation in "The Cornish Mystery." Not only does the device eliminate the need for describing violence, but it also forces Poirot to start at the beginning. He knows only that the person was worried or frightened and that the person is now dead. He must uncover the pre-death circumstances by his reason— and, if the reader is not to be bored, by the ingenuity of his author. Though just one way in which Christie treats an early murder, the letter-from-the-dead ploy is a good example of her preparing for her detective's extended course of discovery.

Though fewer, there are examples of the late first murder, which allows for all suspects to be introduced and their motives explored before the death. The whole purpose of the structure of *Towards Zero* is to build toward the murder, and thus it occurs much later than usual (page 90). The murders in *Endless Night* and *At Bertram's Hotel* are even later; that in the latter does not take place until page 197. However, *Endless Night* has practically no detection, and *At Bertram's Hotel* is one of Christie's novels containing two separate crimes, most of it being concerned with a series of robberies. Since the placement of the murder determines the length of the investigation, the many early and few late murders are evidence of Christie's clear preference for emphasizing the second plot of murderer versus detective, rather than the earlier one of murderer versus victim.

In many works the murderer's timing is crucial for his plan, and the difference between apparent time and real time becomes the key to the solution. In these works the murderer's scheduling of his crime is usually directly related to his establishment of an alibi. The locked-room murders are illustrations. Devices used by murderers to hide or confuse their presence at the time of the murder include skis in *Murder at Hazelmoor*, a dictaphone in *The Murder of Roger Ackroyd*, ventriloquism in "Problem at Sea," and the switching of bodies in "A Christmas Tragedy" and *Evil Under the Sun*. The trite broken watch or clock whose hands have been changed does not help murderers in Christie's fiction; her detectives see through the subterfuge. However, *The Murder at the Vicarage* does contain a significant example of clock hands being adjusted by the murderer to confuse the time of a death. Manipulation of time by Christie's murderers is most often achieved by disguise or the use of an accomplice. Disguise to hide the actual time of the murder and thus provide an alibi occurs in "The Affair at the Victory Ball" and *Funerals Are Fatal,* while accomplices are used in *Murder on the Orient Express* and *Hickory Dickory Death.* In the last the murderer seems to receive a telephone call at the police station from his victim, who is already dead, the call being made by an accomplice. Even more frequent is for the two methods to be combined, as in "Greenshaw's Folly," *The Mystery of the Blue Train, Lord Edgware Dies, An Overdose of Death,* and *Dead Man's Folly.* These tricks of scheduling allow Christie to complicate the murder, whose motive and means may be simple, by twisting the opportunity, thus impeding the final discovery and mystifying the reader.

Christie's ingenuity in disposing of her victims in a mystifying manner is hardly arguable. She always seemed to find some new method—or at least a new variation—for the commission of murder. (The group murder of *Murder on the Orient Express* was suggested by Max Mallowan, to whom the novel is dedicated, while the narrator-murderer premise of *The Murder of Roger Ackroyd* was suggested by a brother-in-law and Lord Louis Mountbatten.) The mystification is usually in the murderer's plan; the actual means, in the sense of the weapon, are rarely spectacular. Though characters are shot, stabbed, strangled, smothered, knocked on the head, pushed over cliffs, run over by automobiles, and even defenestrated, the majority of her victims die by poison. An incomplete list of Christie's poisons includes arsenic, strychnine, stropanthine, potassium cyanide, formic acid, prussic acid, oxalic acid, hydrochloric acid, eserine, aconitine, antimony, digitalin, thallium, nicotine, taxine, yellow jasmine, a variety of sleeping pills, and the venom of *Dispholidus Typus.* Poison may be used to make the death appear to be from natural causes, or it may be used overtly. The murderer may be on the scene, or he may have planted the poison— in the tonic, the sherry, the marmalade, or among the aspirin or sleeping pills—and removed himself from the vicinity. Whatever the circumstances, a death by poisoning is, as Christie so often noted, not "messy." This is one of the two reasons for her preference; the other is her work in hospital dispensaries during the two world wars which gave her a thorough knowledge of toxicology, a knowledge she did not have of firearms or other weapons and their effects.

Without question, poison is Christie's favorite weapon for murder.
There are a few instances of poison being administered by
unexpected means. Though most are not impossible, they are highly
improbable. In *Cards on the Table* murder is committed by infecting
a man's shaving brush with anthrax bacilli. Another man's
shaving cream is treated with atropine sulphate to create symptoms
of madness in "The Cretan Bull," as is a woman's face cream in *A
Caribbean Mystery*. The villain of "The Flock of Geryon" uses
bacterial cultures as his murder weapon, and Poirot comments, "He
had also, I gather, cultivated a substance which had the power of
delaying but intensifying the action of the chosen bacillus" (267)—
which sounds very much like that hackneyed device of the poison
unknown to science. Less unlikely, but quite confusing, is the use by
the murderess of *Sad Cypress,* who is a nurse, of "the quickest and
most powerful emetic known," apomorphine hydrochloride, to save
herself immediately after she and her victim have shared her
sandwiches laced with poisonous morphine hydrochoride (206). The
most fanciful method of murder in all of Christie's works is in the
Quin story "The Face of Helen." The would-be murderer, a chemist,
presents his victim with a thin crystal ornament and urges her to
listen to a new operatic tenor on the radio the same evening. The
ornament is filled with poisonous gas, so that when the tenor hits a
high C, the crystal will shatter, the gas will escape, and the victim
will be asphyxiated. With prompting from Quin, Mr. Satterthwaite
foils the diabolical scheme at the last moment. Happily, Christie
does not make a practice of such improbable murders. One other,
and more effective, unusual type of murder, generally involving
poison, of which she is fond is the public murder: one committed
boldly in the presence of others. Seven novels contain examples:
*Death in the Clouds, Three Act Tragedy, Appointment with Death,
Remembered Death, The Mirror Crack'd from Side to Side,* and,
using a weapon other than poison, *Cards on the Table* and *A Murder
Is Announced.* The presence of the group scatters suspicion, poses
the problem of the concealment of the act, and, in some cases, raises
the question of whether the actual victim was the intended one. Like
so many of her other methods of murder, Christie's public murders
allow for plentiful misdirection before the final solution is
presented.

John Dickson Carr once wrote, "The fine detective story...does
not consist of 'a' clue. It is a ladder of clues, a pattern of evidence."[4]
That ladder of clues becomes the source of the detective's
deductions; without those deductions the clues appear meaningless.
His memory and reasoning must act upon them to discover their
pattern. Any single clue must contribute to the ladder, but it must

also seem not to. Therefore, it is impossible to consider clues without, at the same time, considering misdirection, for it is the interplay between the two which creates mystification while making detection possible. The reader must be directed to miss the clues' significance, which the detective grasps. Like the murderer, they must be hidden and not hidden simultaneously. This dual plot necessity is made somewhat easier since *anything* may be a clue. For the sake of simplicity, most critics divide clues into two large groups: tangible or intangible, physical or psychological, material or human, and so on. The first group consists of objects—dead violets, skiboots, a cut tennis net, etc.—which lead from the crime to a suspect; the second—motive, behavior, statements, etc.—leads from a suspect to the crime. Both groups allow for reader misdirection. Crossing these groups is another type: the absent or negative clue, which should be present but is not. Related to it is the clue by deduction, which the detective assumes has to be if the solution is to be flawless. When the detective presents a list of seemingly unrelated clues, he usually knows that there is another link which must be found to complete that ladder. Whichever type, a true clue must contribute to the sense of inevitability when the final explanation is given.

Christie uses all of the types of clues, but she favors the intangible. Julian Symons finds this preference the "basic difference in plotting between her and most detective story writers": "the central clue in almost all of her best books is either verbal or visual. We are induced to give a meaning to something that has been said, or something that has been seen, which is not the true meaning or not the only possible meaning."[5] Just as Poirot scorns the human foxhound who runs around looking for physical clues, Christie rarely bases a solution on a tangible clue. Poirot's attitude is first expressed in *The Murder on the Links,* his second appearance, and so Christie early decided that tangible clues would take second place to those of character and behavior. There are many tangible clues, but they are not, to use Symons' word, *central,* and quite often they are either discounted or given a behaviorial meaning. For instance, though a suicide note on a scrap of paper is not clearly seen by the amateur detective of *The Moving Finger* to be fake—though it probably is by most readers—it is not an essential clue, while in *Hickory Dickory Death* the same device is immediately spotted. A good example of a tangible clue is the bridge score of *Cards on the Table,* but it is used principally as a clue to the personalities of the four players. When physical clues are significant, they usually appear in a list made by the detective. The list may be of two types: all clues may be given, as in *A Murder Is Announced* and *Postern of*

*Fate,* or, more often, the important clues may be concealed among numerous other objects, as in *Murder at Hazelmoor, Death in the Clouds,* and *Hickory Dickory Death.* The same is true of the absent clue; a list is given with the significant item not included. This is the basis of "Sing a Song of Sixpence," but is also used in "Murder in the Mews" and *Death on the Nile.* Such lists are puzzling fun for the reader. With the first he must fit all of the clues into the correct pattern, with the second he must determine which are significant and which not, and with the third he must decide what is missing and why it is important. Nevertheless, and to repeat, the intangibles of behavior and character presented through statement and action are more commonly the central clues.

When the murderess of *Funerals Are Fatal* unconsciously makes a statement which reveals the basis of her murder plan, the next line is "But nobody was paying any attention to [her] well meant trivialities" (170)—nobody but Poirot. Such verbal clues as her statement, which often seem to be just trivial remarks, are Christie's most frequent type. Their significance is easy to conceal in the midst of conversation. Rarely does she give a signpost to these clues as she does in her first novel. There Poirot, alone knowing the identity of the murderer early but not having proof, says that the victim would never forgive him if the person suspected were arrested now, and *now* is italicized. Of course, his statement seems to exonerate that person, who is the murderer. *A Murder Is Announced,* which contains a plethora of both tangible and intangible clues, indicates the versatility of the verbal ones and their concealment. Four times characters comment that central heat is on early in the season at the murder site. These innocuous remarks are actually important clues to the method of the murder. On four other occasions slips of the tongue when trying to speak of two people as one cause a character to confuse the names Letty and Lotty. The confusion is not mentioned by the person being spoken to and is easily overlooked. Finally, the difference in the spelling of *enquiries* and *inquiries* is, as Miss Marple says, "very significant." The word "indictments" and the phrases "prisoners at the bar" and "red herring" should give readers the identity of the murderer of *And Then There Were None,* but seldom do. Sometimes the verbal clue consists of a single statement; just two examples are Poirot's comment in *Evil Under the Sun* about sunbathers looking like bodies in a morgue and the phrase "smoke screen" in *The Moving Finger.* On the other hand, the number of statements in *The ABC Murders* as to both the unknown murderer *and* the person finally discovered to be that murderer having the qualities of a boy—Poirot even goes so far as to speak of "the boy motif"—provides an extended instance of the verbal clue. The same is true of *There Is a Tide*. The keys to its solution are the comment that Rosaleen Cloade "seems half-witted because she's being so frightfully careful" (38), her repeated statements that she does not deserve her late husband's money, and her enjoyment of "an afternoon out just like a servant" (69). Actual words are not always necessary, for similar to the absent clue is a murderer's silence when general conversation is in progress. In *Peril at End House* the murderess does not enter the discussion about her fiance's overdue flight even though he may have crashed. The silence itself is suspicious, as it also is in *Towards Zero* when at a houseparty a lawyer describes a child who committed murder and everyone present, with one exception, discusses the affair for nearly four pages. The person not speaking is that now grown murderer.

Almost as prevalent as the verbal clues are those of behavior or specific actions. The behavior of characters reveals intentionally or not their true nature, and their actions may contradict their statements, again revealing the truth. The unconscious egoism of the victim in *The Mirror Crack'd from Side to Side,* the exaggerated stupidity of the murderer in *Murder After Hours,* and the curiosity of the murderers in *Death in the Clouds, Three Act Tragedy,* and *Cards on the Table* (as well as the last's bidding at bridge) are illustrations of behavior as clue. Actions as clues vary from the failure of a murderer in *The Moving Finger* to send a poison-pen letter to the woman he loves, a woman's not being dizzy crossing a foot bridge in *Evil Under the Sun,* a small child's dipping shoelaces in water in *N or M?,* to a woman's identification of a corpse as that of her cousin when it is not in *The Body in the Library.* In all of these instances, the behavior or actions of a character, whether the murderer or otherwise, provides essential knowledge for the discovery by the detective of the murderer's identity. However, actions may vindicate the innocent as well as convicting murderers. A weak example occurs in *Appointment with Death.* Because poison is administered by a syringe, Poirot concludes that the victim's family is innocent as they could have put it in her medicine. Better is his clearing the convicted Mrs. Crale in *Murder in Retrospect* of having murdered her husband. When he hears that she wiped fingerprints off a bottle of beer the husband drank before his death, Poirot knows that not only did she not commit the crime but did not even know how it was committed, for the poison was not in that bottle.

These clues of behavior and action join with the verbal ones to form Christie's major type: the intangible or non-material, but whatever type is used, her clues are always accompanied by some form of misdirection. Miss Marple says, "To commit a successful murder must be very much like bringing off a conjuring trick.... You've got to make people look at the wrong thing and in the wrong place—Misdirection, they call it, I believe" (Finger, 197). In this statement Christie permits Miss Marple to reveal one of her standard methods of confounding her readers. As she put it in an interview, "I don't cheat, you know. I just say things that might be taken two ways."[6] Though *The Murder of Roger Ackroyd* and *Endless Night* would probably be most people's choice for the best display of this ability, another fascinating example of it is *Remembered Death*. That novel's solution is openly displayed in the second chapter, which consists of the memories of one of the two murderers. Nowhere else does Christie offer the reader so early and so overtly the premise of a murder plot. But since other characters also have motives—and chapters of their memories—the significance of this murderer's thoughts and statements can be overlooked, especially as they may be "taken two ways." The chapter is principally concerned with Ruth Lessing's account of fulfilling her employer's request to ship an unsavory relative of his wife off to South America. Early in the chapter is the following statement: "That interview with Victor had been the beginning of it all, had set the whole train in motion" (26). She does not state that it is a train of murder. By the end of the chapter, through omissions and statements with double meanings, Christie has outlined the situation which is to lead to two deaths. A passage when Ruth Lessing reports back to her employer illustrates the technique:

"What did you think of him, Ruth?"
Her voice was deliberately colourless as she replied, "Oh—much as I expected. A weak type."
And George saw nothing, noticed nothing! She felt like crying out, "Why did you send me to see him? Didn't you know what he might do to me? Don't you realize that I'm a different person since yesterday? Can't you see that I'm dangerous? That there's no knowing what I may do?" (34).

When Christie or her characters say things that may be taken two ways, she is employing her favorite means of misdirection. There are others, but most are somehow related to the double-edged statement. Her skill lies in presenting a number of clues which seem to lead directly to a solution until new clues surface making that solution impossible and creating more mystification; she repeats this process until the correct solution is finally reached. In order to accomplish this pattern, she must conceal the significant clues from the reader. John Cawelti has stated that readers may be deceived as to person, motive, means, time, place, and "whether it is a crime or not."[7] Christie deceives about all of these elements, but in her works the first two are the most important. Whether double-edged statement or otherwise, the deceptions are nearly always the result of one of the following seven methods of misdirection: (1) everything that is presented is true, but there are vital omissions; (2) clues and their significance are separated by many pages; (3) clues are hidden in a group of unimportant items or statements; (4) the false clue or red herring is used as a distraction; (5) incorrect assumptions about facts or incidents are forced upon the reader—also often upon the detective for a time; (6) the reader—and the detective—are made to view events from a false perspective; (7) the murderer is permitted to conceal, distort, or falsify evidence. The methods are not discrete. There are all sorts of combinations, especially between the seventh and any of the others. A few examples of each will have to serve for hundreds of instances.

Omissions have been noted in Ruth Lessing's account of her meeting with Victor Drake. That account is typical, for it involves the revelation of some information which can be interpreted variously, while omitting what, if included, would provide an immediate solution. Among the many forms the method may take are the omission of a character's name when his or her thoughts are given—especially if the character is the murderer; the omission of part of an overheard conversation—important in *Murder in Retrospect* and *They Do It With Mirrors;* and the unfinished enigmatic statement, such as "There is only one thing to do" or "I must go through with it," which usually occurs at the end of a chapter. One of the simplest omissions, and certainly the most common, is the murderer's name from the detective's list of principal suspects midway in a novel. It is a feature of the least-likely murderer plots of *Murder in Mesopotamia, Peril at End House, The Moving Finger,* and a dozen others, and it serves to concentrate attention on the list and away from the criminal. Another form consists of a person saying that he or she knows the murderer, but cannot announce his name. If the person is not the detective, he or she will probably be the next victim, as is Lavinia Fullerton of *Easy to Kill,* who says that "the person in question is just the last person anyone would suspect" (15), gives no name, and is shortly run over by a Rolls Royce. If the detective makes such a statement, he usually qualifies it by saying he does not have enough proof. All of these omissions fulfill the proper tasks of fictional misdirection; they postpone the solution until the moment decided upon by the author, they are "fair" in that the author has not lied, and they may, if interpreted correctly, turn out to be clues.

The separated clues and the clues hidden within a group of insignificant items are such obvious methods of misdirection that little added comment is necessary. Both depend upon the reader's interest in the action of the story, what will happen next—thus overlooking the small but telling points. For example, in *Murder in Retrospect* Poirot's impression of a character's taste in interior decoration is " 'expense no object,' allied to a lack of imagination" (83); twenty pages later Poirot and another character decide that the murderer is undoubtedly "a person of rather limited imagination." It is unlikely that a first-time reader of the novel would connect the two statements from the different contexts and the distance between them. As previously stated, the clue hidden in a group is most often a tangible clue. Confronted by such a group, the tendency for a reader is not to stop and attempt to judge the significance or lack of it of each item, but to continue reading. The author knows this and mixes the one or two important items with a number of trivial ones so that the reader's perception is spread over the entire group. When the technique is used for intangible clues, it generally consists of some significant statement being lost in the midst of conversation, as noted of *A Murder Is Announced.* What seems like a casual remark may be vital to the solution of the crime, but can easily be ignored in the flow of talk. Also, there is the conversational remark which seems to emphasize one thing while its significance is elsewhere, as when a character in *Easy to Kill* says of his late wife's final illness, "Easterfield sent down grapes and peaches from his hothouses. And the old tabbies used to come and sit with her. Honoria Waynflete and Lavinia Fullerton" (80). Since the wife was poisoned, Lord Easterfield's gifts seem to be the possible clues; in reality, the visits of Honoria Waynflete are.

Just as the separated clue and the clue hidden in a group are standard devices of misdirection for all writers of detective fiction, so are red herrings, anything which distracts from the central problem of solving the murder. In Christie's fiction, red herrings are again more often characters than physical clues. She uses her witnesses and suspects to provide multiple motives, to confuse the investigation by their actions, and to hide the murderer's identity by sending the reader off on tangents. Among the varied types are the non-murderous criminal active at the murder site, such as the thieves in *Murder in Mesopotamia* and *The Murder at the Vicarage;* a suspect's parent or grandparent having been a murderer, as in *Poirot Loses a Client* and *They Do It With Mirrors;* characters other than the murderer in disguise for their own reasons, as in *Hercule Poirot's Christmas* and *A Murder Is Announced;* an attempt on a character's life by someone other than the murderer, as in *Death on the Nile* and *Mrs. McGinty's Dead;* a character who has vowed revenge or is a threat but never appears, as in *A Pocket Full of Rye* and *There Is a Tide;* the presence of characters suspected of a previous, unrelated murder, as in *Cards on the Table* and *A Caribbean Mystery;* and, of course, the person who is being framed, as in *The ABC Murders, Easy to Kill,* and a number of others. These red herrings are another method for Christie to scatter the possibility of guilt among her characters, thus directing the reader's attention away from the murderer whom she is concealing.

It could be said that false assumptions are the basis of all misdirection, but Christie at times forces false assumptions on her characters and therefore on her readers. A character's misunderstanding or lack of knowledge is the cause of the false assumption, which is then accepted by the other characters—and the reader. The members of a family suspecting each other, when the murderer is not one of the family is a frequent type, the false assumption being that there is every reason to suspect the family of the victim, but none for suspecting an outsider. Such novels as *Appointment With Death, What Mrs. McGillicuddy Saw!,* and *Funerals Are Fatal,* among others, depend upon this assumption for their mystification. Another type is the gender mistake. *Person* is assumed to mean *man* in *Easy to Kill,* Evelyn Hope is assumed to be a woman's name in *Mrs. McGinty's Dead,* Pip is assumed to be a man's name in *A Murder Is Announced,* and the writer of poison-pen letters in *The Moving Finger* is assumed to be a woman. Secret relationships may also create false assumptions; whether love affairs or marriages, parentage, illegitimacy, a supposed dead relative still alive, or some other form, impersonation is nearly always involved. A fourth type is the false assumption about the connection between two murders. It is assumed that the death of Cora Lansquenet in *Funerals Are Fatal* is the consequence of something she knew about the death of her brother, which was actually a natural death, and that Joyce Reynolds of *Hallowe'en Party* and Marlene Tucker of *Dead Man's Folly* are murdered because they saw earlier murders, though neither did. Statements which seem to exonerate the murderer are a final major type. The central misdirection in *The Mirror Crack'd from Side to Side* is that Heather Babcock was not the intended victim. This false assumption begins with the spilling of her drink at a party and Marina Gregg's giving her hers, which is poisoned. Everyone assumes that Marina Gregg is the intended victim. Instead, she is the murderer, having deliberately caused the spilling. She kills Mrs. Babcock because of what that lady has just told her, but Mrs. Bantry, another guest, later says, "I don't believe she even heard what Mrs. Babcock was saying" (65). The false assumption is enforced, and the search focuses on a possible killer of Marina Gregg. Occasionally Christie will allow one of the detectives to state or imply that the actual murderer could not have committed the crime. When such a statement is made by a police officer, as it is in *A Pocket Full of Rye* and *They Do It With Mirrors*, the later solution by the amateur detective is made more brilliant. But when Miss Marple in *The Body in the Library* says of a character, who turns out to be one of a murderous pair, that she cannot plot, the statement is later explained as resulting from insufficient evidence at that point. In *N or M?* Tuppence dismisses a woman as a possible spy because she has a child with her and spying is "not the kind of thing you'd bring a child into. I'm quite sure of that.... I *know*" (63). The definite nature of the statement seems to eliminate the woman totally—until it is eventually realized that the child is not hers and is just being used as camouflage. One character's misinformation about another is the cause of all five types of false assumptions. When the assumption is accepted by others, truth is obscured and detection is made difficult. Like the double-edged statement, which is often a part of it, the forced false assumption is a principal Christie method of misdirection—and one of her most skillful.

The last two methods can be considered together, for the false perspective of a case is nearly always arranged by the murderer, *By the Pricking of My Thumbs* being the major exception. There Christie has Tuppence begin with an incorrect assumption, which determines her and the reader's concept of what follows. Otherwise, as Poirot states it in "Triangle at Rhodes," the reader is made to see everything "the wrong way round" by "*very clever stage managing*" of the murderer (189). All of the works which use the supposed-victim-as-murderer plot employ this false perspective. The murderer appears to be the intended victim, and the reader sees the events as the murderer wishes. The same is true of the two narrator-as-murderer novels, and also of *Towards Zero*, in which the murderer's plan consists of his seemingly being framed and then found innocent in order to frame a person he hates. The false perspective as arranged by Christie's murderers misleads the detective for only a time, but until he gives his explanation, most readers view everything "the wrong way round." Fictional murderers also have the right to conceal, distort, and falsify evidence. They can lie, switch bodies, play tricks with time, fake attempts on themselves, or even, in *Three Act Tragedy*, "direct" the investigation of the crime. If he is plausible, the murderer may be believed instead of a witness who tells the truth, *A Murder Is Announced* providing one of the best illustrations. Christie's use of the murderer to misdirect is perhaps most clever when she permits him to lay a trail of false clues, which may lead nowhere, as in *The Moving Finger* and *A Pocket Full of Rye,* or may nearly convict someone else, as in *The ABC Murders* and *Easy to Kill.*

Honoria Waynflete's scheme in *Easy to Kill* to have Lord Easterfield, who once jilted her, convicted of seven murders she has committed is exemplary of the murderer as misdirector. She uses few lies, relying on double-edged statements, veiled suggestions, and calculated facial expressions. She says that she dare not name the killer, while continually dampening suggestions of any possibilities other than Easterfield made by Luke Fitzwilliam, the investigator: "Her eyes met Luke's in an expression that puzzled him. They showed impatience and something closely allied to it that he could not quite place" (116). She secretly encourages Easterfield's pompous notion that anyone who crosses him will suffer retribution; she arranges to push Lavinia Fullerton under a car and then say that its license number is Easterfield's; she asks Easterfield to show her a knife, and then when others enter she shudderingly pleads with him to put it away; and she pretends to be worried for the safety of Luke and Bridget Conway, the woman he loves, and warns them over and over to be careful, even walking Luke home to "protect him." It is not surprising that when she feels safe, she can say of Luke, "I've had such fun with him, leading him along!" (161). Honoria Waynflete is a clever, if insane, killer, who almost succeeds. Bridget's knowledge of Easterfield's character is the one obstacle to that success, but Honoria fools everyone else. *Easy to Kill* is an excellent example of the least-likely murderer, of the murderer as deceiver, and of Christie's skill in constructing a classic detective fiction plot.

Techniques and methods have been considered in this chapter as individual elements of Christie's plots, but it is only when they are combined with each other and with the other principal elements that their true effectiveness for mystification-detection is evident. The intricacy of her plots is developed primarily by her intertwining clues and misdirection to make detection possible but difficult. Since a process of discovery is the essential structure of classic detective fiction, Christie's ability to dramatize the investigation which results in that discovery—by shifting possible guilt amongst the characters, by manipulating time, impersonation, red herrings, methods of murder, etc., and especially by verbal deviousness in misleading the reader with double-edged statements—accounts for a large part of her success in the genre.

# Chapter V
## Devices, Diversions, & Debits

*"Extras" make as much difference to a mystery novel as dressing to a salad.*
**Sutherland Scott**

*Writing a detective story is a good deal like making a sauce. You know you've put in all the right ingredients but so many things can go wrong, you can't tell until it reaches the table if it will be a success or a complete disaster.*
**Agatha Christie**

*The perfect mystery cannot be written. Something must always be sacrificed.*
**Raymond Chandler**

This chapter is an admitted miscellany. John Cawelti was quoted earlier as saying that the major artistic problem for the writer of "the longer classical detective story" is to find "additional narrative interests" to supplement the central plot of mystification and detection. Though a number of critics have stated or implied that Christie was only interested in the working out of that central plot, they exaggerate. Everything in her works is secondary to the plot structure, but her works do include additional narrative interests. Whereas later writers of detective fiction have often used descriptions of violence as a significant addition, Christie and her fellow writers of the Golden Age avoided it. As she told an interviewer, "I specialize in murders of quiet, domestic interest."[1] Her dislike of messy deaths, and her refusal to present the details of them, is a principal reason for her reputation for "cosiness." The elimination of overt violence and the inevitable solution of the plot complications bring Christie's works into the broad genre of comedy. If Christie is cosy, she is cosy as Jane Austen is. Therefore, her humor is one of the additions to be examined. Others are her use of literary allusions, nursery rimes, and titles and her comments, serious and otherwise, on detective fiction appearing in the works, as well as her use of point of view and her narrative style—or, to some, her lack of it. Also, some attention must be given to the debits: the coincidences, anomalies, loose ends, and other lapses that occasionally occur in Christie's fiction.

167

## Allusions, Nursery Rimes, and Titles

Unlike Dorothy Sayers, Michael Innis, or Edmund Crispin, Christie makes no claims to erudition by filling her books with quotations from or references to esoteric literature. Nor does she use literary allusions as significant clues, with the single exception of John Webster's *The Duchess of Malfi* in *Sleeping Murder.* Her attitude seems to have been that in the game of solving the mystery, she should not require any kind of special knowledge of her readers: one of the reasons for her popularity. When she does make allusions, they are never obscure—and always English. They are to works which were a natural part of the childhood and education of the upper middle class of her generation. The catalogue of favorite books, presented through Tuppence and Tommy, in *Postern of Fate* is the most extensive illustration. With the exception of Shakespeare, the most prominent sources of allusions are nineteenth and early twentieth century poets: Blake, Keats, Fitzgerald, Browning, Kipling, Flecker, and especially Tennyson. Tennyson provides two titles: the original British title of *Murder After Hours* is *The Hollow,* which comes from the opening lines of *Maud,* and *The Mirror Crack'd from Side to Side* is from "The Lady of Shalott." The latter poem is also quoted appropriately in "Dead Man's Mirror," while Mr. Satterthwaite quotes from *Idylls of the King* in *Three Act Tragedy.* However, the nineteenth century author most often referred to is Lewis Carroll; there are over two dozen allusions to *Alice in Wonderland* and *Through the Looking Glass* in twenty works. Though obviously she doted on these two works, she still used them for only passing allusions, rather than significant plot devices. The only writer outnumbering Carroll is Shakespeare. Allusions to his plays range from titles and epigraphs to works *(There Is a Tide, By the Pricking of My Thumbs, Sad Cypress, Hercule Poirot's Christmas)* to analogies with the case under investigation *(The Pale Horse, Hallowe'en Party, Curtain),* as well as dozens of passing references. Christie's favorites among the plays are *Othello* and *Macbeth.* The character of Iago fascinated Christie. The many references to him culminate in *Curtain,* where the villain and his method are specifically equated with Shakespeare's schemer and his. There are more quotations from and allusions to *Macbeth* than to any other of the plays. *The Pale Horse* has three witches, *Hallowe'en Party* a Lady Macbeth; *By the Pricking of My Thumbs* receives its title, and *Hercule Poirot's Christmas* its epigraph from the play. What impresses one is the relatively small number of allusions of any kind, and the restricted number of sources, in such a large body of works as Christie's.

Though not as "lowbrow" as she liked to pretend, she kept to the fairly obvious—and what she knew—in literary allusion.

Christie's fondness for employing nursery rimes as a structural device in her fiction has been often noted by critics, but the number is again relatively small considering the attention they have received. Three short stories and six novels—seven, if the child's game title of *Mrs. McGinty's Dead* is included—use lines from nursery rimes as titles. These titles immediately create an expected plot structure: how are the events going to parallel or fit the rime? Christie has several methods. The detective may be given the vital clue by the rime, as in "How Does Your Garden Grow?" and "Sing a Song of Sixpence." On the other hand, from a warped sense of humor, the murderer may be following a nursery rime in his killings; *And Then There Were None* and *A Pocket Full of Rye* are illustrations. In *Crooked House* and *An Overdose of Death* (original title: *One, Two Buckle My Shoe),* the rime serves as the organizing principle; in the first by presenting the basic situation and in the second by outlining Poirot's investigation. Finally, there are those works in which the rime is simply imposed upon the story with little purpose or effect: "Four and Twenty Blackbirds," *Hickory Dickory Death,* and *Murder in Retrospect* (original title: *Five Little Pigs).* In setting up expectations which are not fulfilled, the titles of this last group are rather irritating. The works do not have the sense of careful meshing of the rime and the plot which *And Then There Were None,* Christie's best use of a nursery rime, illustrates so superbly.

Other than those using nursery rimes or allusions, Christie's titles are not particularly distinctive. Her favorite word for a title is *dead* or *death;* one or the other occurs in titles of sixteen works. *Mystery* or *mysterious* appears in fourteen, and *murder* in thirteen. Anyone seeing a title with one of these words knows what to expect, and that is their intent. (Surprisingly, "The Case of," so prevalent among other writers of detective fiction, appears for no novels and only ten short stories, nearly all about Parker Pyne. The next most common phrase in her short story titles is "The Adventure of," appearing in eight.) This practice of announcing the nature of her works declines toward the end of her career, where she seems to prefer "meaningless" titles as far as the content is concerned. Such titles as *Third Girl, Elephants Can Remember,* and *Postern of Fate* could easily serve for non-detective novels. Within works, though some of her Golden Age colleagues evolved elaborate parallel or connected chapter titles, Christie generally stayed with simplicity. As many of her novels have numbered chapters as those with titles. The simplicity was obviously a choice. One has only to examine *The*

*Labours of Hercules* to see that she could carry through a complicated set scheme when she wished. There are also the chapters according to the agricultural year of ancient Egypt in *Death Comes as the End,* but the novel that best indicates her awareness of her colleagues' tricks is *Three Act Tragedy,* which is not only divided into three sections, entitled "First Act—Suspicion," "Second Act—Certainty," and "Third Act—Discovery," but also includes the following prefatory matter:

*Directed by*
SIR CHARLES CARTWRIGHT
*Assistant Directors*
MR. SATTERTHWAITE
MISS HERMIONE LYTTON GORE
*Clothes by*
AMBROSINE LTD
*Illumination by*
HERCULE POIROT

This conceit is singular in her works. It verges on the pseudo-clever—as do so many of the similar verbal tricks of her fellow writers of the twenties and thirties.

## Humor

References have been made throughout this study to the assumption that Golden Age detective fiction is essentially in the comic mode. The comic characteristics of Christie's detectives, especially those of Poirot and the Beresfords, have been examined, as have the comic thrillers, Christie's own term. Less attention has been given to the overtly comic short stories, but there are a number of them, including among others, "The Girl in the Train," "The Nemean Lion," "Strange Jest," "The Rajah's Emerald," and all of Parker Pyne's London cases. Christie's humorous comments on her genre will be considered in the next section of this chapter; here explicitly comic scenes, comic minor characters, and the effect of Christie's humor are the subjects.

Setting aside the incidents of the comic thrillers, overtly comic scenes or episodes occur in most of the other Christie novels. They are of two types: in some way integral to the plot or strictly unnecessary additions for narrative interest. What is significant of the first type is that Christie did not have to treat them with humor; they could have fulfilled their function without it. The discussion of the case amidst the bickering chatter of the Mah Jong game in *The*

*Murder of Roger Ackroyd,* Julia Upjohn's tennis racket filled with jewels in *Cat Among the Pigeons,* the semi-parodic ambience and afternoon tea at Bertram's Hotel, the incongruous finding of the corpse in the first chapter of *The Body in the Library* (which Christie considered her best opening), and the delightful meeting of Colin Lamb with Geraldine Mary Alexandra Brown and the *au pair* girl Ingrid in *The Clocks* are just a few of the many comic scenes which carry forward the plot, misdirect the readers, or supply needed information in "non-comic" novels. The second type is frequently related to minor characters and consists of short vignettes when a witness is questioned—whether flighty lady, pompous gentleman, or addled maid—or when the village gossips begin their talk, as in the Miss Marple works; however, occasionally, important information may also result from these scenes. The other major form of the second type is the comic romance. Charles Enderby's pursuit of Emily Trefusis in *Murder at Hazelmoor* is typical, but the best example is in *What Mrs. McGillicuddy Saw!*. There Lucy Eyelesbarrow receives proposals from an elderly gentleman, two of his sons, and his daughter's son, the last on behalf of his father, and the end of the novel is left open, with only the "twinkling" Miss Marple apparently knowing Lucy's final choice. The same novel includes a third form of the strictly unnecessary type in the sleuthing of the ever hungry, ever curious schoolboys Alexander Eastley and James Stoddart-West; though not as developed, the play of the Ramsay boys of *The Clocks* is similar. Of whichever type, these comic scenes are nearly always seamless in the totality of a work; they do not have the appearance of being inserted for comic purposes. They are a natural element of Christie's mode of writing.

Minor comic characters fill Christie's pages. They may be grotesque, wacky, satiric, whimsical, or, to some—since the human sense of humor seems infinite—merely absurd or silly. Their role is similar, in one sense, to that of comic characters in Shakespearean tragedy, providing moments of relief from tension. But they also have another quite different, and more important, function. They provide a comic "coloring" to the events, reassuring the reader that, sooner or later, the mystery will be solved and these people will be able to return to their usual pursuits, no matter how ridiculous those pursuits may be. A few examples will have to represent hundreds. Christie's extravagant Americans are one group, including Mrs. Hattie West, "the California Cucumber King's Wife" of "The Case of the Middle-Aged Wife," and Mr. and Mrs. Odell C. Gardner, the bossy wife and long-suffering husband of *Evil Under the Sun.* Then there is the insufferably earnest Rupert Bateman, nicknamed "Pongo" by his contemporaries, who for much of *The Seven Dials*

*Mystery* seems the obvious suspect, and in the same novel is George
Lomax, permanent Under Secretary of State for Foreign Affairs,
"who was shunned by many because of his inveterate habit of
quoting from his public speeches in private. In allusion to his
bulging eyeballs, he was known to many...as Codders" (36). In
*Poirot Loses a Client,* Christie offers the Misses Tripp, who are
"vegetarians, theosophists, British Israelites, Christian Scientists,
spiritualists and enthusiastic amateur photographers" (83). Major
Horton of *Easy to Kill* is a John Bull type breeder of bulldogs, who
though henpecked by his wife, after her death ironically has
nothing but praise for her, saying, "Fellow needs a wife to keep him
up to scratch," and of marriage, "Young people make me sick. No
stamina, no endurance" (78). The actress Rosina Nunn of "The
World's End" is characterized solely by her love of food; her director
says, "She can't think of anything else. I remember in *Rider* [sic] *to
the Sea*—you know 'and it's the fine, quiet time I'll be having.' I
could *not* get the effect I wanted. At last I told her to think of
peppermint creams—she's very fond of peppermint creams. I got the
effect at once—a sort of far-away look that went to your very soul"
(114). As a final illustration, there is Lady Lucy Angkatell of *Murder
After Hours.* Lady Angkatell is a woman of vivid, and unbelievably
accurate, imagination, who makes outrageous statements, and yet
is utterly vague in her reasoning processes. One can only agree with
an inspector, who, after talking with her, feels "all tangled up in
thistledown" (187). For family reasons, she considers an "accident"
for a man who is raising havoc among the younger womenfolk, but
she discards the idea on the following basis: "One can't ask someone
to be a guest and then arrange accidents. Even Arabs are most
particular about hospitality" (189). A dozen more pages could be
filled with such characters, who while serving as suspects or
witnesses, also provide humor in Christie's fiction, and in so doing
significantly contribute to its tone.

That intangible quality of literature known as tone is the result
of many things, but one of its bases is an author's attitude toward
his subject. To state that Christie's attitude toward crime is comic is
misleading, but the humorous leavening which she employs in the
presentation of crime's investigation is evidence that she views her
works as entertainment. They entertain primarily by mystery-
detection, but they also entertain by the humor whose presence
lightens the grimness of murder. Her humor is not raucous, but
gentle. Though she often expressed admiration for the fiction of P.G.
Wodehouse, to whom she dedicated *Hallowe'en Party,* and though
their characters have similarities, her humor is less waggish. There
is little wit and little farce. Her humor consists essentially of parody,

comic characterization, humorous understatement, and exaggeration which rarely goes too far. Most of all, her humor is the result of detachment, a characteristic of comic writing; in fact, it is Christie's detachment that makes it possible for her to employ humor at all. If she identified strongly with her characters, she could not laugh at them. Works of mystery and detection are often described as "light fiction," and much of the lightness of Christie's fiction comes from its humor.

## Comments on Detective Fiction

Peter Carmody, aged nine, says, "Do you like detective stories? I do. I read them all and I've got autographs from Dorothy Sayers and Agatha Christie and Dickson Carr and H.C. Bailey" (Library, 57). Master Carmody is far from alone among Christie's characters; most seem to have at least some acquaintance with the genre, though no other claims to have gotten Christie's autograph. The habit of characters in detective fiction mentioning other characters, other works or authors of the genre is not confined to Christie. Indeed, George Dove has said, "References by people in detective stories to other people in other detective stories have been made so frequently that they constitute at least a minor convention of the genre."[2] This reference-convention is first an attempt to create a sense of verisimilitude: those other characters or works belong to fiction; *this is real.* At the same time, they serve as additional humor, as well being a general guide to the author's concept of the genre, particularly when there are as many as in Christie's works. Her only work based upon this convention is *Partners in Crime,* with its parodies of writers of the twenties, but since many of them are now forgotten, much of the critical effect is lost. Aside from the more than a hundred casual references, the major comments on detective fiction are provided by Poirot in *The Clocks,* Daniel Clancy in *Death in the Clouds,* and, most extensively, Ariadne Oliver in work after work.

The casual references vary considerably, but most are satiric or facetious. They show Christie's awareness of the conventions and the cliches of detective fiction and her enjoyment in playing with them. The satire is always mild. For instance, whenever something is sensational, the usual comment in the early works is "rather Edgar Wallace stuff," though Japp in *An Overdose of Death* goes so far as to exclaim, "Shades of Phillips Oppenheim, Valentine Williams, and William leQuex!" (100): such comments are as much a tribute to the once great popularity of these writers as it is criticism. Similarly, when Christie decides to have fun at the expense of her readers, she is gentle. In *Murder in Mesopotamia* Nurse Leatheran provides Christie the opportunity to mock readers who look only for technical errors, while not being smart enough to solve the mystery:

> I was reading *Death in a Nursing Home*—really a most exciting story—though I don't think the author knew much about the way nursing homes are run! At any rate I've never known a nursing home like that! I really felt inclined to write to the author and put him right about a few points.
> ...I put the book down at last (it was the red haired parlormaid and I'd never suspected her once!)... (66).

By far the most common type of passing reference is one character's saying to another that present circumstances are similar to or different from those in detective fiction. The comment may be about the course of events or about the characters addressed and is nearly always facetious. Here are ten examples:

I see that you are that favorite character of fiction, the amateur detective. I don't know that they really hold their own with the professional in real life (Vicarage, 131).

"You're not going to tell me one of my poor desert mutts bumped her off after all? Because," added Colonel Carbury sternly, "if so, that would be *cheating*" (Appointment, 139).

Your position certainly seems impeccable. In a work of fiction you would be strongly suspected on that account (Appointment, 181).

You're talking like a thriller by a lady novelist (Overdose, 88).

"This," said Dr. Constantine, "is more wildly improbable than any *roman policier* I have ever read" (Orient, 236).

I suppose her body might have been lowered into a tank of acid by a mad scientist—that's another solution they're very fond of in books! But take my word for it, these things are all my eye and Betty Martin (Overdose, 90).

That's it, clues.... That's what I like in detective stories. Clues that mean everything to the detective—and nothing to you—until the end when you fairly kick yourself (McGinty, 101).

"And to think," said Tuppence, finding her voice, "that those two young idiots were only suspecting each other in that weak way they do it in books" (Partners, 42).

Do you mean to tell me, Superintendent, that this is one of those damned cases you get in detective stories where a man is killed in a locked room by some apparently supernatural agency? (*Christmas*, 86).

"How long has she been dead?"
"She was killed at eleven-thirty-three yesterday evening," said Brett promptly.
Then he grinned as he saw Japp's surprised face.
"Sorry, old boy," he said. "Had to do the super-doctor of fiction!" (Mews, 105).

Though such comments gently ridicule the cliches of the genre, Christie is not averse to using them herself, sometimes humorously and sometimes not. The opening chapter of *The Body in the Library* is a parody of its title's convention, and that is made explicit by Colonel Bantry: "Bodies are always being found in libraries in books. I've never known a case in real life" (11). The use of identical twins as a solution is mocked by Tuppence in "The Unbreakable Alibi" and by Inspector LeJeune in *The Pale Horse,* but it is the key to *Elephants Can Remember.* Poirot in *Murder on the Orient Express* and Superintendent Spence in *There Is a Tide* are not taken in by a smashed watch as an indication of the time of death, the latter calling it, "a well-known hoary old trick" (109), yet Battle accepts it in *The Secret of Chimneys* as marking "the crime as having been committed at exactly a quarter to twelve" (83). More jokes are made about rare untraceable poisons, usually the arrow poison of some obscure South American indian tribe, than any other cliche—Dr. Sheppard even calls such a poison "the essence of a detective story" (22). Though Christie never employs arrow poison, the murder in *Death in the Clouds* is committed by a dart "dipped in the venom of *Dispholidus Typus,* better known as the boomslang or tree snake," which if not South American is South African (49). From the evidence of the many casual comments on detective fiction, one can be sure that when Christie used a cliche, she was aware of what she was doing.

Poirot's comments are most evident in *The Clocks,* though he makes occasional jokes about detective fiction in other works, as when he teases Hastings in *The Big Four* about all celebrated detectives having smarter brothers and parodying Mycroft Holmes with Achille Poirot. But in *The Clocks* Poirot is studying detective fiction for his book on the subject, and he gives Colin Lamb his views on a number of authors and works, views which coincide with those of Christie (106-09). He praises the period charm of Anna Katharine Green's *The Leavenworth Case* and the panache of Maurice Leblanc's *Adventures of Arsene Lupin* and calls Gaston Leroux's *The Mystery of the Yellow Room* a masterpiece for its logic and escaping cheating by a hair. For Poirot, Conan Doyle is *"Maitre,"* not because of his plotting, which Poirot finds "far-fetched, full of fallacies and contrived," but for "the art of the writing" and, above all, for the creation of Dr. Watson (Christie's homage to the literary sire of Hastings). He dismisses the hard-boiled school as dull violence for violence's sake and the thriller writers for producing "melodrama stirred up with a stick." Four other writers are presented through pseudonyms. Cyril Quain, the master of the alibi and the railway time-table is obviously Freeman

Wills Crofts, who, though dull, is praised for his order and method. Two American women writers—who could be any of four or five now writing—are praised under the names Florence Elks and Louisa O'Malley. The fourth pseudonymous author is Ariadne Oliver. Through Poirot's comment on Mrs. Oliver, Christie gives a short but candid overview of her own work, without shirking deficiencies:

I do not wholly approve of her works, mind you. The happenings in them are highly improbable. The long arm of coincidence is far too freely employed. And, being young at the time [she started to write], she was foolish enough to make her detective a Finn, and it is clear that she knows nothing about Finns or Finland except possibly the works of Sibelius. Still, she has an original habit of mind, she makes an occasional shrewd deduction, and of later years she has learnt a good deal about things which she did not know before. Police procedure for instance. She is also now a little more reliable on the subject of firearms. What was even more needed, she has possibly acquired a solicitor or a barrister friend who has put her right on certain points of the law.

While presented in his most pompous manner, Poirot's comments reflect directly the taste of his author, her likes and dislikes, with reasons given, in detective fiction, as well as a clear-sighted appraisal of her own abilities.

Daniel Clancy appears only in *Death in the Clouds*. Like Mrs. Oliver, who takes his place two books later, he is a writer of detective stories. He is a comic figure, and his fiction, such as *The Clue of the Scarlet Petal*, is satirized. His detective is Wilbraham Rice, who eats bananas and bites his nails: "I don't know why I made him bite his nails to start with—it's really rather disgusting—but there it is. He started by biting his nails, and now he has to do it in every single book" (158)—another parodic comment on Poirot. Mr. Clancy does not believe that detective fiction can be too sensational. He tells Poirot, "After all, you don't want a detective story to be like real life. Look at the things in the papers—dull as ditchwater" (161). Of course, his problem, one which Christie knew well, is to come up with something new in every work. He gives as one instance the perennial matter of the young woman who will not tell what she knows: "There's never any real reason, of course, why she shouldn't blurt the whole thing at once, but you have to try to think of something that's not too definitely idiotic" (164). Mr. Clancy is too overdrawn to make many sensible comments; rather, he is meant to be laughed at.

He could be considered a preliminary sketch for Mrs. Oliver if she had not preceded him in a couple of Parker Pyne stories. In them she differs with Mr. Clancy on the need for always being original; as she puts it, "The public is conservative, Mr. Pyne; it likes the old well-worn gadgets" (Soldier, 44). Her policy at this point in her career is to give the public what it wants, accounting for her bestsellers. In spite of the early appearances, Mrs. Oliver does not become Christie's spokeswoman on detective fiction until she meets Poirot in *Cards on the Table*. That she is a self-caricature of Christie in her appearance, taste, shyness, and number of works has already been noted. Christie also makes the identification through specific works of Mrs. Oliver. She has written a novel entitled *The Body in the Library*, and both *The Lotus Murder* and *The Clue of the Candle Wax* have the same plot premise as *The Murder on the Links*. In *Mrs. McGinty's Dead* it is suggested to her that she kill off Sven Hjerson in a swan-song book to be published after her death; when Christie included the suggestion, she had already written *Curtain*. Also, just as Christie tired of Poirot, so does Mrs. Oliver of Hjerson. She says that she must have been mad to invent "the revolting man," but that if you try something as a writer and the public approves, "then you go on—and before you know where you are, you've got someone like that maddening Sven Hjerson tied to you for life.... If I met that bony gangling vegetable eating Finn in real life, I'd do a better murder than any I've ever invented" (McGinty, 109). A change of nationality and the adjectives is all that is necessary for the statement to be Christie's, at times, on Poirot. Mrs. Oliver has Christie's aversion to talking about her writing, but when she thinks about her work, her view is identical to that of Christie's in interviews and *An Autobiography:* "She thought the detective stories she wrote were quite good of their kind. Some were not so good and some were much better than others.... She was a lucky woman who had established a happy knack of writing what quite a lot of people wanted to read. Wonderful luck that was... (Elephants, 7).

Christie's statement that she specializes in "murders of quiet domestic interest" is matched by Mrs. Oliver's "I only write very plain murders.... Just about people who want other people out of the way and try to be clever about it" (Horse, 62). However, this statement is often contradicted by the satiric descriptions of Mrs. Oliver's novels. Like Mr. Clancy, she considers her fiction superior to actual crime: "I could invent a better murder *any* day than anything *real*. I'm never at a loss for plot" (Cards, 43). Nor does she worry very much about making errors. She becomes irritated when people write to tell her that she has used the wrong flowers or vegetables for a particular season, given the wrong length of a blowpipe, or stated that sulphonal is soluble in water. She states her attitude in *Cards on the Table:*

"I don't see that it matters if I mix up police ranks and say a revolver when I mean an automatic, and a dictograph when I mean a phonograph, and use a poison that just allows you to gasp one dying sentence and no more. What really matters is plenty of *bodies!* If the thing's getting a little dull, some more blood cheers it up. Somebody is going to tell something—and then they are killed first. That always goes down well. It comes in all my books—camouflaged different ways, of course. And people *like* untraceable poisons, and idiotic police inspectors and girls tied up in cellars with sewer gas or water pouring in (such a troublesome way of killing any one really) and a hero who can dispose of anything from three to seven villains single-handed" (71).

Allowing for the comic exaggeration, Mrs. Oliver is not unfairly presenting many Golden Age writers' concept of their craft.

In a long passage of *Hallowe'en Party,* Mrs. Oliver explains to Poirot her method of finding her characters. Like Christie, she does not use persons she knows, but she can see a stranger who will give her an idea which she can develop. She says that she would never want to meet the person after using him or her, and Poirot understands: "The story must be yours, the character is yours. She is your child. You have made her, you begin to understand her, you know how she feels, you know where she lives and you know what she does" (187). Poirot states that however much a character may be considered a stereotype, he or she is still the creation of the author. This kind of "serious" statement about the nature of detective fiction is most clearly seen when Rhoda Dawes gushes in *Cards on the Table* about how wonderful it must be to be a writer. Mrs. Oliver gives a straightforward answer for her author:

One actually has to *think,* you know. And thinking is always a bore. And you have to plan things. And then one gets stuck every now and then. . . . Writing's not particularly enjoyable. It's hard work, like everything else.
\*\*\*
I can always think of things. . . . What is so tiring is writing them down. I always think I've finished, and then when I count up I find I've only written thirty thousand words instead of sixty thousand, and so then I have to throw in another murder and get the heroine kidnapped again. It's all very boring (146 & 147).

Boring as it may be, she perseveres, and she learns as she does. By the time of *The Pale Horse,* she is becoming more "realistic." She finds the master criminal no longer satisfactory, because when he is revealed, he always seems inadequate: "It's much easier if you just have a bank manager who's embezzled the funds, or a husband who wants to get rid of his wife and marry the children's governess [as in *The Moving Finger].* So much more natural—if you know what I mean" (52).

In the same novel, Mark Easterbrook interrupts Mrs. Oliver at work, and she spends three pages explaining the writing of detective fiction (7-10), the longest of her statements. She discusses a plot snag and an unsatisfactory heroine and worries about interviewers asking embarrassing questions. She states, however, that her major problem in writing is the fact that usually murder is obvious and that she must find a means of hiding it. She says, "The murder part is quite easy and simple. It's the covering up that's so difficult. I mean why *should* it be anyone else but the [murderer]? [He] stick[s] out a mile." She goes on to point out that the usual method of multiple suspects is an arbitrary answer: "Say what you like, it's not natural for five or six people to be on the spot when B is murdered and all have a motive for killing B—unless, that is, B is absolutely madly unpleasant and in that case nobody will mind whether he's been killed or not, and doesn't care in the least who's done it." Christie's ability in covering that unnaturalness and making the reader care is a major factor in her success as a writer. Mrs. Oliver's final point is concerned with subject matter. Again supporting Christie, she refuses to write about matters with which she is unfamiliar: "It's safer, I think, to stick to what you know." She then gives a list of characters she might use—almost none of which appear in Christie's works. Nevertheless, Mrs. Oliver's principle is still that of her creator: stick to what one knows.

As stated at the beginning of this section, Christie is not the only writer of detective fiction to incorporate comments on the genre into her works. Nevertheless, it is doubtful if any other writer has made as many statements about the structure, characters, conventions, difficulties, and absurdities of the fictional type which he or she writes within their works themselves as Christie. They are evidence of her deep and wide knowledge of the genre's requirements, however inadequately individual examples of her work may fulfill those requirements.

## Point of View

The question of fairness arises in any discussion of detective fiction's point of view. It involves both the detective and the murderer. The detective's investigation must be followed by the reader, but the detective's solution and his reasoning to that solution must be hidden in some way. In 1929 Dorothy Sayers presented four "viewpoints" of detective fiction, relating to the detective's role, and they are apposite to Christie's method of narration: (1) the reader may be given only the detective's external actions, (2) the reader may be given what the detective sees, but not what he observes, (3) the reader may be given what he sees and, at once, his conclusions, and (4) the reader may be taken inside the mind of the detective.[3] If the omniscient or third-person point of view is used, all four of these may appear in the same novel, for that method is the loosest. The author can include or exclude whatever he desires. Also, by its nature, this point of view distances the reader from the characters; he is not receiving the story from the consciousness of one of them. On the other hand, the use of a narrator not the detective eliminates the fourth of Sayers' viewpoints—at least until the detective decides to reveal his thoughts. The Watson-narrator provides the information the detective has, but cannot detail his reasoning. The reader receives the words, the actions, and perhaps even the expressed emotions of the detective, but his mind remains closed. It has to be if the story is to continue.

Christie began by following Conan Doyle, with Hastings as Watson to Poirot's Holmes. As a dense narrator, Hastings is reliable only as to facts—what is seen and what Poirot tells him: that is, Sayers' first, second, and occasionally third viewpoints. He is not reliable as to the interpretation of those facts. Other narrators, such as the Vicar of *The Murder at the Vicarage* and Nurse Leatheran of *Murder in Mesopotamia,* are more intelligent than Hastings, but they are not detectives and so are also limited to the first three viewpoints and may misinterpret. Quite different are Dr. Sheppard of *The Murder of Roger Ackroyd* and, forty-one years later, Michael Rogers of *Endless Night;* they are murderers. Rogers is psychopathic and tells his story from a cell. In spite of the novel's being a superb mystery, the cleverness of Rogers' narration is artificial: why should or would he present the story *as a mystery?* Dr. Sheppard is the most famous murderer-narrator in detective fiction. The outcry over Christie's not playing fair in allowing him to narrate the events has long since died away. One wonders now why it ever occurred. With Hastings in South America, Poirot needs a Watson to record the case. His choice of his nextdoor neighbor, the local doctor, is a logical one. Sheppard, like his author in other works, omits; he does not make false statements. As Poirot says to him, "A very meticulous and accurate account. You have recorded all the facts faithfully and exactly—though you have shown yourself becomingly reticent as to your own share in them" (257). Christie repeats the same idea in answering those who accuse her of cheating: "if they read it carefully they will see that they are wrong. Such little lapses of time as there have to be are nicely concealed in an ambiguous sentence, and Dr. Sheppard, in writing it down, took great pleasure in writing nothing but the truth, though not the whole truth."[4] And when, after being confronted with Poirot's knowledge, Sheppard explains the final details, he takes pride in his careful wording, as obviously did Christie.

A general principle in allowing the reader into the murderer's mind is that the murderer cannot be mystified or "think innocently." He can lie, but his thoughts cannot. Christie never violates this principle, though she nearly does so in *What Mrs.*

*McGillicuddy Saw!* (especially chapter nineteen), which comes closest among all of her works to being unfair. Aside from it and the two novels with murderer-narrators, Christie has three other major methods of including the murderer's thoughts. They may be given without any attribution as to the character thinking them. All that the reader knows is that one of the characters is thinking. This method is used in *And Then There Were None, Towards Zero,* and *Funerals are Fatal.* The second method is to present the murderer's thoughts when he is not thinking about the murder; then, of course, his name can be given. *Cards on the Table* and *Sad Cypress* contain examples. Both of these methods have obvious advantages for misdirection: the first leaves open all possibilities, and the second leads the reader elsewhere, for surely a murderer thinks of nothing but his murder.

The third method is employed in five of the eight novels in which Christie combines first-person and third-person narration. The clumsiest illustration is *The Man in the Brown Suit.* It opens with a third-person chapter, six chapters consist of the villain's diary, and the others are told by the heroine Anne Beddingfeld. It is an unsuccessful experiment, but a forerunner of *The Murder of Roger Ackroyd. The ABC Murders* intersperses into Hastings' account the wanderings of Alexander Bonaparte Cust, the chief suspect—one of Christie's most obvious red herrings. More successfully, Mark Easterbrook narrates *The Pale Horse,* with the exception of four chapters, while *The Clocks* alternates chapters of narration by Colin Lamb with third-person chapters. The other four novels—*Remembered Death, Murder in Retrospect, Murder After Hours,* and *Ordeal by Innocence*—are basically third-person, but all include chapters of the thoughts, memories, or narratives of the suspects, including the murderers. These chapters are again advantageous for misdirection, as noted earlier of *Remembered Death,* for, with their careful wording, the reader will have all of the suspects' versions of the murder and the surrounding events, but will not be able to determine which of them is the murderer. As with the use of narrators, the following of the detective's investigation, and the presentation of murderers' thoughts, even when as literary technique they may not be faultless, Christie's methods of combined points of view are fair and contribute materially to her mystifying the reader.

## Style

Opinions vary greatly on Christie's narrative style. Edmund Wilson dismisses it completely: "her writing is of a mawkishness and banality which seem to me literally impossible to read."[5] Frank Behre, a linguist, finds it natural: "the dialogue of Agatha Christie's stories is, beside being 'careless' in the choice of structure and wording, brimful of hackneyed phrases and cliches, and disdainful of elegant variation; in short, like everyday conversation."[6] Edmund Crispin only partially agrees: "She wrote dialogue very well—a lot of her books are dialogue almost entirely, with relatively little action—but I wouldn't say she was a particularly good stylist."[7] The greatest praise is that of Anthony LeJeune, who says, "The real secret of Agatha Christie is...not in the carpentering of her plots, excellent though that is, but in the texture of her writing; a texture smooth and homely as cream. Her books are the easiest of reading. They 'go down a treat', as the saying is."[8] Christie herself was humble about her ability as a writer, saying, "If I could write like Elizabeth Bowen, Muriel Spark or Graham Greene, I should jump to high heaven with delight, but I know that I can't, and it would never occur to me to attempt to copy them. I have learned that I am *me,* that I can do the things that, as one might put it, *me* can do, but I cannot do the things that *me* would like to do."[9]

No attempt will be made here to supply a stylistic analysis of Christie's fiction (I pity the person who attacks the mass of material for such a purpose); rather a general discussion of her style and a brief survey of what Christie's *me* does with some of the basic elements of English diction and grammar, supported by minimal examples, will be offered.

If one word can describe Christie's style, that word is *ingenuous.* Others might prefer easy, colloquial, or readable, but ingenuous, in its sense of artless or innocent, seems to capture most closely the quality of her best writing. Its unpretentious, direct, even prosaic nature is the result of the underlying ingenuousness. She is not trying to impress, just tell a story. Her already mentioned lack of descriptions of violence and of recondite allusions is matched by a lack of pseudo-sophisticated or ultra-clever dialogue and of Latinate, high-flown language. Fine writing is not Christie's forte, and she does not attempt it. She may be cumbersome and repetitious in diction—as Behre says, "disdainful of elegant variation"—but until the works of her last years her writing displays an economy of wording. Those last works, however, such as *Third Girl, Elephants Can Remember,* and *Postern of Fate,* indicate a slackening of her skill at construction, with an inordinate amount of repetition and padding, much of which is also confused and confusing. Before advanced age caused this loss of control, she could use language for effect, but did so sparingly. Her playing with Poirot's speech has already been discussed. His problems with syntax, diction, and idiom demonstrate her awareness of the possibilities of language for characterization. She could also parody the excesses of other writers. The treacly prose of Miss Pamela Horsefall in *Mrs. McGinty's Dead* is an example. Another occurs in the comic thriller *The Big Four* when a villain's description of possible tortures to Mrs. Hastings brings the following reaction from Hastings: "You fiend! Not that—you wouldn't do that—"; this outburst ends with "with a cry of horror I clapped my hands to my ears" (112). The sensationalism of Edgar Wallace and his like are her obvious targets in this quotation. The byplay of Tuppence and Tommy in *Partners in Crime* is another example of this kind of parody. "Yellow Iris" even provides a parodic popular song:

> There's nothing like Love for driving you crazy
> There's nothing like Love for making you mad
> Abusive
> Allusive
> Suicidal
> Homicidal
> There's nothing like Love
> There's nothing like Love...(115).

Other instances could be mentioned, but definite evidence of her consciousness, within her limits, of the effects of language and how to achieve them is provided by her attitude toward her publisher's making editorial revisions for "correctness": "she objected to sentences being re-arranged to be more grammatically correct, especially in the case of spoken conversation, for this would make all the characters sound alike and not like ordinary variable human beings."[10]

Her ingenousness gave her the insight that ordinary human beings speak in cliches and stock phrases and use a small vocabulary and short sentences, and she does not attempt to make her characters speak otherwise. She also uses a minimum of punctuation and short paragraphs. All of these stylistic features lead to easy reading and contribute to her massive popularity. It would be foolish, however, to deny that there are solecisms in her works. At times she seems to become stuck on a word. For example, Miss Van Schuyler of *Death on the Nile* never speaks; she always "snaps" or "snapped." Perhaps Christie's intent is satirical characterization, but no one *always* "snaps," and the repetition becomes tiresome. She can be guilty of an occasional genteelism, as in "We reposed ourselves most of the morning" (Brown, 142), or of tautology, as in "She went out from the bar on to the terrace outside" (Baghdad, 98). Her images and figures of speech are hardly original.

Most are domestic in nature and used for description of characters' appearance or personality. She is particularly fond of "boiled gooseberry eyes" for men and "a wistful dog-like expression" for almost anyone. In fact, animal imagery, especially relating to dogs, is her favorite type, as noted of the presentation of Tuppence Beresford and Megan Hunter. She also reverses the process in the chatty anthropomorphizing of the dogs in *Poirot Loses a Client* and *Postern of Fate,* the latter being both boring and silly. Her humorous figures of speech are often rather ponderous. Miss Marple's spying in *A Caribbean Mystery* is described thusly: "With all the care of a big game hunter approaching upwind of a herd of antelope, Miss Marple gently circumnavigated Mr. Rafiel's bungalow" (184). Rarely does she use extended figures of speech. The following from *Hallowe'en Party* is about as long as any: "Judith Butler was a woman of about thirty-five, and while her daughter resembled a dryad or a wood nymph, Judith had more the attributes of a water spirit. She could have been a Rhine maiden. Her long blonde hair hung limply on her shoulders, she was delicately made with a rather long face and faintly hollow cheeks, while above them were big sea-green eyes fringed with long eyelashes" (112-13). Much more common is the single phrase, as in the description of a young man in *Hercule Poirot's Christmas,* whose face "has the mild quality of a Burne-Jones knight. It was, somehow, not very real" (27). (Both of these are non-literary allusions and are as arcane as she allows herself to be.)

In spite of weaknesses, Christie's ingenuous style is a serviceable one. It is simple and direct; its purpose is to tell a story without flourishes. Her propensity for adverbs is the result of wanting to tell the story quickly, of identifying reactions in a word. Her favorites are *sharply* and *dryly,* followed by *bluntly, shrewdly, curiously, abruptly,* and *thoughtfully.* They are ordinary—as well as being adaptable to misdirection—and typical of the linguistic blocks with which she constructs her maze-like fictions. Therefore, as a general statement, it can be said that Christie has an ingenuously serviceable style, one which serves for 184 very popular works.

## Coincidences, Anomalies, and Loose Ends

No writer's technique is perfect. Christie supposedly took great pains to get her facts right about poisons, legal procedures, and other matters necessary for her fiction. This is not the place to quarrel with her knowledge or lack of same about such matters. However, there are narrative weaknesses and contradictions which mar her fiction, and even though many are minor in the total effect of their works, they must be noted. Some will say that to take such notice is to be picayune, but detective fiction exists by its carefulness to detail.

Some of them are simply the result of her writing so much. She occasionally forgets what has happened or been said in a previous work. Poirot's investigation in *Lord Edgware Dies* being interrupted by his leaving the scene to solve the case of "The Ambassador's Boots," a Tuppence and Tommy case in *Partners in Crime,* can only be explained by Christie's forgetfulness. The same is true of a later inconsistency. Joan West says in *At Bertram's Hotel* that Miss Marple enjoyed her trip to the Caribbean in spite of a murder, but in *Nemesis* Miss Marple says that she did not tell Joan or Raymond about the murder. As previously stated, more serious narrative weaknesses appear in such late novels as *By the Pricking of My Thumbs, Elephants Can Remember,* and *Postern of Fate.* All three novels are concerned with past crimes, and they become confused because having happened "so long ago" no one is sure of anything, even when closely involved. For example, the Ravenscroft murders of *Elephants Can Remember* occur fifteen years before the novel's opening. Mrs. Oliver is the godmother of the Ravenscroft child, yet knows practically nothing about the family. That same child, now grown, is amazingly vague about the supposed murder-suicide of her mother and father, saying, "You see, I never read any account of the inquest or anything like that or the inquiry into it" (61). Then two pages later, she provides specific details and says, "I think about it [the murder-suicide] nearly all the time" (63). Age, rather than forgetfulness, is the culprit in such instances.

It is expected that a detective story will tie up all loose ends. In the vast majority of her works, Christie does, but there are exceptions, minor and major. A minor instance is the disappearance without explanation from *The Moving Finger* of the Symmington boys, after their parents have been disposed of. Failure of the detective to explain fully or his contradicting earlier facts is not minor. The principal illustration is in *Towards Zero.* Much is made of water being on the floor of the murderer's room the morning after the murder (138). In his explanation Superintendent Battle mentions it again: "a good deal of water on the floor as we noticed (but without seeing the point, I'm sorry to say)," but then a few paragraphs later he says of the murderer, "he had all night to clear up his traces and fix things" (215). If so, why did he not clear up the water?

*Towards Zero* also contains a striking example of coincidence. The murderer chooses at random a name from a hotel register as an alias for having his suit cleaned. The name chosen just happens to belong to a man who is also having a suit cleaned, and he receives the murderer's suit, leading directly to the murderer's exposure. Coincidence such as this is often called the unforgiveable sin of detective fiction, but it appears over and over in Golden Age works, including Christie's. She was aware of using it, as evidenced by Poirot's dictum that at least one coincidence is permissible in any case and Tuppence Beresford's statement in *The Secret Adversary:* "I've often noticed that once coincidences start happening they go on happening in the most extraordinary way. I dare say it's some natural law that we haven't found out" (38). The weakness of coincidence is not so much in someone accidentally finding a clue or over-hearing an important conversation; after all, the word *serendipity,* the faculty of making fortunate or unexpected discoveries by accident, was coined by Horace Walpole from what is considered a precursor of detective fiction. The weakness arises when the effect is that the author could not plan or complete the work without using coincidence and when that need of the author is obvious. The most irritating example (to me) in all of Christie's fiction is Elspeth McGillicuddy's supposedly having to leave England for Ceylon immediately after having witnessed a murder. It is a contrived coincidence by Christie to leave center stage to Miss Marple and to be able to bring in Mrs. McGillicuddy at the end to verify what she saw. Many other examples of coincidence— including other examples of the contrived variety—can be found, but perhaps no work of Christie's is so based upon coincidence as *Sleeping Murder.* Househunting in England, the heroine newly arrived from New Zealand chooses unknowingly the very house in which she lived as a small child and witnessed a murder. One must accept the coincidence or reject the novel. Realizing the unlikelihood of such a coincidence, Christie provides the following as an answer to critics of it:

[Gwenda:] "But surely it's quite impossible that I should come to England and actually buy the identical house I'd lived in long ago?"
[Miss Marple:] "It's not *impossible,* my dear. It's just a very remarkable coincidence—and remarkable coincidences do happen" (32).

The London *Times* reviewer of *Poirot Loses a Client* in 1937 asked, "Who in their senses would use hammer and nails and varnish in the middle of the night within a few feet of an open door [to commit murder]? And do ladies wear large brooches in their dressing-gowns [while committing murder]?"[11] This type of inexplicable or anomalous situation occurs more frequently than might be expected in Christie's fiction. From nearly fifty found, here are twenty-four, presented as questions. Readers are free to attempt to find the answers.

Why in *Dead Man's Folly* does no one recognize the son of the most prominent local family when he returns, an army deserter, disguised only by a beard and change of name?

Why in *Why Didn't They Ask Evans?* is Roger Bassington-ffrench not called to testify at the inquest, or even be present, since he remained with the body until the police arrived?

How does the murderess in *Nemesis* know that Elizabeth Temple is investigating an earlier death and is to be at a convenient spot to become another victim?

Why in *Elephants Can Remember* is the murderess's hand covered with blood from pushing her victim over a cliff?

How can Poirot still have the "bullet pencil" on page 74 of "Dead Man's Mirror" when he has given it to Colonel Bury on page 65?

What is the explanation for Martin Dering's being married to Sylvia Pearson on page 65 and then to Martha Elizabeth Rycroft on pages 194 and 207 in *Murder at Hazelmoor?*

Why in *They Came to Baghdad* does the powerful anarchist organization fail to investigate the sister of Anna Scheele, its greatest threat?

How can Anne Johnson of *Murder in Mesopotamia* say, "The window—, Nurse—the window'," after drinking a glass of hydrochloric acid?

How and with what does the hidden murderer bore air-holes in the chest of "The Mystery of the Spanish Chest"?

How does Poirot arrange in *Third Girl* to have Dr. Stillingfleet on the scene when an attempt is made on Norma Restarick's life?

Why is the "anarchistic" Emlyn Price on a tour of historic homes and gardens in *Nemesis?*

Can one accept the following answer in *Murder After Hours* to Poirot's question of how strange fingerprints were placed on a gun: "An old blind man who sells matches in the street. He didn't know what it was I asked him to hold for a moment while I got some money out!" (248)?

Would a teenage girl in 1960, as stated in *Cat Among the Pigeons,* not know the difference between a fat woman and a pregnant one?

Why in *Hercule Poirot's Christmas* is the single clue an unrecognizable piece of a balloon? Where is the rest? Why did it burst?

Could, as happens in "The Adventure of Johnny Waverly," one leave a three-year old boy in a totally dark, enclosed space for a length of time—even with toys—without the child's becoming terrified and announcing his presence?

If the murderer in *Sleeping Murder* is so obsessed with Helen Kennedy, why does he allow her to go to India to be married to someone else?

In the same novel, after strangling Helen Kennedy, the murderer carries her body upstairs; where is the small child who has watched the murder from the top of the stairs?

Since Derek Kettering of *The Mystery of the Blue Train* has been offered £100,000, why does Poirot say that he "was in a tight corner, a very tight corner, threatened with ruin" (185-86)?

Is it possible, as in *The Mysterious Affair at Styles,* that a murderer would never have the opportunity, or nerve, over a period of months to gain the only incriminating evidence against himself, which he has hidden? Or not have his accomplice obtain it?

Are people so unaware of place—or the food on their plates—as those of *Remembered Death,* who on their return to a restaurant table sit one place over because of a moved purse?

Why in *Third Girl* does a murderess engage in art forgery and dope smuggling when she and her male cohort have already gained millions by their murder?

How can that same murderess be active in a business, which takes her all over England, and at the same time be mistress of a country house? Poirot's explanation is hardly acceptable: "Two women—never, at any time, seen together. Their lives so arranged that no one noticed the large gaps in their time schedules when they were unaccounted for" (241).

What happens in *Curtain* after Poirot serves hot chocolate laced with sleeping tablets, to which he has tolerance, to himself and the murderer? All that Poirot says is "His portion took effect in due course, mine had little effect upon me" (233). Since Poirot has already told the murderer of his knowledge, which is not denied, what happens during that "due course," just calm chocolate sipping?

Finally, how in *Curtain* does Poirot get the packet detailing his death to practically the last moment to his lawyers for transmission to Hastings?

Anyone reading with care all 184 works could find other examples of coincidences, anomalies, and loose ends. They are there, but hidden in the massive bulk of Christie's fiction, and her ability to obfuscate—the only appropriate word—them for the vast majority of her readers is not a weakness, but a triumph.

\*   \*   \*

The devices, diversions, and even the debits of this chapter are part of the texture of Christie's fiction. They could be removed or changed, and the fundamental structure of mystification-detection would still be present, but the remaining work would not be Christie's. As she says, writing a detective story is like making a sauce, and these are among the spices which give it flavor—whether good or bad the reader must decide.

# Chapter VI
## Theme

*In a perfect world there will be no need for detective stories, but then there will be nothing to detect.*

**Erik Routley**

*In your books you condemn all that is foul and mean*
*Many's the party, but always kept clean.*
*Yours is the role of Morality Play*
*Wherein all the wicked find crime doesn't pay.*
*Blackmailer, killer, scoundrel and crook*
*Sooner or later are brought to book.*

**Max Mallowan**

*Always underneath the smooth surface there was some black mud. There wasn't clear water down to the pebbles, down to the shells, lying on the bottom of the sea. There was something moving, something sluggish somewhere, something that had to be found, suppressed.*

**Tommy Beresford.**

Those who see classic detective fiction as mere puzzle would argue, as Edmund Wilson did, that it is not literature, and, therefore, the question of theme is irrelevant. To others, the concept of theme in the genre is hardly worth consideration because of its obviousness. The attitude is that, of course, the theme is good versus evil, innocence versus guilt, and nothing more need be said except that in the conflict good *always* prevails. Such a view places detective fiction within the larger genre of melodrama, with its eternal theme of virtue triumphant. Persons holding this view would probably add that if any other themes are present, they are the results of sub-structure, second text, deep text, the author's unconscious, or some other theory supplied by the critic who wishes to find them. The problem with this type of easy dismissal is that nearly all of the world's literature is based in some way on the conflict of good and evil. The two valid points implicit in this "of course, the theme is obvious" concept are that detective fiction is moral and that its ultimate outcome—however confusing the way to it—is predictable. Perhaps these are the reasons for Erik Routley's description of detective fiction as "entertainment for puritans," as surely they are the basis of Christie's statement that her belief when she began to write was that detective fiction was "very much a story with a

190

moral; in fact it was the old Everyman Morality Tale, the hunting down of Evil and the triumph of Good."[1] To understand more fully "the triumph of Good" in Christie's fiction, more does need to be said, first, on theme in the genre generally and, second, on some of the prominent themes of her works.

There are a number of seeming paradoxes in the themes of detective fiction: pervasiveness of evil and optimism, catharsis and renewal, free will and the dictates of cause and effect, and life and death. The concept of evil always present but unseen below the surface of human existence is not a pretty one, but the insistence in Christie's works that anyone can commit murder is evidence of its thematic importance. The identification of the guilty person is a necessity for removing the pervasiveness: then evil is no longer "everywhere," but within a single individual. At the same time, the grimness of this view of pervasive evil is softened by the genre's optimism. Order can be created out of a situation which appears to be chaotic, nightmarish, or inexplicable. The expulsion of the evildoer recreates harmony or brings renewal. That harmony is based upon the social and moral values of the community in which disruption has occurred. This equation of the good with established systems, as has been noted, is the principal reason for the genre's conservative reputation. The second paradox also involves the ends of works. The catharsis provided by detective fiction is the discovery of the truth and the deliverance of the innocent. The reader expects a morally acceptable and intellectually satisfying solution. The pinpointing of guilt frees the reader, as well as the innocent characters, from any stigma of that guilt. This catharsis, which comes with the detective's explanation, prepares the way for the renewal of life, to repeat, an instance of the genre's optimism. The third paradox is that in detective fiction nothing happens without a reason—cause and effect rule—while concurrently free will is implied in the idea that man can solve his problems. The apparent conflict is resolved if one accepts that man's free will, even a murderer's, is the result of his reason (hence, the importance of motive). The detective chooses to exercise his free will for the good of the society, and in so doing demonstrates not only the "cause" of the murder, but also that murder as cause inevitably leads to the revelation of its perpetrator as effect. The problem is that detective fiction provides absolute poetic justice, and that, as many critics have noted, can lead to the trivializing of life and death. The assumption that guilt is always specific does not recognize the ambiguity so often present in human conduct. This simplification is largely the result of detective fiction's similarity to comedy: everything eventually "works out for the best," and everyone—

except victim and murderer—lives happily ever after. The formula of detective fiction does offer the potential for trivializing vital issues of existence, but it also presents the optimistic theme of the affirmation of life.

One method of expressing this affirmation is in the treatment of death. The sanctity of life is violated by murder. Even if the victim is less than honorable, the murderer is presuming to play God by his irrevocable act. The message is that no life is unimportant. To emphasize that message, Christie's most unequivocal statements of it are made not about murder, but about suicide. The Harley Quin story "The Man from the Sea" and *Towards Zero* state that a person's life is not his own to dispose of at will, for each person's life touches many others. In the first Mr. Satterthwaite asks a woman planning suicide how she can dare to ignore the possibility that she is "part of a gigantic drama under the orders of a divine Producer?" (227). Neither she nor anyone else can foresee what the significance of that part may someday be. The identical point is made in *Towards Zero*, the only difference being that it occurs after a failed attempt at suicide. When Angus MacWhirter attempts to explain to a hospital nurse why he tried to kill himself, the following dialogue ensues:

> "My dear girl, what use am I to anybody?"
> She said confusedly:
> "You don't know. You may be—someday—"
> ***
> "It may be just by *being* somewhere—not doing anything—just by being at a certain place at a certain time—oh, I can't say what I mean, but you might just—just walk along a street some day and just by doing that accomplish something terribly important—perhaps even without knowing what it was" (18 & 19).

Though the comments in these two works are the most explicit of Christie's statements on the sanctity of human life, there are many others throughout the works. The only exceptions to this governing attitude appear in two other Quin stories, "The Bird With the Broken Wing" and "Harlequin's Lane," which present the view that death can be a release from a life of unhappiness. Otherwise, in Christie's fiction life is to be lived, and the extinguishing of a human life is the ultimate crime.

Christie's most prevalent single theme is directly related to the affirmation of life. It might be called save-the-innocents. Christie said that one of the most rewarding forms of detective fiction is that which "has a kind of passion behind it—that passion being to help save innocence. Because it is *innocence* that matters, not *guilt*." She went on to say that the only reason for removing the "plague-stricken" person of evil is that "the *innocent* must be protected."[2] (Thus, she provides a justification—inadequate to some—for the taking of the lives of murderers: it is not retribution so much as prevention of further harm to the innocent.) The innocents who require protection are not just those who may be physically endangered. Again and again, Christie makes the point that the innocent who are placed under suspicion because of murder suffer. The suffering takes two forms: the innocent person cannot trust those around him, in Christie's fiction usually his family and friends, and he himself is suspected by the other innocents involved. Such an unstable situation demands a resolution; the truth must be known and the guilty one revealed, so that the innocents can be freed from this double burden of fear and mistrust. In *The ABC Murders,* Poirot says, "There is nothing so terrible as to live in an atmosphere of suspicion—to see eyes watching you and the love in them changing to fear—nothing so terrible as to suspect those near and dear to you.... It is poisonous—a miasma" (122). Similar statements appear in "Sing a Song of Sixpence" and *Hercule Poirot's Christmas,* and the theme of save-the-innocents is the sole basis of "The Four Suspects," "The Coming of Mr. Quin," and *Ordeal by Innocence.* The latter is the most extended treatment of the theme. Arthur Calgary returns to England to find that he could have saved a man now dead from prison for a murder he did not commit: the murder of his mother. Calgary believes it his duty to inform the man's family; however, when he does, the family is not happy with his information, for its members must undergo suspicion a second time. He comes to realize that his attempt to see justice done has not only not convicted the guilty, but that "it has not delivered the innocent from the shadow of guilt" (36). (Almost the same phrase is used in *Hercule Poirot's Christmas* to explain what will happen if the murderer is not uncovered: "The shadow will remain on all alike..." [189].) *Ordeal by Innocence* is Christie's best example of the mental and emotional torment of a family not knowing *who* among them is guilty, but the same theme appears implicitly in nearly all of her fiction. The detective's task is to answer the question of *who,* and the necessity of answering it is to save the innocent from that shadow of guilt. In an essay comparing *Endless Night* to Henry James's *Wings of the Dove,* Abigail Ann Hamblen says that in that novel Christie "seems to be saying what James is saying—that life and love built on victimized innocence cannot endure."[3] It is not extravagant to extend that statement about *Endless Night* to make it serve as the principal underlying theme of all of Christie's fiction: innocence must be saved if life is to go on.

At the time of Christie's death, the leading Communist newspaper in Hong Kong attacked her for having "described crimes committed by the middle and lower classes of British Society without ever exposing their social causes," that failure, therefore, making her a "running dog for the rich and powerful."[4] Others less politically oriented have also criticized her for a lack of social awareness, characterizing her as a champion of the *status quo*. It is more accurate to say that she is a champion of traditional values. Though she strived to be "up-to-date," as in *Funerals Are Fatal* where there is no condemnation of a sympathetic character's illegitimate child, she continued to hold Edwardian, if not Victorian, attitudes toward moral and social values. Never as snobbish in her writing as Dorothy Sayers or Georgette Heyer, she, nevertheless, held the upper middle class social attitude of *noblesse oblige*, with both its inherent idealism and patronization. This attitude grew—as is true of most people—as she aged. Writing her last novel, *Postern of Fate*, in her eighties, she gave to Colonel Pikeaway, one of her recurring characters, words which she obviously believed: "You don't want equality in the world, you want the strong to help the weak. You want the rich to finance the poor. You want the honest and the good to be looked up to and admired" (194-95). The idealism is there, but so are the class divisions. As social values changed during her lifetime, so did moral values. The decline in what some see as moral rigidity and others as a sense of sin had very little effect on Christie. Essentially, she never abandoned those concepts of right and wrong which she had been taught as a child. As a consequence, two thematic currents run continually through her later novels: a fear of and for the modern world, with an expected concurrent nostalgia for an earlier, simpler, and "more moral" society, and a related—and often unfortunately strident—distrust of modern youth.

Just as she was horrified by the violence in post-World War II crime fiction, the increase in actual violence, as well as changing moral standards, filled Christie with dread as to the world's direction. Her late unhappy world view is most clearly present in *Third Girl, Postern of Fate*, and especially *Passenger to Frankfurt*, but there are many other statements in the late novels, as well as *An Autobiography*, to indicate her concern. She is particularly distrustful of those who claim they have a map to utopia; to her, their real purpose is the acquisition òf power. The concept of a criminal mastermind attempting to control the world through others has long been a cliche of sensational fiction, but the example of Hitler and the disruptions by terrorism in the sixties give it a meaning for Christie in *Passenger to Frankfurt* quite different from the burlesques of *The Secret Adversary* and *The Big Four* in the twenties. She calls *Passenger to Frankfurt* an "extravaganza," but she ends the "Introduction" to the novel with

> But most of the things that happen in it are beginning or giving promise of happening in the world today.
> It is not an impossible story—it is only a fantastic one (xiii).

Rather than a burlesque, the novel is her commentary on what she considers insanities present in modern life. Her anti-utopianism is based upon her belief that people do not change; Mary Ann, the heroine spy of *Passenger to Frankfurt,* says, "You can create a third world now, or so everyone thinks, but the third world will have the same people in it as the first world or the second world or whatever names you like to call things. And when you have the same human beings running things, they'll run them the same way" (153). Rather than faith in some suspect utopia to come, Christie's general optimism that the good in the world as it is—or at least has been—can still defeat the forces that wish to destroy it is at the center of her "political philosophy." This conservative stance is nowhere stated more positively than in a scene of *So Many Steps to Death.* There, after listening to a group of political dreamers and schemers, Hilary Craven thinks,

> Why do you decry the world we live in? There are good people in it. Isn't muddle a better breeding ground for kindliness and individuality than a world order that's imposed, a world order that may be right today and wrong tomorrow? I would rather have a world of kindly, faulty, human beings, than a world of superior robots who've said goodbye to pity and understanding and sympathy (77).

As many comments in her autobiography show, Christie is undoubtedly presenting her own view through her heroine.

A major cause of her late fears was her unease about youth. Her own increasing age obviously contributed to the feeling, but the swinging 'sixties brought permissiveness, rebelliousness, terrorism, and increased juvenile crime: trends which could only intensify her sense of alienation—as they did for many others—from a generation so different from her own. However, the first novels expressing her fears of youth appear in the 'fifties. In *They Do It With Mirrors,* Miss Marple attacks what she considers over-concern for rehabilitating juvenile delinquents and presents her ideal of the young: "the young people with a good heredity, and brought up wisely in a good home. . . well, they are really, when one comes down to it—the sort of people a country *needs*" (120), and she is supported by other sympathetic characters. Also from the 'fifties are *They Came to Baghdad* and *So Many Steps to Death,* both of which present a mastermind attempting to use the young to gain world domination. The disapproval of the life style of the young and the fear of its being manipulated by unscrupulous elders continue, together and separately, in *The Pale Horse, Hallowe'en Party, By the Pricking of My Thumbs,* and again *Third Girl, Passenger to Frankfurt,* and *Postern of Fate.* The demagogic speech on the glories of youth by The Director of the evilly planned scientific complex in *So Many Steps to Death,* the attacks on youth culture in *The Pale Horse* and *Third Girl,* and Superintendent Spence's long speech on the permissive morals of the young in *Hallowe'en Party* are just three instances of the forms Christie's disapproval takes. *Passenger to Frankfurt* is the most direct example of the manipulation of youth. In that novel a strategy conference of the "good guys," all but one at least middle-aged, takes place, and the following pronouncement is delivered:

> What is being promoted, you must understand, is the growing organization of youth everywhere against their mode of government; against their parental customs, against very often the religions in which they have been brought up. There is the insidious cult of permissiveness, there is the increasing cult of violence. Violence not as a means of gaining money, but violence for the love of violence (111).

Later, the proliferation in the use of drugs by the young is explained as a deliberate technique "to finish off the weaklings" (176). Though the young are given their licks for their life style and for being dupes, the emphasis in *Passenger to Frankfurt* is upon those who are older and manipulate them for their own ends. Christie includes not only the power-hungry fictional villains, but also those whom she considers to be the shapers of the minds of today's youth. The "preachings and tenets by the modern prophets of the world," among whom she names Marcuse, Guevara, Levi-Strauss, and Fanon (184), are, for Christie, as much to blame for the unbelief, immorality, and violence of the young as the machinations of any diabolical villain. Both permissiveness and ideology are present, and she considers the second worse: unrestrained youth is bad enough, but the mobilization of youth for some "unholy" cause is more dangerous for the survival of civilization. Youth requires direction, but that direction must be aimed at the preservation of what is good in society, not in the destruction of "everything" to create a hopeful new earth that if no different from the present can only be worse. For Christie, a harmonious society is not to be gained by imposed utopias, but by good will and reason.

As repeatedly noted, the detective's explanation in Christie's novels, as in those of her Golden Age colleagues, reveals the truth, exposes the guilty, and absolves the innocent. At the end the nightmare is over, fear is dispelled, and life begins anew. In the last lines of *Easy to Kill,* Luke Fitzwilliam expresses the general theme of Christie's conclusions when he says to Bridget Conway, "We've been close to death for a long time. Now that's over! Now we'll begin to live" (174). As in traditional comedy, various symbols of celebration and renewal mark the end of confusion and trouble. There are celebratory dinners in *The Secret Adversary, Appointment with Death,* and *Postern of Fate,* announcements of coming births in *Partners in Crime* and *Murder at the Vicarage,* and impending marriages of young lovers in more than a dozen novels. The conclusion of *A Murder Is Announced* has more of such symbols of new life than any other Christie novel. First, two young women, twin sisters, marry the young men of their choice, as well as sharing an inheritance of millions. Second, the novel begins and ends with the newspapers read in the village of Chipping Cleghorn. Since the murder is "announced" in the *North Benham News and the Chipping Cleghorn Gazette,* at the end we see one of the young couples refusing to take it, while ordering six other papers at the stationer's. They are putting the murder behind them. Then Christie plays ironically with the symbol by giving the stationer's wife the last word after the couple leave: "Of course they want the *Gazette!* Everybody has the *Gazette.* How else would they know what's going on around here?" (288). Third, the vicar has to prepare a sermon. When he refuses the text "Thou Shall Do No Murder," his wife suggests not quite accurately "a much nicer text, a happy text" from The Song of Solomon: "For lo the Spring is here and the Voice of the Turtle is heard in the Land" (285). Two weddings, an inheritance, rejection of reminders of murder, and a joyous Biblical text—all of these are used to express the theme of optimism, of new life, and of the end of the shadow of death and suspicion. The same theme is expressed more simply in the last words of *Death on the Nile:* "it is not the past that matters but the future" (318), but that statement summarizes it: the episode of murder is past; life can go on.

This brief discussion of Christie's themes does not attempt to be exhaustive; rather, it presents a few of her obvious concerns which appear prominently in her fiction. Nor does it try to be esoteric in method. I leave to others the task of examining her works by structuralism, semiotics, phenomenology, or any of the other fashionable critical schools, and I wish them luck. They will need it, for theme is not as important in detective fiction as plot or the three central characters, and it can be conservative, simplistic, or even trivial. However, its overall moral that evil can be detected and defeated by human reason is not trivial, but a concept that cannot be repeated too often. Such other Christie themes as the necessity of protecting the innocent and the affirmation of life, as well as her fiction's inherent optimism—in spite of those late fears—give that fiction a humane quality. They are another justification for describing her art of murder as *gentle*.

# Chapter VII

## The Achievement of Agatha Christie

*I had formed a habit of writing stories by this time. It took the place, shall we say, of embroidering cushion covers or pictures taken from Dresden china flower-painting.*

**Agatha Christie**

*...she domesticated murder, made an etiquette out of it, which isn't quite the same thing as making a banality out of it, a 20th-century specialty.*

**John Leonard**

*...the champion deceiver of our time.*

**Julian Symons**

Agatha Christie received twenty-five pounds for *The Mysterious Affair at Styles,* a tiny sum for the writer who was to become the subject of an oft-repeated cliche: she made more money by crime than any woman since Lucrezia Borgia. The popularity of her 184 works of mystery and detective fiction, as well as 13 mystery plays (the night she died, *The Mousetrap* had its 9,612th performance) and 5 other plays and 20 films based upon her works, made her rich and famous. Some of the facts of that popularity are staggering. By the time of her death, she was, according to a UNESCO report, the most widely read British author of all time, translated into 103 languages—14 more than William.Shakespeare. Her total readership was estimated then at 2,000,000,000 and her total earnings at $20,000,000, which is probably too low (her will left an estate of less than $250,000—another mystery). Her agent Edmund Cork stated in 1975: "Her sales go up every year. A million and a half paperbacks a year in Britain alone. She is unquestionably the bestselling author of all time. Every estimate of her sales I have seen is a gross under-estimate."[1] The following year at her death, *Curtain* was on the bestseller list in England, the United States, and Japan, and a few months later the American paperback rights to *Sleeping Murder* were bought for $1,000,000.

Other facts less financial are just as telling: a musical version of *And Then There Were None* called *Something's Afoot,* Christie's statue in Madame Tussaud's Wax Museum, the veneration of a paperback cover of *Evil Under the Sun* by New Guinea cultists, and the adoption of the little grey cells as a totem by a West African tribe. The result of a 1972 poll of critics and editors, writers, and readers of detective/mystery fiction by *Ellery Queen's Mystery Magazine* to select the twelve most famous detectives for a set of Nicaraguan stamps was Poirot second—surpassed by only Sherlock Holmes— and Jane Marple thirteenth (she was seventh among readers); Christie was the only author to have two detectives on the lists. [2] Her fans have ranged from the anonymous millions—including a Persian writing to her of her "nobility" and an African wishing to be adopted—to Tupamaro guerillas in Argentina and their captive, a British ambassador, on to such notables as T.S. Eliot, John Updike, Ayn Rand, Charles deGaulle, Helmut Schmidt, Queen Mary, and Queen Elizabeth II, as well as most of her fellow mystery writers. She received the first Grand Masters Award of the Mystery Writers of America in 1954 and was elected president of The Detection Club in England, succeeding Dorothy Sayers, in 1957. She had already become a Fellow of the Royal Society of Literature in 1950 and later received an Honorary Doctorate of Letters from Exeter University in 1961. Having been named Commander of the Order of the British Empire by the Queen in 1956, she was raised to Dame Commander in 1971.

Such wealth, fame, and honors could give many people the egotism of Poirot, but not his creator. Though her preeminent position in her field was established by the end of the thirties, when John Strachey could already call her "an old master" and "the most prolific and efficient professional of them all," [3] she remained unusually modest about her work. She called herself a "tradesman" and a "sausage machine," repeatedly said "I am a lowbrow," and claimed that her high mark of fame was having one of her characters in a London *Times* crossword puzzle. Such remarks were not totally serious, but they show that she never allowed herself to become overly impressed by the nature of her fiction or her abilities as a writer. Near the end of her life, the Earl of Snowdon asked her what she hoped to be remembered for; her answer was simple: "Well, I would like it to be said that I was a good writer of detective and thriller stories" [4]—hardly an unreasonable request from the woman known around the world as the Queen of Crime and Mistress of Mystery.

Setting aside financial success and fame, we are left with two questions: what is her achievement in the works themselves? and what are the reasons for their popularity? The second question is ultimately unanswerable. However, in the answer to the first may be found at least a partial explanation for that enormous popularity, and that answer consists of eight principal points.

*Christie accepts the formulas and conventions of her genre and yet is able to find seemingly numberless variations within and for them.* Her genius—the first time that word has been used—for taking the mystification-detection formula as developed from Poe to Conan Doyle and using it in so many works in so many ways, while finding methods of concealing repetitions and reversals of the same patterns, techniques, and devices, is remarkable. The many comments in the works themselves on the nature, requirements, and expectations of classic detective fiction are evidence of her thorough knowledge of her genre, a genre to which she remained loyal to her death. She knew its limits, but, even more important, she was able to find enormous variety within those limits. She also added new conventions to the genre, two obvious instances being the narrator as murderer, which *The Murder of Roger Ackroyd* made famous, and the husband-and-wife detective team, for which Tuppence and Tommy Beresford are the prototype. Her emphasis on verbal and behavioral, rather than physical, clues and misdirection is a significant change from earlier detective fiction. It shifts the solution from objects to the characters, thus making the process of discovery less puzzle and more fiction. Christie's achievement is in great part her ability to use an essentially rigid form and, while staying within it, still create a large, distinctive, and varied body of work.

*Christie is a superb storyteller.* To some, such a statement may seem facile, but it must be made. Though by their nature her stories are quite complex in structure, she may confound but she very rarely confuses. Her skill in plot construction rests in her balancing of mystification and detection, in covering any anomalies and loose ends, and in not allowing other elements to detract excessively from the central process of discovery. She fulfills readers' expectations of what her fiction will be, by staying within the boundaries of her genre, while surprising them with new twists and turns of plot and characterization. This duality of predictability and variation has always been a characteristic of great—and popular—tellers of tales, and Christie has it. She is the Dickens of detective fiction.

*Christie demands no specialized knowledge of her readers but, at the same time, makes them want to join a process of discovery of the truth.* The few reader requirements play a major role in her popularity. Esoteric and technical matters are kept to a minimum, a probable reason for Christie's insistence that she wrote only about "simple murders." Also, there are no stylistic obstacles; her ingenuous style makes for easy reading. Since her aim is to tell a story which is filled with misdirection for the reader, she puts nothing else in his way. That misdirection is, on the other hand, the principal element of her fiction's "intellectual" nature as a process of discovery. The necessity of reason to accomplish that discovery—even when it is not actually used—is emphasized continuously. *Reason, discovery,* and *truth* are the keynote words of Christie's fiction. Her ability to create within the reader a desire for truth and a willingness to test his reason against hers is unparalleled. She is able to satisfy an innate psychological need of human beings: the need to know, while deliberately hindering that need through misdirection. Her success is enhanced by the reader's awareness that she always *plays fair;* the phrase itself is significant: her works are not so much puzzles as games. They are intellectual games between author and reader, fictional games in which truth is discovered by reason.

*Christie has created two extraordinarily memorable characters: Hercule Poirot and Jane Marple.* The eccentric little Belgian and the late Victorian spinster are known to millions. Poirot especially has taken on supra-fictional status. In spite of their personal differences, reader response to both is the same: admiration for their detectival skills, their sense of justice, and their protection of the innocent; and amusement at their idiosyncrasies and minor frailties. Filmed, quoted, parodied, imitated and alluded to in all sorts of circumstances, they are known to people who have never read a Christie work—though the number of those cannot be large. They are members of a very small company of fictional detectives—led by Sherlock Holmes and including Lord Peter Wimsey, Charlie Chan, Ellery Queen, and Perry Mason—who have transcended the works in which they originally appeared and become a part of twentieth-century popular culture, and they are not least in that company. It is no small accomplishment for a writer to create one internationally famous character, who "lives" for readers outside his works; Christie's creation of two such characters in Poirot and Miss Marple is, indeed, an achievement.

*Christie provides a social history of England from World War I to the 1970s.* From an upper middleclass viewpoint, she records the changes of those years and their meaning for her class, not on any large political or economic level, but in the day-to-day existence of her characters. This social history is limited by its class view, but since the values of that class have dominated English life for much of the century, it is not a distorted record. Her basic conservatism is another plus as social historian. As her views do not fundamentally change, she does not fluctuate with current faddish ideas. She has nostalgia for the past, as everyone does, but she is also amused by her own nostalgia, and she realizes that change, however unpleasant, is a fact of life and inevitable. Changes are perhaps less noticeable because of the unchanging nature of her detectives; however, her use of series detectives and other recurrent characters over such a long period of time gives a sense of continuity to the changes, permitting a reader to follow those changes through those characters' lives. Someday a historian or sociologist will examine Christie's fiction as a record of English life in the first half of the twentieth century. Though that social record has little, if any, relation to her popularity during the period it covers, it is another achievement.

*While being thoroughly English, Christie's fiction has great appeal across national lines.* A principal reason is that very lack of description for which she has occasionally been criticized. It gives the reader freedom to fill in details as he wishes. A reader in Germany may see her characters and settings differently from a reader in India, but both can fit them into their own concepts of England, even when those concepts may be totally erroneous. If sometimes bewildered by the social norms, a non-English reader has no difficulty in identifying the social norms present. He can also see reflections of his own friends and acquaintances—and perhaps himself—in the typical, or stereotypical, behavior of her characters, particularly when they are involved in an event as universally distressing as murder. By not attempting to probe too deeply into her characters, Christie provides the opportunity to her readers of "completing" them. That freedom to complete as one's imagination can is a principal source of her worldwide popularity. (One can only wonder as to how many native peoples of Nigeria, Kenya, Burma, Malaya and other former possessions of the British empire first imagined England and its daily life to be as pictured in a Christie novel.) Christie's popularity around the world is another achievement, one which other writers, whatever their genre, can hardly help but envy.

*Christie's works are essentially optimistic.* Though that characteristic in itself is not necessarily an achievement, it qualifies as such in that the optimistic nature of her fiction is a contributing factor in its popularity. Even her late novels which express fears for society are resolved by the defeat of evil and the restoration of harmony. Her lack of violent action, her belief that human beings can solve their problems, and her strict morality are comforting to readers. Though she does not deal with the ultimate mysteries of life and death, her fiction affirms life. Murder is an act against man and God, and whoever commits it must be removed from society. The specifying of guilt enables the society to return to normal pursuits. A reader finishing a Christie work has the satisfaction of knowing that the guilty have been exposed for what they are and that the innocent are saved. Human existence is not always so neatly arranged, so "cosy" if one prefers, but as she said, her works are meant to be morality tales. As such, they make clear distinctions between good and evil, and the final resolution for good is inevitable, no matter what the difficulty in reaching it. Her fiction's optimistic view that mankind's reason and goodwill will always triumph is not only moral but cheering, and it has certainly had appeal to readers.

That basic optimism is a factor in the last point: *Christie's art is gentle.* When she combines all of the elements of her genre to create a novel or short story, she also adds her own special quality of gentleness. Along with the optimism, her sense of humor, mild but pervasive, contributes to this quality, lightening the gloom of murder and suspicion. Her refusal to indulge in violence for violence's sake is another factor, as is her serene detachment from the unpleasantness her characters experience. Evil is present in her fiction, but it is hidden beneath the surface. It is there to be discovered and eliminated, and it always is. Her detectives see to that, while she gently guides readers through her fictional mazes. She lays traps and false paths for those readers, but they are harmless. She never hurts, and the readers never worry, for though her subject is murder, her art is gentle.

# Notes

## Chapter I

[1] Quoted in Elliot L. Gilbert, ed., *The World of Mystery Fiction*, Del Mar, CA, 1978, p.xxii; [as S.S. Van Dine], "Twenty Rules for Writing Detective Stories," *The Art of the Mystery Story*, ed. Howard Haycraft, New York, 1975 (rpt.), p.189, and "The Great Detective Stories," *The Art of the Mystery Story*, p. 35.

[2] *The Detective Story in Britain*, London, 1962, p.8; "Introduction," *The Omnibus of Crime*, New York, 1929, p.31.

[3] "Murder and Karl Marx," *The Nation*, 25 March 1936, p.382; "An Etiquette of Murder," *New York Times*, 13 January 1976, p.40.

[4] "The Algebra of Agatha Christie," *The Sunday Times*, 27 February 1966, p.25. Mathematics fascinated Christie all of her life; her husband has written that "she had a natural mathematical brain" and that "this capacity appears in her books and in the neat solution of the most complex tangles, an ability in analysis as well as synthesis" (Max Mallowan, *Mallowan's Memoirs*, London, 1977, p.196).

[5] "The Mystery Versus the Novel," *The Mystery Story*, ed. John Ball, Del Mar, CA, 1976, p.70; "Emma Lathen: Murder and Sophistication," *The New Republic*, 31 July 1976, p.25.

[6] "The Moment of Violence," *Crime in Good Company*, ed. Michael Gilbert, London, 1959, pp.108-09.

[7] "The Christie Nobody Knows," *Agatha Christie: First Lady of Crime*, ed. H.R.F. Keating, New York, 1977, p.127.

[8] Quoted in Arlette Baudet, "Simenon Hates Fiction But Loves the Muppets," *Macon Telegraph & News*, 26 March 1978, p.3E.

[9] "Casual Notes on the Mystery Novel," *Writing Detective and Mystery Fiction*, rev. ed., ed. A.S. Burack, Boston, 1967, p.84.

[10] For Van Dine's rules, see footnote 1; the five which Christie does not break are 1, 5 (debatable), 6, 14, and 15. Knox's list is in *The Art of the Mystery Story*, pp.194-196; of these Christie does not break I, III, and IV.

[11] *The Art of the Mystery Story*, p.188.

[12] "The Grandest Game in the World," *The Mystery Writer's Art*, ed. Francis M. Nevins, Bowling Green, 1970, pp.243-245.

[13] *Mystery Fiction: Theory and Technique*, New York, 1943, p.99.

[14] *Mortal Consequences: A History from the Detective Story to the Crime Novel*, New York, 1972, p.17.

[15] Robert Champigny, *What Will Have Happened*, Bloomington, 1977, p.18. Champigny also says, "The mystery in a mystery story is a narrative secret, not a conceptual mystery; it is physical, not transcendental" (13).

[16] *Adventure, Mystery, and Romance*, Chicago & London, 1976, p.99.

[17] *Mortal Consequences*, p.104.

[18] Quoted in Nigel Dennis, "Genteel Queen of Crime," *Life*, 14 May 1956, p. 101; Quoted in "Agatha Christie Dies at 85," Atlanta *Constitution*, 13 January 1976, p.12. Max Mallowan has written, "Agatha never gloats over [murder], or describes it beyond the necessary minimum detail—there are no obscenities" *(Mallowan's Memoirs*, p.222).

[19] *Masters of Mystery*, Norwood, PA, 1976, (rpt.), p.21.

[20] "Death as a Game," *Ellery Queen's Mystery Magazine*, November 1965, pp.50-51 & 53.

[21] *Blood in Their Ink*, London, 1953, p.45.

[22] *Adventure, Mystery, and Romance*, p.19. The same idea is expressed by George N. Dove: "the special ability of the detective story to create its own illusion of reality" ("The Criticism of Detective Fiction," *The Popular Culture Scholar*, 1 [Winter 1977], 5).

[23] *The Puritan Pleasures of the Detective Story*, London, 1972, p.51. Routley is writing specifically of Conan Doyle, but the concept has wider application. Two almost identical statements are "It is the element of fantasy in detective fiction—or rather, the juxtaposition of fantasy with reality—that gives the genre its identity" (Nicholas Blake, "The Detective Story— Why?," *The Art of the Mystery Story*, p.402), and "Modern escape fiction is romantic fiction

modified by the general fictional tendency to realism" (Rodell, p.109).

[24]Barzun and Wendell Hertig Taylor, *A Catalogue of Crime*, New York, 1971, pp.7-8.

[25]"The Nonbeliever's Comeuppance," *Murder Ink: The Mystery Reader's Companion*, ed. Dilys Winn, New York, 1977, p.18.

[26]Jeanne F. Bedell, "A Pair of Box Sets: Class-Oriented Attitudes and Values in English Popular Drama and Detective Fiction, 1880-1939," paper presented before the Popular Culture Association, Cincinnati, April 1978, p.13. Copy provided by the author.

[27]Grella's essay is included in *Dimensions of Detective Fiction*, ed. Larry N. Landrum et al., Bowling Green, 1976, pp.37-57. The quotation is from p.41.

[28]*Adventure, Mystery, and Romance*, p.108.

[29]"The Art of the Detective Story," *The Art of the Mystery Story*, p.14.

[30]*Mystery Fiction: Theory and Technique*, p.28. Subsequent quotations will be cited in the text by page number.

[31]"Detective Fiction: A Modern Myth of Violence?," *Hudson Review* 18 (1965), 12. Subsequent quotations will be cited in the text by page number.

[32]Auden's essay has often been reprinted. The easily available text used here is in *Detective Fiction: Crime and Compromise*, ed. Dick Allen and David Chacko, New York, 1974, pp.400-410. Quotations will be cited in the text by page number.

[33]*English*, 1 (1936), pp.23-25. Quotations will be cited in the text by page number.

[34]*Adventure, Mystery, and Romance*, p.1. Subsequent quotations will be cited in the text by page number.

[35]*An Autobiography*, New York, 1977, p.329.

[36]*An Autobiography*, p.329.

[37]*An Autobiography*, p.398.

[38]Elizabeth Walter, "The Case of the Escalating Sales," *Agatha Christie: First Lady of Crime*, p.21.

[39]"Five Writers in One: The Versatility of Agatha Christie," *The Times Literary Supplement*, 25 February 1955, p.x. As all quotations are from the same page, no further citations will be given.

[40]*An Autobiography*, p.398.

# Chapter II

[1]*An Autobiography*, p.323.

[2]Jacques Barzun and Wendell Hertig Taylor, *A Book of Prefaces*, New York, 1976, p.67. See also their *A Catalogue of Crime*, p.18.

[3]Hugh Douglas, "Commuting: An Unscheduled Stop at an Isolated Junction," *Murder Ink*, pp.483-484. Christie enthusiastically expressed her love of trains in *Come, Tell Me How You Live*, New York, 1946, pp.21-25. Her favorite was, naturally, the Orient Express: "it has become an old familiar friend, but the thrill [of travelling by it] has never quite died down" (21).

[4]"Cornwallis's Revenge," *Agatha Christie: First Lady of Crime*, p.91.

[5]*Mallowan's Memoirs*, pp.222 & 206-207.

[6]*Snobbery with Violence*, London, 1971, p.171.

[7]Quoted in Francis Wyndham, "The Algebra of Agatha Christie," p.25.

[8]Quoted in "Dame Agatha: Queen of the Maze," *Time*, 26 January 1976, p.75.

[9]George Grella finds that the social forms of the society provide "the observable clues to human behavior by which the detective hero can identify the culprit" ("Murder and Manners: The Formal Detective Novel," p.47). Auden's view is similar: "The detective story writer is also wise to choose a society with an elaborate ritual and to describe this in detail.... The murderer uses his knowledge of the ritual to commit the crime and can be caught only by someone who acquires an equal or superior familiarity with it" ("The Guilty Vicarage," p.403).

[10]" 'Grannie' Read Him Her Crime Stories," Atlanta *Constitution*, 11 November 1977, p.20-A.

[11]Elizabeth Walter, "The Case of the Escalating Sales," *Agatha Christie: First Lady of Crime*, p.24.

[12]"Cornwallis's Revenge," *Agatha Christie: First Lady of Crime*, p.88.

[13]Quoted in Francis Wyndham, "The Algebra of Agatha Christie," p.25.

[14]After quoting a passage from *Cards on the Table*, in which one character describes another

as "that damned Dago," Colin Watson comments, "The passage shows Mrs. Christie's awareness of how widespread in the England of 1936 was xenophobia, her own disapproval of which she implied in the phrase 'with a singular lack of originality'. But it would have taken someone with a little more subtlety than that of the average reader to notice that hers was not just another routine sneer at the foreigner" (*Snobbery with Violence*, pp.174-175). At the same time, Christie can include such unpleasant little bits as "Mary Grey was being firm with a stout Jewess who was enamoured of a skintight powder-blue evening dress" (Finger, 208) or "He had a distinctly Jewish cast of countenance.... His manner was affected to the last degree (Edgware, 133).

# Chapter III

[1] "Introduction," *The Omnibus of Crime*, p.33.

[2] "Detection and the Literary Art," *The Mystery Writer's Art*, p.260.

[3] Cawelti, *Adventure, Mystery, and Romance*, p.118.

[4] W.H. Wright, "The Great Detective Stories," *The Art of the Mystery Story*, p.40.

[5] *Bloodhounds of Heaven*, Cambridge and London, 1976, p.21. Ousby's study of the detective in English fiction through Conan Doyle is highly recommended for the pre-history of Christie's genre.

[6] Aaron Marc Stein says that "the detective represents an abstraction, namely scientific method" ("The Mystery Story in Cultural Perspective," *The Mystery Story*, p.54). D.F. Rauber's similar comment is that "the 'great detective' can be seen as a vulgarization of the scientist.... Indeed, at bottom the 'great detective' is a fantasy figure of the perfectly functioning mind, pure intellect proceeding inexorably onward, indifferent to, or rather oblivious of, emotional considerations. But on a larger cultural scale this is also the ideal of the scientist" ("Sherlock Holmes and Nero Wolfe: The Role of the 'Great Detective' in Intellectual History," *Dimensions of Detective Fiction*, p.89).

[7] Brigid Brophy, "Detective Fiction: A Modern Myth of Violence?," p.25.

[8] "The Guilty Vicarage," p.406.

[9] *An Autobiography*, p.244.

[10] Quoted in Celia Fremlin, "The Christie Everybody Knew," *Agatha Christie: First Lady of Crime*, pp. 115-116. In *An Autobiography* Christie says, "Hercule Poirot, my Belgian invention, was hanging round my neck, firmly attached there like the old man of the sea" (263).

[11] Quoted in Francis Wyndham, "The Algebra of Agatha Christie," p.26. She also felt that *Murder After Hours* was ruined by inclusion of Poirot, and she omitted him from the dramatic version; see *An Autobiography*, p.458.

[12] "The Mistress of Simplicity," *Agatha Christie: First Lady of Crime*, p.43, and "Introduction," ibid., p.8.

[13] Robin G. Collingwood, "Who Killed John Doe? The Problem of Testimony," *The Historian as Detective: Essays on Evidence*, ed. Robin W. Winks, New York, 1968, p.59.

[14] *An Autobiography*, pp.420-421.

[15] Quoted in G.C. Ramsey, *Agatha Christie: Mistress of Mystery*, New York, 1967, p.57.

[16] Mary Jane Jones, "The Spinster Detective," *Journal of Communication*, 25 (Spring, 1975), 108.

[17] "The Autonomy of History: R.G. Collingwood and Agatha Christie," *Clio*, 7 (Summer 1978), 260.

[18] "Murder She Says," *The New Republic*, 26 July 1975, p.27.

[19] *An Autobiography*, p.266.

[20] *An Autobiography*, p.420.

[21] Max Mallowan's defense of *Postern of Fate* is actually an attack: "The chronology of this book was imperfectly worked out, but one of the delights of Agatha's works is that occasionally and rarely the sharp know-all, incapable of writing an imaginative work himself, is able to detect a flaw" (*Mallowan's Memoirs*, p.211).

[22] Quoted in Ramsey, p.94.

[23] *An Autobiography*, pp.419-420.

[24] Derrick Murdoch, *The Agatha Christie Mystery*, Toronto, 1976, p.91.

[25]Celia Fremlin gives the details of an actual series of murders eleven years after *The Pale Horse* using the same poison and of Christie's being upset by the similarity ("The Christie Everybody Knew," *Agatha Christie: First Lady of Crime*, p.120). Christie must have been cheered by the letter she received in 1975, in which a woman told her of reading *The Pale Horse* and realizing that another woman's husband was being poisoned with thallium by his wife *(Mallowan's Memoirs,* p.207). Also, in 1977 an English nurse read the novel and recognized the symptoms of thallium poisoning in a child near death, thus leading to the child's life being saved ("Poisoning: Nurse Reads Mystery and Saves Child," Atlanta *Constitution,* 24 June 1977, p.2-A).

[27]This discussion of the unsympathetic elderly victim is indebted to George Grella, "Murder and Manners: The Formal Detective Novel," pp.49-50.

[28]Quoted in Francis Wyndham, "The Algebra of Agatha Christie," p.26. For Christie's long statement on her attitude toward actual crime and criminals, see *An Autobiography*, pp.424-427.

[29]Emma Lathen has commented thusly on the murderous duos: "This Christie penchant for exhaustive combinations and permutations really blossoms whenever two people conspire to commit a crime. Outlandish yokings of every description abound" ("Corwallis's Revenge," *Agatha Christie: First Lady of Crime,* p.87).

[30]For an excellent feminist analysis of the motives of Christie's women murderers, see Agate Nesaule Krouse and Margot Peters, "Why Women Kill," *Journal of Communication,* 25 (Spring 1975), 98-104.

[31]Bedell, pp.2-3.

[32]*Mallowan's Memoirs,* pp.208-209.

[33]*Murder Must Appetize,* London, 1975, p.42.

[34]"The Decline and Fall of the Detective Story," *The Vagrant Mood* (rpt.), Port Washington, NY, 1969, p.107. While accepting the convention, Christie agreed with Maugham: "I myself always found the love interest a terrible bore in detective stories. Love, I felt, belonged in romantic stories. To force a love motif into what should be a scientific process went much against the grain. However, at that period detective stories always had to have a love interest—so there it was" *(An Autobiography,* p.246).

[35]*Murder on the Menu,* New York, 1972, p.xiii.

# Chapter IV

[1]"Casual Notes on the Mystery Novel," p. 86.

[2]Quoted in Francis Wyndham, "The Algebra of Agatha Christie," p.26.

[3]Two recent critics agree with me that the limitations of the short story prevent it from being as effective a form for classic detective fiction as the novel: LeRoy Panek, *Watteau's Shepherds: The Detective Novel in Britain 1914-1940,* Bowling Green, 1979, p.33, and David I. Grossvogel, *Mystery & Its Fictions: From Oedipus to Agatha Christie,* Baltimore, 1979, p.95n. ·

[4]"The Grandest Game in the World," *The Mystery Writer's Art,* p.231. My discussion of clues and misdirection is indebted to Marie F. Rodell, "Clues," *The Art of the Mystery Story,* pp.264-72.

[5]"The Mistress of Complication," *Agatha Christie: First Lady of Crime,* pp.33-34.

[6]Quoted in Peter J. Shaw, "Agatha Christie: Top Crime Writer to be 80 Tomorrow," Charleston (SC) *Evening Post,* 14 September 1970, p.3-B.

[7]*Adventure, Mystery, and Romance,* p.114.

# Chapter V

[1]Quoted in Nigel Dennis, "Genteel Queen of Crime," p.88. Another similar statement is "I avoid violence whenever possible...I should not like to read it. It's like being forced to go into a hospital and watch an operation" (Quoted in Robert G. Deindorfer, "Agatha Christie at 84; Still Getting Away With Murder," *Parade,* 8 December 1974, p.9).

[2]"Shades of Dupin: Fictional Detectives on Detective Fiction," *The Armchair Detective,* 8

(November 1974), 12. See also Jane Gottschalk, "The Games of Detective Fiction," *The Armchair Detective*, 10 (January 1977), 76.

³"Introduction," *The Omnibus of Crime*, pp.28-30.

⁴*An Autobiography*, p.330. One of Christie's staunchest defenders in the controversy over Dr. Sheppard as narrator was Dorothy Sayers. In her Introduction to *The Omnibus of Crime*, she says that the critics are guilty of "resentment at having been ingeniously bamboozled," that "All the necessary data are given," and that "It is, after all, the reader's job to keep his wits about him and, like the perfect detective, to suspect *everybody*" (28). In "Aristotle on Detective Fiction" she says that "moral worth and Watsonity are by no means inseparable...nor, when the Watson in Roger Ackroyd turns out to be the murderer, has the reader any right to feel aggrieved against the author—for she has vouched only for the man's Watsonity and not for his moral worth" (33).

⁵"Why Do People Read Detective Stories?," *Classics & Commercials: A Literary Chronicle of the Forties*, New York, 1962, p.234.

⁶*Studies in Agatha Christie's Writings: The Behaviour of a Good (Great) Deal, A Lot, Lots, Much, Plenty, Many, A Good (Great) Many*, Goteborg: University of Gothenburg, 1967, p.32.

⁷"The Mistress of Simplicity," *Agatha Christie: First Lady of Crime*, p.41.

⁸"The Secret of Agatha Christie," *The Spectator*, 19 September 1970, p.294.

⁹*An Autobiography*, p. 394.

¹⁰Elizabeth Walter, "The Case of the Escalating Sales," *Agatha Christie: First Lady of Crime*, p.20.

¹¹Quoted in Celia Fremlin, "The Christie Everybody Knew," *Agatha Christie: First Lady of Crime*, p.116.

# Chapter VI

¹*The Puritan Pleasures of the Detective Story*, p.226; *An Autobiography*, p.424.

²*An Autobiography*, p.425.

³"The Inheritance of the Meek: Two Novels by Agatha Christie and Henry James," *Discourse*, 12 (Summer 1969), 413.

⁴Celia Fremlin, "The Christie Everybody Knew," *Agatha Christie: First Lady of Crime*, p.119. On the other hand, Pamela Hansford Johnson states that "Agta," as she is called, is so popular in the U.S.S.R. that a serialization of one of her novels can "save a magazine from collapse" *(Important to Me*, New York, 1974, p.224).

# Chapter VII

¹Quoted in Gregory Jensen, "Crime Queen Began on Dare," *Atlanta Journal and Constitution*, 31 August 1975, p.13-C. For the history of Christie's popularity, see Elizabeth Walter, "The Case of the Escalating Sales," *Agatha Christie: First Lady of Crime*, pp.13-24; for Christie's success in the United States, see Emma Lathen, "Cornwallis's Revenge," ibid., pp.79-94. In *The New York Times Book Review*, Ray Walters reported the following statistics for 1977: 1,250,000 copies of *Sleeping Murder*, 2,500,000 copies of *Curtain*, 79 paperback titles of other works in print in the United States, and total sales of 95 million in the United States and 400 million worldwide ("Paperback Talk," 2 October 1977, p.49).

²"The 12 Most Famous Detectives," *Ellery Queen's Mystery Magazine*, February 1973, pp.140-143.

³"The Golden Age of English Detection," *The Saturday Review*, 7 January 1939, p.13.

⁴Lord Snowdon, "The Unsinkable Agatha Christie," *Toronto Star*, 14 December 1974, p.G1.

# Bibliography

## I. The Detective and Mystery Fiction of Agatha Christie

This bibliography is divided into seven sections. Each of the first six presents the works featuring one of Agatha Christie's series detectives; the seventh presents works of mystery or detection not employing a series detective. All sections are arranged chronologically, with, where applicable, novels and short stories listed separately. As there have been so many editions of Christie's works, only the edition of a novel or collection of short stories used for this study is listed, with its original date of publication preceding it. Alternate titles of novels follow the entry in parentheses. Also, since the various groupings of short stories in collections overlap, only the collections and the specific stories from those collections used for the study are listed. Since only works of detective and mystery fiction are examined, Christie's six "Mary Westmacott" novels and her stories of the supernatural are omitted. For further information, one should consult Nancy Blue Wynne, *An Agatha Christie Chronology* (New York: Ace Books, 1976), which is the most nearly complete bibliography.

A.  *Hercule Poirot*
    *Novels*
    1920                The Mysterious Affair at Styles. New York: Bantam Books, 1961.
    1923                The Murder on the Links. New York: Dell Publishing Co., 1964.
    1926                The Murder of Roger Ackroyd. New York: Dodd, Mead & Company, 1967 (Greenway Edition).
    1927                The Big Four. New York: Dell Publishing Co., 1968
    1928                The Mystery of the Blue Train. New York: Dodd, Mead & Company, 1973 (Greenway Edition).
    1932                Peril at End House. New York: Pocket Books, 1959
    1933                Lord Edgware Dies. New York: Dodd, Mead & Company, 1970, (Greenway Edition). (*Thirteen at Dinner*)
    1934                Murder on the Orient Express. New York: Dodd, Mead & Company, 1968 (Greenway Edition). (*Murder in the Calais Coach*)
    1935                The ABC Murders. New York: Dodd, Mead & Company, 1977 (Greenway Edition).
    1935                Death in the Clouds. New York: Dodd, Mead & Company, 1974 (Greenway Edition). (*Death in the Air*)
    1935                Three Act Tragedy. New York: Dodd, Mead & Company, 1973 (Greenway Edition) (*Murder*

|      | *in Three Acts)* |
|------|------------------|
| 1936 | *Murder in Mesopotamia.* New York: Dell Publishing Co., 1961. |
| 1936 | *Cards on the Table.* New York: Dodd, Mead & Company, 1968 (Greenway Edition). |
| 1937 | *Death on the Nile.* New York: Dodd, Mead & Company, 1970 (Greenway Edition). |
| 1937 | *Poirot Loses a Client.* New York: Avon Books, n.d. *(Dumb Witness, Mystery at Littlegreen House, Murder at Littlegreen House)* |
| 1938 | *Appointment with Death.* New York: Dell Publishing Co., 1963. |
| 1938 | *Hercule Poirot's Christmas.* New York: Dodd, Mead & Company, 1974 (Greenway Edition). *(Murder for Christmas, A Holiday for Murder)* |
| 1940 | *Sad Cypress.* New York: Dell Publishing Co., 1963. |
| 1940 | *An Overdose of Death.* New York: Dell Publishing Co., 1967. *(The Patriotic Murders; One, Two, Buckle My Shoe)* |
| 1941 | *Evil Under the Sun.* London: Fontana Books, n.d. |
| 1943 | *Murder in Retrospect.* New York: Dell Publishing Co., 1961. *(Five Little Pigs)* |
| 1946 | *Murder After Hours.* New York: Dell Publishing Co., 1960. *(The Hollow)* |
| 1948 | *There Is a Tide.* New York: Dell Publishing Co., 1961. *(Taken at the Flood)* |
| 1952 | *Mrs. McGinty's Dead.* New York: Pocket Books, 1953. *(Blood Will Tell)* |
| 1953 | *Funerals Are Fatal.* New York: Pocket Books, *(After the Funeral)* |
| 1955 | *Hickory Dickory Death.* New York: Pocket Books, 1956. *(Hickory, Dickory, Dock)* |
| 1956 | *Dead Man's Folly.* New York: Pocket Books, 1961. |
| 1959 | *Cat Among the Pigeons.* New York: Pocket Books, 1961. |
| 1963 | *The Clocks.* London: Fontana Books, 1966. |
| 1966 | *Third Girl.* New York: Dodd, Mead & Company, 1967. |
| 1969 | *Hallowe'en Party.* New York: Dodd, Mead & Company, 1969. |
| 1972 | *Elephants Can Remember.* New York: Dodd, Mead & Company, 1972. |
| 1975 | *Curtain.* New York: Dodd, Mead & Company, 1975. |
| *Short Stories* | |
| 1924 | *Poirot Investigates.* New York: Bantam Books, 1961. |

The Adventure of "The Western Star"
The Tragedy of Marsdon Manor
The Adventure of the Cheap Flat
The Mystery of Hunter's Lodge
A Million Dollar Bond Robbery
The Adventure of the Egyptian Tomb

The Jewel Robbery at the Grand Metropolitan
The Kidnapped Prime Minister
The Disappearance of Mr. Davenheim
The Adventure of the Italian Nobleman
The Case of the Missing Will
The Veiled Lady
The Lost Mine
The Chocolate Box

1937      *The Incredible Theft.* New York: The American Mercury, n.d.
The Incredible Theft

1937      *Dead Man's Mirror.* New York: Dell Publishing Co., 1966
Murder in the Mews
Triangle at Rhodes
Dead Man's Mirror

1939      *The Regatta Mystery.* New York: Dell Publishing Co., 1964.
Problem at Sea
Yellow Iris
The Dream
How Does Your Garden Grow?
Mystery of the Baghdad Chest

1947      *The Labours of Hercules.* New York: Dodd, Mead & Company, 1967 (Greenway Edition).
The Nemean Lion
The Lernean Hydra
The Arcadian Deer
The Erymanthean Boar
The Augean Stables
The Stymphalean Birds
The Cretan Bull
The Horses of Diomedes
The Girdle of Hyppolita
The Flock of Geryon
The Apples of the Hesperides
The Capture of Cerberus

1950      *The Mousetrap and Other Stories.* New York: Dell Publishing Co., 1969. *(Three Blind Mice and Other Stories)*
The Third-Floor Flat
The Adventure of Johnnie Waverly
Four and Twenty Blackbirds

1951      *The Under Dog and Other Stories.* New York: Dell Publishing Co., 1969.
The Under Dog
The Plymouth Express
The Affair at the Victory Ball
The Market Basing Mystery
The Lemesurier Inheritance
The Cornish Mystery
The King of Clubs
The Submarine Plans

|  | The Adventure of the Clapham Cook |
| 1960 | *The Adventure of the Christmas Pudding.* London: Pan Books, Ltd., 1969. |
|  | The Adventure of the Christmas Pudding |
|  | The Mystery of the Spanish Chest |
| 1961 | *Double Sin.* New York: Dell Publishing Co., 1964 |
|  | Double Sin |
|  | The Double Clue |
|  | Wasps' Nest |
|  | The Theft of the Royal Ruby |

B. *Miss Jane Marple*

*Novels*

1930 *Murder at the Vicarage,* New York: Dodd, Mead & Company, 1977 (Greenway Edition).

1942 *The Body in the Library.* New York: Pocket Books, 1968.

1943 *The Moving Finger.* New York: Dodd, Mead & Company, 1968 (Greenway Edition).

1950 *A Murder Is Announced.* New York: Dodd, Mead & Company, 1967 (Greenway Edition).

1952 *They Do It With Mirrors.* New York: Dodd, Mead & Company, 1970 (Greenway Edition). *(Murder with Mirrors)*

1953 *A Pocket Full of Rye.* New York: Pocket Books, 1963.

1957 *What Mrs. McGillicuddy Saw!.* New York: Dodd, Mead & Company, 1957. *(The 4:50 from Paddington, Eyewitness to Murder)*

1962 *The Mirror Crack'd from Side to Side,* London: Fontana Books, 1970. *(The Mirror Crack'd)*

1964 *A Caribbean Mystery.* New York: Dodd, Mead & Company, 1964.

1965 *At Bertram's Hotel.* New York: Dodd, Mead & Company, 1965.

1971 *Nemesis.* New York: Dodd, Mead & Company, 1971.

1976 *Sleeping Murder.* New York: Dodd, Mead & Company, 1976.

*Short Stories*

1932 *Thirteen Problems.* New York: Dodd, Mead & Company, 1973 (Greenway Edition). *(Tuesday Club Murders)*

   The Tuesday Night Club
   The Idol House of Astarte
   Ingots of Gold
   The Bloodstained Pavement
   Motive v. Opportunity
   The Thumb Mark of St. Peter
   The Blue Geranium
   The Companion

The Four Suspects
A Christmas Tragedy
The Herb of Death
The Affair at the Bungalow
Death by Drowning

|      |      |
|------|------|
| 1939 | *The Regatta Mystery.* New York: Dell Publishing Co., 1964. |
|      | Miss Marple Tells a Story |
| 1966 | *13 Clues for Miss Marple,* New York: Dell Publish- Co., 1966. |
|      | Tape-Measure Murder |
|      | Strange Jest |
|      | The Case of the Perfect Maid |
|      | The Case of the Caretaker |
|      | Sanctuary |
|      | Greenshaw's Folly |
|      | (The other seven stories in this volume are also in *Thirteen Problems.)* |

C. *Tuppence and*
*   Tommy Beresford*
*   Novels*

|      |      |
|------|------|
| 1922 | *The Secret Adversary.* New York: Bantam Books, 1967. |
| 1941 | *N or M?.* New York: Dodd, Mead & Company, 1974 (Greenway Edition). |
| 1968 | *By the Pricking of My Thumbs.* New York: Dodd, Mead & Company, 1968. |
| 1973 | *Postern of Fate.* New York: Dodd, Mead & Company, 1973. |

*Short Stories*

|      |      |
|------|------|
| 1929 | *Partners in Crime.* New York: Dell Publishing Co., 1971. (This is a collection of related short stories, set in a frame.) |

D. *Superintendent Battle*
*   Novels*

|      |      |
|------|------|
| 1925 | *The Secret of Chimneys.* New York: Dell Publishing Co., 1964. |
| 1929 | *The Seven Dials Mystery.* New York: Bantam Books, 1964. |
| 1936 | *Cards on the Table.* New York: Dodd, Mead & Company, 1968 (Greenway Edition). |
| 1939 | *Easy to Kill.* New York: Pocket Books, 1945. *(Murder Is Easy)* |
| 1944 | *Towards Zero.* New York: Dodd, Mead & Company, 1974 (Greenway Edition). |

E. *Harley Quin*
*   Short Stories*

|      |      |
|------|------|
| 1930 | *The Mysterious Mr. Quin.* New York: Dell Publishing Co., 1968. (*The Passing of Mr. Quin)* |
|      | The Coming of Mr. Quin |

The Shadow on the Glass
At the Bells and Motley
The Sign in the Sky
The Soul of the Croupier
The World's End
The Voice in the Dark
The Face of Helen
The Dead Harlequin
The Bird with the Broken Wing
The Man from the Sea
Harlequin's Lane

1950    *The Mousetrap and Other Stories.* New York: Dell Publishing Co., 1969.
The Love Detectives

1971    *Ellery Queen's Murdercade,* ed. Ellery Queen. New York: Random House, 1975, pp.149-80.
The Harlequin Tea Set

F.  *Parker Pyne*
   *Short Stories*
   1934    *Mr. Parker Pyne, Detective.* New York: Dell Publishing Co., 1962. *(Parker Pyne Investigates)*
The Case of the Middle-Aged Wife
The Case of the Discontented Soldier
The Case of the Distressed Lady
The Case of the Discontented Husband
The Case of the City Clerk
The Case of the Rich Woman
Have You Got Everything You Want?
The Gate of Baghdad
The House at Shiraz
The Pearl of Price
Death on the Nile
Oracle at Delphi

   1939    *The Regatta Mystery.* New York: Dell Publishing Co., 1964.
The Regatta Mystery
Problem at Pollensa Bay

G.  *Works Without a*
   *a Series Detective*
   *Novels*
   1924    *The Man in the Brown Suit.* New York: Dell Publishing Co., 1962.

   1931    *Murder at Hazelmoor.* New York: Dell Publishing Co., 1966. *(The Sittaford Mystery)*

   1934    *Why Didn't They Ask Evans?* New York: Dodd, Mead & Company, 1968 (Greenway Edition). *(The Boomerang Clue)*

   1939    *And Then There Were None.* New York: Pocket Books, 1959. *(Ten Little Niggers, Ten Little Indians)*

   1945    *Remembered Death.* New York: Pocket Books, 1947. *(Sparkling Cyanide)*

| 1945 | *Death Comes as the End.* New York: Pocket Books, 1959. |
| 1949 | *Crooked House.* New York: Dodd, Mead & Company, 1967 (Greenway Edition). |
| 1951 | *They Came to Baghdad.* New York: Dodd, Mead & Company, 1970 (Greenway Edition). |
| 1954 | *So Many Steps to Death.* New York: Pocket Books, 1956. (*Destination Unknown*) |
| 1958 | *Ordeal by Innocence.* New York: Pocket Books, 1959. |
| 1961 | *The Pale Horse.* New York: Pocket Books, 1963. |
| 1967 | *Endless Night.* New York: Dodd, Mead & Company, 1968. |
| 1970 | *Passenger to Frankfurt.* New York: Dodd, Mead & Company, 1970. |

*Novel in Collaboration*

| 1932 | *The Floating Admiral.* Garden City, NY: The Crime Club, Inc., 1932 (with G.K. Chesterton, Canon Whitechurch, G.D.H. & M. Cole, Henry Wade, John Rhode, Milward Kennedy, Dorothy Sayers, Ronald A. Knox, Freeman Wills Crofts, Edgar Jepson, Clemence Dane, and Anthony Berkeley). |

*Short Stories*

| 1934 | *The Listerdale Mystery.* London: Pan Books Ltd., 1970. |
| | Sing a Song of Sixpence |
| | Mr. Eastwood's Adventure |
| 1948 | *The Witness for the Prosecution.* New York: Dell Publishing Co., n.d. |
| | The Witness for the Prosecution |
| | The Red Signal |
| | S.O.S. |
| | Where There's a Will |
| | The Mystery of the Blue Jar |
| | Philomel Cottage |
| | Accident |
| 1950 | *The Mousetrap and Other Stories.* New York: Dell Publishing Co., 1969. |
| | Three Blind Mice |
| 1971 | *The Golden Ball and Other Stories.* New York: Dodd, Mead & Company, 1971. |
| | The Listerdale Mystery |
| | The Girl in the Train |
| | The Manhood of Edward Robinson |
| | Jane in Search of a Job |
| | A Fruitful Sunday |
| | The Golden Ball |
| | The Rajah's Emerald |
| | Swan Song |

## II. Other Works Consulted

"Agatha Christie Dies at 85," Atlanta *Constitution,* 13 January 1976, pp. 1 & 12.

Allen, Dick & David Chacko, eds. *Detective Fiction: Crime and Compromise.* New York: Harcourt Brace Jovanovitch, Inc., 1974.

Allingham, Margery. "Mysterious Fun for Millions of Innocent Escapists," *New York Times Book Review,* 4 June 1950, p. 3.

Anderson, Lou Ann. "Agatha Christie's Poisons," unpublished study, 15 pp. (provided by Dr. Kathleen Klein).

Athanason, Arthur Nicholas. *"The Mousetrap* Phenomenon," *The Armchair Detective,* 12 (Spring 1979), 152-157.

Ball, John, ed. *The Mystery Story.* San Diego: University Extension, University of California, San Diego, 1976.

Bander, Elaine. "The English Detective Novel Between the Wars: 1919-1939," *The Armchair Detective,* 11 (July 1978), 262-273.

Barsley, Michael *The Orient Express.* New York: Stein & Day, 1967.

Barzun, Jacques & Wendell Hertig Taylor. *A Catalogue of Crime.* New York: Harper & Row, 1971.

—————. *A Book of Prefaces.* New York & London: Garland Publishing, Inc., 1976.

Baudet, Arlette. "Simenon Hates Fiction But Loves the Muppets," *Macon Telegraph & News,* 26 March 1978, p. 3E.

Bedell, Jeanne F. "A Pair of Box Sets: Class-Oriented Attitudes and Values in English Popular Drama and Detective Fiction, 1880-1939." paper presented before the Popular Culture Association, Cincinnati, 1978.

Behre, Frank. *Studies in Agatha Christie's Writings: The Behaviour of A Good (Great) Deal, A Lot, Lots, Much, Plenty, Many, A Good (Great) Many.* Goteborg: University of Gothenburg, 1967.

"Book Ends," *New York Times Book Review,* 23 March 1975, p. 41

"Bood Ends," *New York Times Book Review,* 26 October 1975, p. 61.

Booth, Wayne C. *The Rhetoric of Fiction.* Chicago & London: University of Chicago Press, 1961.

Boucher, Anthony. "Criminals at Large," *New York Times Book Review* 25 September 1966, p. 61.

—————. *Multiplying Villainies: Selected Mystery Criticism, 1942-1968.* ed. Robert E. Briney & Francis M. Nevins, Jr. Boston: A Boucheron Book, 1973.

Brophy, Brigid. "Detective Fiction: A Modern Myth of Violence?," *Hudson Review,* 18 (Spring, 1965), 11-30.

Burack, A.S., ed. *Writing Detective and Mystery Fiction.* Boston: The Writer, Inc., 1945.

—————. *Writing Suspense and Mystery Fiction.* Boston: The Writer, Inc., 1977.

Butcher, S.H. trans. *Aristotle's Theory of Poetry and Fine Art.* New York: Dover Publications, 1951.

Byrne, Evelyn B. & Otto M. Penzler, eds. *Attacks of Taste.* New York: Gotham Book Mart, 1971.

Callendar, Newgate. "Criminals at Large," *New York Times Book Review,* 12 January 1972, p. 34.

—————. "We Care, Roger," *New York Times Books Review,* 23 July 1978, pp. 3 & 33.

Cary, Cecile Williamson. "Images of Women in Mysteries by Three Women: Sayers, Christie, and Marsh," paper presented before the Popular Culture Association, Indianapolis, 1973.

Cawelti, John. *Adventure, Mystery, and Romance.* Chicago & London: University of Chicago Press, 1976.

—————. "Emma Lathen: Murder and Sophistication," *The New Republic,* 31 July 1976, pp. 25-27.

Champigny, Robert. *What Will Have Happened: A Philosophical and Technical Essay on Mystery Stories.* Bloomington: Indiana University Press, 1977.

Christie, Agatha. *An Autobiography.* New York: Dodd, Mead & Company, 1977.

—————. *The Mousetrap and Other Plays.* New York: Dodd, Mead, 1978.

Cone, Edward T. "Three Ways of Reading a Detective Story—or a Brahms Intermezzo," *The Georgia Review,* 31 (Fall 1977), 554-574.

"Dame Agatha Christie: Queen of the Maze," *Time,* 26 January 1976, p. 75.

Deegan, Mary Jo. "The Myth of Miss Marple," unpublished study provided by the author.

Deindorfer, Robert G. "Agatha Christie at 84: Still Getting Away With Murder," *Parade,* 8 December 1974, pp. 9-11.

Dennis, Nigel. "Genteel Queen of Crime," *Life,* 14 May 1956, pp. 87-88, 91-92, 97-98, 101-102.

Dove, George N. "Shades of Dupin: Fictional Detectives on Detective Fiction," *The Armchair Detective,* 8 (November 1974), 12-14.

—————. "The Criticism of Detective Fiction," *The Popular Culture Scholar,* 1 (Winter 1977), 1-7.

—————. "The Rules of the Game," unpublished study provided by the author.

Duffy, Martha. "The Sweet Sleuth Gone," *Time,* 15 September 1975, pp. 88-89.

—————. "Grand Dame," *Time,* 28 November 1977, pp. 127-128.

East, Andy. *The Agatha Christie Quizbook.* New York: Pocket Books, 1976.

Egloff, Gerd. *Detektivroman und englisches Burgertum: Konstruktionsschema und Gesellschaftbild bei Agatha Christie.* Dusseldorf: Bertelsmann Universitatsverlag, 1974.

"Entertaining Inquiry: The Nature of the Detective Story," *The Times Literary Supplement,* 25 February 1955, p. iv.

"The Escape of Agatha Christie," *Christianity Today,* 13 February 1976, p. 38.

Feinman, Jeffrey. *The Mysterious World of Agatha Christie.* New York: Award Books, 1975.

Fishman, Katherine Davis. "Professionals in Crime," *New York Times Book Review,* 26 April 1970, pp. 2 & 32.

Fletcher, Connie. "The Case of the Missing Criminal: Crime Fiction's Unpaid Debt to Its Ne'er-Do-Wells," *The Armchair Detective,* 10 (January 1977), 17-20.

Frye, Northrop. *Anatomy of Criticism.* Princeton: Princeton University Press, 1957.

Gilbert, Elliot L., ed. *The World of Mystery Fiction.* Del Mar, CA: University Extension, University of California San Diego, 1978.

Gilbert, Michael, ed. *Crime in Good Company.* London: Constable, 1959.

Gottschalk, Jane. "The Games of Detective Fiction," *The Armchair Detective,* 10 (January 1977), 74-76.

" 'Grannie' Read Him Her Crime Stories," *Atlanta Constitution,* 11 November 1977, p. 20-A.

Grant, Ellsworth. "A Tribute to Agatha Christie," *Horizon,* 18 (Autumn 1976), 106-109.

Graves, Robert. "After a Century, Will Anyone Care Whodunit?" *New York Times Book Review,* 25 August 1957, pp. 5 & 24.

Graves, Robert & Alan Hodge. *The Long Week-End: A Social History of Great Britain 1918-1939.* New York: W.W. Norton & Company, 1940 (rpt. 1963).

Green, Mars. "An Elegantly Executed 'Death on the Nile'," *The Chronicle of Higher Education,* 30 October 1978, pp. R24-25.

Grimes, Larry E. "Doing, Knowing and Mystery: A Study of Religious Types in Detective Fiction" *The Popular Culture Scholar,* 1 (Winter 1977), 24-35.

Groff, Mary. "Friday, February 25, 1955," *The Armchair Detective,* 10 (July 1977),

232-234.

Grossvogel, David I. *Mystery and Its Fictions: From Oedipus To Agatha Christie.* Baltimore & London: John Hopkins University Press, 1979.

Hackett, Alice Payne. *70 Years of Best Sellers: 1895-1965.* New York & London: R.R. Bowker, 1967.

Hamblen, Abigail Ann. "The Inheritance of the Meek: Two Novels by Agatha Christie and Henry James," *Discourse,* 12 (Summer 1969), 409-413.

Hartman, Geoffrey. "The Mystery of Mysteries," *The New York Review of Books,* 18 May 1972, pp.31-34.

Haycraft, Howard. *Murder for Pleasure: The Life and Times of the Detective Story.* Enlarged Edition. New York: Biblo and Tannen, 1968.

—————, ed. *The Art of the Mystery Story.* New York: Biblo and Tannen, 1975 (rpt.)

Hayne, Barrie, "Robert Barr: A Europeo-Canadian Rival to Conan Doyle," paper presented before the Popular Culture Association, Chicago, 1976.

Hays, R.W. "More 'Shades of Dupin!' " *The Armchair Detective,* 8 (August 1975), 228-229, 274.

Herman, Linda & Beth Stiel. *Corpus Delicti of Mystery Fiction: A Guide to the Body of the Case.* Metuchen, NJ: The Scarecrow Press, 1974.

Holquist, Michael. "Murder She Says," *The New Republic,* 26 (July 1975), pp.26-28.

Hubin, Allen J. "Criminals at Large," *New York Times Book Review,* 13 December 1970, p.42.

Innes, Michael. "Death as a Game," *Ellery Queen's Mystery Magazine,* November 1965, pp.48-54 (reprinted from *Esquire*).

"In the Best Tradition: Mystification and Art," *The Times Literary Supplement,* 25 February 1955, p.viii.

Jensen, Gregory. "Crime Queen Began on Dare," *Atlanta Journal and Constitution,* 31 August 1975, p.13-C.

Johnson, Pamela Hansford. *Important to Me.* New York: Charles Scribner's Sons, 1974.

Jones, Mary Jane. "The Spinster Detective," *Journal of Communication,* 25 (Spring 1975), 106-112.

Keating, H.R.F. *Murder Must Appetize.* London: Lemon Tree Press, 1975.

—————, ed. *Agatha Christie: First Lady of Crime.* New York: Holt, Rinehart and Winston, 1977.

King, Margaret J. "Binocular Eyes: Cross-Cultural Detectives," paper presented before the Popular Culture Association, Cincinnati, 1978.

Kitchin, C.H.B. "Five Writers in One: The Versatility of Agatha Christie," *The Times Literary Supplement,* 25 February 1955, p.x.

Kramer, Peter G. "Mistress of Mystery," *Newsweek,* 26 January 1976, p.69.

Krouse, Agate Nesaule & Margot Peters. "Why Women Kill," *Journal of Communication,* 25 (Spring 1975), 98-105.

—————. "Murder in Academe," *Southwest Review,* 62 (Autumn 1977), 371-378.

Krutch, Joseph Wood," 'Only a Detective Story,' " *The Nation,* 25 November 1944, pp.647-48 & 652.

la Cour, Tage & Harald Mogensen. *The Murder Book.* New York: Herder and Herder, 1971.

Lambert, Gavin. "Review of *Sleeping Murder," New York Times Book Review,* 19 September 1976, p.1.

Landrum, Larry N., Pat Browne & Ray B. Browne, eds. *Dimensions of Detective Fiction.* Bowling Green, Ohio: The Popular Press, 1976.

Larmoth, Jeanine. *Murder on the Menu.* New York: Charles Scribner's Sons, 1972.

Legars, Brigitte and Jean Thibaudeau, "Agatha Christie," *La Nouvelle Critique,* 96 (November 1976), 46-52. (in French)

LeJuene, Anthony. "The Secret of Agatha Christie," *The Spectator,* 19 September

1970, p.294.

Leonard, John. "I Care Who Killed Roger Ackroyd," *Esquire,* August 1975, pp.60-61, 120.

————. "An Etiquette of Murder," *New York Times,* 13 January 1976, p.40.

Levine, Joseph M. "The Autonomy of History: R.G. Collingwood and Agatha Christie," *Clio,* 7 (Summer 1978), 253-264.

"Line of Heroes: Some Detectives of Character," *The Times Literary Supplement,* 25 February 1955, p.ix.

Lingeman, Richard R. "Book Ends," *New York Times Book Review,* 11 December 1977, p.55.

Lord Snowdon, "The Unsinkable Agatha Christie," *Toronto Star,* 13 December 1974, p. G1.

Lowenthal, Max. "Agatha Christie: Creator of Poirot, Dies," *New York Times,* 13 January 1976, pp. 1 & 40.

Mallowan, Agatha Christie. *Come, Tell Me How You Live.* New York: Dodd, Mead & Company, 1946.

Mallowan, Max. *Mallowan's Memoirs.* London: Collins, 1977.

Maugham, Somerset. "The Decline and Fall of the Detective Story," *The Vagrant Mood.* Port Washington, NY: Kennikat Press, 1969, pp.91-122.

McCarthy, Mary. "Murder and Karl Marx," *The Nation,* 25 March 1936, pp.381-383.

McCleary, G.F. *On Detective Fiction and Other Things.* London: Hollis & Carter, 1960 (rpt. 1974).

Moore, Violet. "Who-Dun-It Addicts: Just Who Are They?" *The Macon Telegraph* 5 November 1975, p.6A

Murch, A.E. *The Development of the Detective Novel.* New York: Greenwood Press, 1958.

Murdoch, Derrick. *The Agatha Christie Mystery.* Toronto: Pagurian Press Limited, 1976.

Neimark, Paul G. "Human Nature Is the Culprit," *New York Times Book Review,* 17 March 1968, p.49.

Nevins, Francis M., ed. *The Mystery Writers Art.* Bowling Green, Ohio: The Popular Press, 1970.

Nightingale, Benedict. "Not So Much a Whodunit as a Whydunit," *New York Times,* 2 October 1977, 2:17.

"Obituary: Dame Agatha Christie," *The Times* (London), 13 January 1976, p.16.

Ousby, Ian. *Bloodhounds of Heaven: The Detective in English Fiction from Godwin to Doyle.* Cambridge: Harvard University Press, 1976.

Pace, Eric. "Mysteries More Real," Atlanta *Constitution,* 30 November 1972, p.20-B.

Panek, LeRoy. *Watteau's Shepherds: The Detective Novel in Britain 1914-1940,* Bowling Green, Ohio: The Popular Press, 1979.

"Paper Book Talk," *New York Times Book Review,* 17 October 1976, p.51.

Penzler, Otto. *The Private Lives of Private Eyes.* New York: Grosset & Dunlap, 1977.

————, ed. *The Great Detectives.* Boston: Little, Brown, 1978.

"People Who Read and Write," *New York Times Book Review,* 12 January 1947, p.8.

"Poirot, Famed Detective, Dies," Atlanta *Constitution,* 6 August 1975, p.11-A.

"Poisoning: Nurse Reads Mystery and Saves Child," Atlanta *Constitution,* 24 June 1977, p.2-A.

Prescott, Peter H. "Looking at Books," *Look,* 9 June 1968, p.12.

Queen, Ellery, ed. *101 Years' Entertainment: The Great Detective Stories 1841-1941.* New York: The Modern Library, 1941.

————. *In the Queen's Parlor.* New York: Biblo and Tannen, 1969.

————. "The 12 Most Famous Detectives," *Ellery Queen's Mystery Magazine,* February 1973, pp. 140-143.

Ramsey, G.C. "Perdurable Agatha," *New York Tims Book Review,* 21 November 1965, pp.2 & 84.
—————. *Agatha Christie: Mistress of Mystery.* New York: Dodd, Mead & Company, 1967.
Reilly, John M. "Classic and Hard-Boiled Detective Fiction," *The Armchair Detective,* 9 (October 1976), 289-91, 334.
Robertson, Nan. "Phyllis Dorothy White Uncovers the Secret Face of P.D. James," *New York Times,* 11 December 1977, p.86.
Rodell, Marie F. *Mystery Fiction: Theory and Technique.* New York: Duell, Sloan and Pearce, 1943.
Routley, Erik. *The Puritan Pleasures of the Detective Story.* London: Victor Gollancz Ltd., 1972.
Sayers, Dorothy, ed. *The Omnibus of Crime.* New York: Harcourt, Brace and Company, 1929.
—————. "Aristotle on Detective Fiction," *English,* 1 (1936), 23-35.
Schickel, Richard. "Camping in Style," *Time,* 2 October 1978, p.66.
Scott, Sutherland. *Blood in Their Ink.* London: Stanley Paul and Co., 1953.
"The Secret Attraction," *Times Literary Supplement,* 25 February 1955, p.i.
Shaw, Peter J. "Agatha Christie: Top Crime Writer to be 80 Tomorrow," Charleston *Evening Post,* 14 September 1970, p.3-B.
"The Silver Age: Crime Fiction from Its Heyday Until Now," *The Times Literary Supplement,* 25 February 1955, p.xi.
Slung, Michele B., ed. *Crime on Her Mind.* New York: Pantheon Books, 1975.
Steinbrunner, Chris & Otto Penzler, eds. *Encyclopedia of Mystery & Detection.* New York: McGraw-Hill, 1976.
Stoppard, Tom. *The Real Inspector Hound.* New York: Grove Press, 1968.
Strachey, John. "The Golden Age of English Detection," *The Saturday Review,* 7 January 1939, pp.12-14.
Symons, Julian. *The Detective Story in Britain.* London: Longmans, Green & Co., 1962.
—————. *Mortal Consequences: A History from the Detective Story to the Crime Novel.* New York: Harper & Row, 1972.
—————. "Review of *Curtain,*" *New York Times Book Review,* 12 October 1975, p.3.
"The Talk of the Town," *The New Yorker,* 29 October 1966, pp.51-52, and 26 January 1976, p.24.
Thompson, Leslie M. & Jeff Banks. "When Is This Stiff Dead?—Detective Stories and Definitions of Death," paper presented before the Popular Culture Association, Cincinnati, 1978.
Thomson, H. Douglas. *Masters of Mystery.* Norwood, PA: Norwood Editions, 1976 (rpt.)
"Tram Cars or 'Dodgems'," *The Times Literary Supplement,* 25 February 1955, p. ii.
Tynan, Kathleen. *Agatha.* New York: Ballantine Books, 1978.
Ulam, Adam. "Agatha Christie: Murder and Class," *The New Republic,* 31 July 1976, pp.21-23.
Walters, Ray. "Paperback Talk," *New York Times Book Review,* 2 October 1977, pp.49-50.
Watson, Colin. *Snobbery with Violence.* London: Eyre & Spottiswoode, 1971.
Waugh, Auberon. "Murder at Newlands Corner," *Esquire,* July 1976, p.140.
Wells, Carolyn. *The Technique of the Mystery Story.* Springfield, Mass.: The Home Correspondence School, 1913 (rpt. 1976).
White, William. "Agatha Christie: A First Checklist of Secondary Sources," *Bulletin of Bibliography and Magazine Notes,* 36 (January-March 1979), 14-17, 49.
"Who Killed Agatha Christie?," *National Review,* 6 February 1976, p.78.

Wilson, Edmund. *Classics & Commercials*. New York: Vintage Books, 1962.

Wingate, Nancy. "Getting Away With Murder: An Analysis," *Journal of Popular Culture*, 12 (Spring 1979), 581-603.

Winks, Robin W., ed. *The Historian as Detective: Essays on Evidence*. New York: Harper & Row, 1968.

Winn, Dilys, ed. *Murder Ink: The Mystery Reader's Companion*. New York: Workman Publishing Company, 1977.

Wren-Lewis, John. "Adam, Eve and Agatha Christie," *New Christian*, 16 April 1970, pp.9-10.

Wuyek, George. "End of the Golden Age," *The Armchair Detective*, 10 (July 1977), 263-267.

Wyndham, Francis. "The Algebra of Agatha Christie," *The Sunday Times* (London), 27 February 1966, pp.25-26.

Wynne, Nancy Blue. *An Agatha Christie Chronology*. New York: Ace Books, 1976.

Zacharias, Lee. "Point of View and the Nature of Truth in Detective Fiction," paper presented before the Popular Culture Association, St. Louis, 1975.

# Index of Characters

**223**

# Index of Novel and Short Story Titles

# Key to Documentation

Listed below in alphabetical order are the key words from the titles of Agatha Christie's detective fiction which will be used with page numbers in parentheses, where necessary after quotations, for internal documentaion. The complete title is given after the key word.

| | |
|---|---|
| ABC | *The ABC Murders* |
| Ackroyd | *The Murder of Roger Ackroyd* |
| Adversary | *The Secret Adversary* |
| Announced | *A Murder is Announced* |
| Appointment | *Appointment with Death* |
| Bagdad | "The Gate of Bagdad" |
| Baghdad | *They Came to Baghdad* |
| Baghdad Chest | "The Mystery of the Baghdad Chest" |
| Bertram's | *At Bertram's Hotel* |
| Brown | *The Man in the Brown Suit* |
| Cards | *Cards on the Table* |
| Caribbean | *A Caribbean Mystery* |
| Cerberus | "The Capture of Cerberus" |
| "Christmas" | "A Christmas Tragedy" |
| *Christmas* | *Hercule Poirot's Christmas* |
| Clerk | "The Case of the City Clerk" |
| Client | *Poirot Loses a Client* |
| Clocks | *The Clocks* |
| Clouds | *Death in the Clouds* |
| Cornish | "The Cornish Mystery" |
| Crack'd | *The Mirror Crack'd from Side to Side* |
| Crooked | *Crooked House* |
| Croupier | "The Soul of the Croupier" |
| Curtain | *Curtain* |
| Cypress | *Sad Cypress* |
| Dials | *The Seven Dials Mystery* |
| Distressed | "The Case of the Distressed Lady" |
| Eastwood | "Mr. Eastwood's Adventure" |
| Easy | *Easy to Kill* |
| Edgware | *Lord Edgware Dies* |
| Egyptian | "The Adventure of the Egyptian Tomb" |
| Elephants | *Elephants Can Remember* |
| End | *Death Comes as the End* |
| Endless | *Endless Night* |
| Evans | *Why Didn't They Ask Evans?* |
| Everything? | "Have You Everything You Want?" |
| Express | *Murder on the Orient Express* |
| Finger | *The Moving Finger* |
| Folly | *Dead Man's Folly* |

| | |
|---|---|
| Sleeping | *Sleeping Murder* |
| Soldier | "The Case of the Discontented Soldier" |
| St. Peter | "The Thumb Mark of Saint Peter" |
| Steps | *So Many Steps to Death* |
| Styles | *The Mysterious Affair at Styles* |
| Sun | *Evil Under the Sun* |
| Theft | "The Incredible Theft" |
| Tide | *There Is a Tide* |
| Tragedy | *Three Act Tragedy* |
| Train | *The Mystery of the Blue Train* |
| Triangle | "Triangle at Rhodes" |
| Tuesday | "The Tuesday Night Club" |
| Vicarage | *Murder at the Vicarage* |
| Western | "The Adventure of 'The Western Star' " |
| Wife | "The Case of the Middle-Aged Wife" |
| Wing | "The Birde with the Broken Wing" |
| World | "The World's End" |
| Zero | *Towards Zero* |